The rise and fall of the Scottish cotton industry, 1778–1914

MANCHESTER
1824
Manchester University Press

The rise and fall of the Scottish cotton industry, 1778–1914

'The secret spring'

Anthony Cooke

Manchester University Press

Manchester and New York

distributed in the United States exclusively by Palgrave Macmillan

Published by Manchester University Press
Oxford Road, Manchester M13 9NR, UK
and Room 400, 175 Fifth Avenue, New York, NY 10010, USA
www.manchesteruniversitypress.co.uk

Distributed in the United States exclusively by
Palgrave Macmillan, 175 Fifth Avenue, New York,
NY 10010, USA

Distributed in Canada exclusively by
UBC Press, University of British Columbia, 2029 West Mall,
Vancouver, BC, Canada V6T 1Z2

British Library Cataloguing-in-Publication Data
A catalogue record for this book is available from the British Library

Library of Congress Cataloging-in-Publication Data applied for

ISBN 978 0 7190 8082 1 *hardback*

First published 2010

Typeset in Minion
by Servis Filmsetting Ltd, Stockport, Cheshire
Printed in Great Britain
by the MPG Books Group, UK

To Ian Donnachie, for his friendship and encouragement

Contents

Acknowledgements

Most of the primary sources for this book are located in Edinburgh, Glasgow or Paisley. My thanks are due to the Pasold Research Fund for a travel grant and the Carnegie Trust for the Universities of Scotland for a grant towards colour illustrations. I have made heavy use of the National Archives of Scotland and the National Library of Scotland in Edinburgh, and of Glasgow University Archives and the Mitchell Library in Glasgow. I have also used the excellent Reference Library in Paisley, the Signet Library in Edinburgh, the University Libraries in Dundee, Edinburgh and St Andrews, the A. K. Bell Library in Perth and the Atholl Manuscripts in Blair Castle. I would like to thank the librarians and archivists in all these places for their help and support. I would also like to thank Jim Bell of the Dornoch Heritage Society, Sutherland for supplying photocopies of the Gilchrist of Ospidale Manuscripts.

I have received a good deal of help, encouragement and guidance from fellow academics. Dr Douglas Lockhart of Keele University generously drew my attention to the Lennox of Woodhead and the Houston of Johnstone Papers in the Mitchell Library, as well as to newspaper advertisements by Scottish cotton mills looking for labour. The late Bob Fitton of Manchester Metropolitan University guided me many years ago to the Glasgow Chamber of Commerce records in the Mitchell Library, while Prof. Stanley Chapman of Nottingham University pointed me towards the Sun Fire Office Company records in the Guildhall Library and the Board of Trade Records in London. Prof. Ian Donnachie of the Open University in Scotland has offered friendship, support and encouragement in my researches and has generously shared with me his unrivalled knowledge of New Lanark and Robert Owen. A number of colleagues and friends have read chapters in draft and made many helpful comments and criticisms. I would like to thank Prof. Stanley Chapman of Nottingham University, Prof. Ian Donnachie of the Open University, Prof. Katrina Honeyman of Leeds University, Dr Bill Knox of St Andrews University and two anonymous referees for their help in these matters. I have been fortunate to work with Historic Scotland during its restoration of Stanley Mills, Perthshire. Its staff have provided much stimulating and questioning conversation during our association, particularly Chris McGregor, Dr Mark Watson, Jim Broughton and Michael Terwey. Emma Brennan and Kim Walker of Manchester University Press have guided me through the publication process with great efficiency and support. I would also like to thank my Copy Editor, Judith Oppenheimer, for her meticulous work on the manuscript of the book.

My family have been supportive as always. My sons Alistair and Michael and their wives, Louise and Gill, have offered good company, hospitality and accommodation during my researches in Glasgow. My wife, Judith, has offered her usual love and support after I had a major operation in 2005. Friends who have offered support and encouragement include Antony Black, Roy Partington, Russell Meek and John Cheyne, who was born and brought up in Grandholm, Aberdeen, opposite the former Woodside cotton mills. Finally, I would like to thank the members of my Wednesday night symposium in Dundee for their stimulating and argumentative company over a number of years.

List of tables

List of illustrations

Plates

The plates can be found between pp. 80 and 81.

Figures

List of abbreviations

Atholl Mss.	Atholl Manuscripts, Blair Castle, Blair Atholl, Perthshire
CC	Commissary Court
CS	Court of Session
GCC	Glasgow Chamber of Commerce
GUA	Glasgow University Archives
ML	Mitchell Library, Glasgow
NAS	National Archives of Scotland, Edinburgh
NLS	National Library of Scotland, Edinburgh
NMRS	National Monuments Record of Scotland, Edinburgh
NSA	New Statistical Account of Scotland
OSA	(Old) Statistical Account of Scotland
PP	Parliamentary Papers
SC	Sheriff Court
SL	Signet Library, Edinburgh
UGD	University of Glasgow Deposits

Introduction

In 1792, the Rev. John Snodgrass described the rapid growth of textile manufactures in the town of Paisley, Renfrewshire, including silk, linen and the 'new' fabric – cotton – introduced into the area in 1783. Unlike the Rev. Robert Boog, his opposite number in Paisley Abbey parish, Snodgrass took a positive view of the impact of manufactures, arguing that their growth had acted as a stimulus to agriculture and that land prices had increased in consequence. He concluded with almost Keynesian logic:

> The spirit of manufacture is the secret spring that puts all in motion; and the weaver upon his loom, while he provides a comfortable subsistence for himself and his family, may be considered as administering to the ease and to the elegance even of the gentleman who lives upon his country estate.[1]

A similar metaphor had been used some years earlier by William Sandeman, who owned a large bleachfield at Luncarty and became a partner in the cotton mills at Stanley, Perthshire. Writing in 1784 from Birmingham to Gilbert Hamilton, the Secretary of Glasgow Chamber of Commerce, Sandeman reported that to Birmingham manufacturers 'the principal of taxing manufactures at all, appears to them in such an alarming view, as stricking at the very Source and Spring of all the wealth of the nation arising from the profitable employment of the people'.[2]

Industrialisation, its causes and consequences, have been of central concern to social critics and historians since the late eighteenth century. The cotton industry has traditionally played a central role in this debate, epitomised by historians such as Eric Hobsbawm, who claimed, 'Whoever says Industrial Revolution says cotton' and characterised the industry as 'the pacemaker of industrial change'.[3] More recently, an increasing number of historians have questioned this view, arguing that cotton was atypical and that much of the British economy was slower to change in areas such as mechanisation, sources of power, industrial organisation, size of firm etc. Indeed, a central argument in this book is that even within the cotton industry itself, there were widely varying rates of change between different processes. There has also been increasing scepticism about the speed of industrial change in Britain during this period and more emphasis on evolution and continuity in the British economy, as opposed to rapid change.[4] Other historians have highlighted regional diversity in the British economy, as well as diversity between different sectors of the economy.[5] In England, the cotton industry was a heavily regionalised industry, largely confined to Lancashire and a few surrounding counties, Cheshire, Derbyshire and Nottinghamshire.[6]

In Scotland, recent historiography has reaffirmed the fundamental importance of the cotton industry to the economy from 1760 to 1830. Knox has asserted, 'it was cotton which more than any other Scottish industry stimulated moves towards industrialisation, particularly in the West of Scotland'.[7] Devine has described the situation in 1830, when the textile industries constituted 'the jewel in the nation's economic crown', with cotton manufacturing having 'a pre-eminent role' in the increasing urbanisation of the country.[8] Whatley has stressed the later onset of industrialisation in Scotland and the rapid speed of change thereafter, as compared to England: 'within two decades, cotton had overtaken linen as Scotland's premier textile product, as measured by employment, volume of output and capital formation'.[9]

This book is an account of the 'secret spring' of cotton manufacturing in Scotland from 1778, when the first spinning mill was established by Sir John Clerk at Penicuik, to 1914, by which time the Scottish industry was reduced to a mere nine cotton spinning firms, excluding cotton thread. In a post-industrial world, where manufacturing industry in Scotland is no longer the major player it once was, it is perhaps not surprising that whilst the decline of the Scottish cotton industry from c. 1850 to 1914 has been the subject of a recent book,[10] no one has written a book on the industry in its heyday, in spite of its key role in Scotland's early industrialisation. Most recent longer work on the cotton industry in Scotland has focussed on the paternalistic factory villages such as New Lanark[11] and Stanley,[12] or on the broader contribution made by Robert Owen, managing partner at New Lanark.[13] Other historians have written books, chapters or articles about capital formation, gender, labour relations, or about the industry in specific locations and specific periods.[14] A number of general social and economic histories of Scotland have included valuable material on the cotton industry.[15] Earlier work focussed on family dynasties such as the Houldsworths and the Finlays.[16]

However, no one has made a close study of the Scottish cotton industry in its heartland of Glasgow and Paisley, where it was the dominant player until the rise of heavy industries based on coal, iron and steel from the 1830s. This is partly due to the nature of the surviving primary sources for the cotton industry in Scotland. Many more business records have survived for factory villages such as Catrine, Deanston and New Lanark than for the more numerous but often shorter-lived cotton firms in Glasgow, Paisley and their industrial suburbs. The exception to this generalisation is the survival of extensive records relating to the giant J. and P. Coats Company in Paisley, which in its different way was also untypical, focussing as it did mainly on the manufacture of cotton thread.

This means that the history of the industry in Scotland cannot be written purely from business records, which are too patchy and incomplete. In this book, I have used a variety of sources, including Parliamentary Papers, Court of Session records, Sheriff Court records (including wills and probate inventories), census records, newspapers, early histories of Glasgow and Paisley and the rich collection of miscellaneous records in the Mitchell Library, Glasgow, including the Glasgow Chamber of Commerce correspondence. I have also tried to place the Scottish industry in a wider context, to draw comparisons with the cotton industry in Lancashire and the North of England and in other countries such as the USA.

The origins of the Scottish cotton industry lie in the fine linen industry in the west of Scotland and in Glasgow's Asian and Atlantic trading links. Chapter 1 examines the origins and pre-history of the industry from 1700 to 1778. In the first half of the eighteenth century, linen was the major textile industry in Scotland, as it also was in Lancashire. Many years ago, two historians of the English cotton industry pointed out, 'it is significant that the feature common to the two centres of Manchester and the West of Scotland, where the cotton industry expanded and flourished, was the prior and continuous existence of a linen industry by the side of cotton'.[17] The west of Scotland specialised in finer yarns and more complex weaving patterns. Paisley was a centre of silk gauze weaving for a time and was noted for the skills of its spinners and weavers. Glasgow specialised in fine muslins and these workforce skills were relatively easily transferred to cotton.[18] Similarly, many of the merchants who organised and financed the linen industry were well placed to transfer their skills to cotton. David Dale was the most prominent of the linen merchants who made this transition. He founded New Lanark in a brief partnership with Richard Arkwright and went on to have interests in many other Scottish cotton mills, from Newton Stewart in the south-west to Spinningdale in Sutherland.[19]

The other major factor in the development of the cotton trade in Scotland was the Atlantic trade built up by Glasgow and the ports of the Clyde estuary. After the Union of 1707 the Scots began to move in to the North American tobacco trade on a large scale, and eventually to dominate it until American Independence. Some of the wealth generated by this trade found its way back into manufacturing industry in Scotland, including the cotton industry.[20] More important, however, was the expertise in long-distance shipping, overseas trade, credit, insurance and finance developed from this trade by Glasgow and, to a lesser extent, Paisley merchants and manufacturers, often cemented by overseas kinship networks. Scots also played a prominent role in the East India Company and turned this to good account in trade and commerce.

Chapter 2 looks at the expansion of the industry from 1778 to 1830. In the late eighteenth century there was a wide geographical spread of cotton spinning mills in Scotland, from Newton Stewart in the south to Spinningdale in the north, but as the nineteenth century advanced the more marginal mills began to drop out of the picture. The Edinburgh region may have boasted Scotland's first cotton mill at Penicuik, but few others followed in its wake. Dundee, like Paisley, had its Cotton Street, but there the similarity ended. The seven Dundee companies engaged in cotton manufacturing in 1799, which the Rev. Robert Small thought 'will probably soon become a very important branch of business',[21] had vanished by the late 1830s and the burgh returned to manufacturing coarse linens. A similar picture applied in Fife, where the four spinning mills for cotton and flax in Kinghorn parish, built in the early 1790s, failed to develop into anything more substantial and the region reverted to linen production.[22] For a time, Perth boasted a thriving cotton industry but a crash in 1810 bankrupted some sixty firms and the industry was never the same again, with obvious exceptions such as the spinning mills at Stanley, which only finally closed down in 1989, although by then they were producing artificial fibres.[23] Aberdeen had a mixture of water-powered linen, cotton and woollen mills, bleachfields and printworks on the River Don, although north of here there was only the ill-fated cotton mills at Spinningdale on the Dornoch Firth in Sutherland, which burned down in 1806, never to re open.[24]

Cotton was arguably more important to the Scottish economy as a whole in this period than its counterpart in Lancashire was to the English economy. Chapman has warned against overemphasising the importance of cotton in the English economy, claiming that it was untypical in the speed of its technological development as compared with other industries such as brewing or construction, and that its contribution to total gross domestic product in England was probably never more than 5%, similar to the contribution of the English iron industry.[25] In Scotland, this figure is likely to have been higher. In 1812, Sir John Sinclair estimated that the Scottish cotton industry employed about 150,000 people, mainly in their own homes, produced goods valued at £6,500,000 and boasted 120 spinning mills with a capital of £1.4m.[26] As late as the 1851 census, textiles employed 257,127 people in Scotland (20% of the total workforce of 1,271,169), with cotton claiming some 60% of total textile employment. By contrast, mining and quarrying employed 53,631, metal manufacture 36,210 and shipbuilding a mere 4,396.[27] This was despite the introduction of the hot blast process in 1829, generally thought to mark the beginnings of the dominance of heavy industry in the Scottish economy.

Table 1 Population (in thousands) of the largest towns in Scotland, 1755–1821

	1755	**1801**	**1821**
Aberdeen	15.6	27.4	44.6
Dundee	12.4	26.8	30.5
Edinburgh	57.0	81.6	138.0
Glasgow	31.7	83.7	147.0
Paisley	6.8	31.2	47.0
Perth	9.0	14.8	19.1

Source: T. C. Smout, *A History of the Scottish People, 1560–1830.*

However, the cotton industry had an importance in Scottish society over and above its economic contribution. It generated large numbers of jobs, particularly for the young, unskilled migrants flooding into urban centres such as Glasgow and Paisley from the Scottish Lowlands, the Highlands and from Ireland. Cotton factories, bleachfields, dyeworks and printworks, and the weaving trade had a voracious appetite for female and child labour and many contemporaries saw them as fulfilling a useful function in keeping the children of the poor in gainful employment and off the streets for twelve or fourteen hours a day, six days a week. Rose has highlighted the 'intimate relationship between eighteenth century social policy and the recruitment of labour by mill owners' and demonstrated how in England 'factories became vehicles for the employment of the poor'.[28] This was equally true in Scotland, where factories were referred to as 'public works'. For the Sabbath, when factories were closed, Sunday Schools were set up on a large scale in Glasgow from 1787 onwards and in Paisley some ten years later.[29]

The cotton industry was the major engine of economic growth in Scotland during the early industrialisation of the country. The cotton manufacturing heartland of Glasgow and Paisley experienced Scotland's fastest rates of population growth in the second half of the eighteenth century. By 1801 Glasgow had overtaken Edinburgh as the largest city and Paisley had grown from the smallest of the six urban centres in 1755 to the third largest in 1801. Between 1755 and 1801, the fastest growing counties in Scotland were Lanarkshire, whose population grew by 80.7%, and Renfrewshire, where it grew by a staggering 194.6%.[30]

The growth of the cotton industry in the west of Scotland, with closely associated developments in the bleaching and finishing trades and in shipping, insurance and finance, is a major factor in explaining why Glasgow's population overtook Edinburgh's in this period. By the late eighteenth century, Glasgow was not only the largest manufacturing centre in the country but had also emerged as the dominant shipping port. In many ways, it combined the roles of Manchester (the manufacturing and commercial centre of the Lancashire industry) and Liverpool (the port of entry for raw cotton). However, the cotton industry and the consequent level of port activity in Scotland were on a smaller scale than south of the border.

The Scottish cotton industry provides an early example of industrial decline and Chapter 3 examines the reasons for this. As the nineteenth century progressed, the industry faced growing competition from Lancashire and the USA, France, Germany and Switzerland. As early as 1784, Glasgow Chamber of Commerce had warned of the dangers of competition with manufacturers of linen and cotton in France, Switzerland and Ireland.[31] By the 1830s, the Parliamentary Commissioners were well aware of the threat of international competition and quizzed witnesses about the price and quality of foreign cotton goods, about labour costs and about their personal experience of labour and working conditions in France and the USA. The greatest crisis faced by the British cotton industry in the nineteenth century was the American Civil War, waged over the rich cotton fields of the American South, which led to the Cotton Famine of 1861–1862. Although both Lancashire and Lanarkshire recovered from this, the Scottish industry had begun to lose its momentum. The book finishes in 1914, on the eve of the First World War, by which time only nine cotton spinning firms were left in Scotland, excluding the highly profitable cotton thread industry in Paisley.

Chapter 4 explores the changing technology of the industry. There was a generational time lag, in the application of technology, between the preparatory and spinning phases of the industry, and weaving. The preparation and spinning of cotton in water-powered mills in Scotland began with the opening of the first spinning mill at Penicuik in 1778, followed the next year by one at Rothesay on the Isle of Bute. This was followed by a whole string of water-powered mills, mainly in Lanarkshire and Renfrewshire, but also in Aberdeenshire, Angus, Ayrshire, Fife, Perthshire and Stirlingshire, as well as in the south-west. Steam-powered spinning mills began to be built in Glasgow from 1792 onwards, which led to the development of Glasgow and Paisley as major centres of cotton manufacturing. On the weaving side, power looms began to be used in Glasgow in the early 1800s but were slow to catch on. By 1811, the firm of James Finlay was using them on a large scale at its factories in Catrine, Ayrshire and Deanston, Perthshire.[32] However, they were only suitable for certain types of cotton cloth and most fancy goods continued to be produced on hand looms. Employing hand loom weavers also offered flexibility to cotton manufacturers, as they required minimal capital investment by employers and home workers were easier to lay off than factory workers.

Originally all the technology of cotton preparation and spinning was imported from England, where James Hargreaves, Richard Arkwright and Samuel Crompton had developed the 'new' spinning machinery – respectively the spinning jenny, the water frame and the mule. Sometimes this technology transfer took the form of formal licensing, as in the case of Arkwright at New Lanark, Woodside, Aberdeen and Stanley, Perthshire. At other times it was more a case of industrial espionage. A French traveller visiting Perth in 1784 reported how machines for carding and spinning cotton had recently been established there by an individual who had them made in Manchester but had 'found it impossible, however, to convey them out of that town except by night; so jealous are the manufacturers of Manchester of this happy invention of Arkwright'.[33]

The greatest technological contribution made by Scots in the cotton industry was in the bleaching and finishing trades. The use of chlorine as a bleaching agent was introduced into Scotland by James Watt in 1786 and by the Aberdeen firm of Gordon, Barron and Company the following year.[34] Twelve years later, Charles Tennant of St Rollox works in Glasgow developed a portable version of chlorine in the form of a dry bleaching powder. The process of Turkey red dyeing was commercialised in 1785 by George Macintosh in partnership with David Dale at Dalmarnock on the Clyde. Macintosh and his son Charles developed many related processes, including cudbear manufacture and the manufacture of textile ancillaries such as alum, copperas, lead and aluminium acetates and, most famously, waterproofing.[35]

The condition of the workforce and wages and working conditions are examined in Chapter 5. Employment in cotton manufacturing was heavily gendered. In the preparing and spinning phases, men dominated the better-paid elite areas of mule spinning and supervision, but the rest of the workforce was mainly composed of lower-paid women and children. The Scottish industry was more female dominated than Lancashire. In 1818, women and girls made up 61% of the workforce in the Scottish cotton industry, compared with 50% in Lancashire.[36] In the water-powered country mills the figure was much higher. Deanston in Perthshire employed 365 workers in 1816, of whom 82% were female, whilst Ballindalloch Mills in Stirlingshire had 289 workers, of whom 79% were female.[37] Initially, mule spinning was under the control of highly paid male spinners, who were supported by children and female piecers. By the late nineteenth century, the Scottish industry was almost entirely feminised, with both spinning and weaving dominated by female labour.

Hand loom weaving had a higher proportion of male labour, with men doing the heavy weaving work and boys employed as drawboys and runners. However, power loom weaving, which began to take off in the 1830s, became an overwhelmingly female occupation as a result of employer pressure for cheaper and more 'docile' female labour, and male dislike of working in power loom factories. Accounts of the running battles to replace men by women in the weaving process are given in the Parliamentary Papers of the

1830s. There was even a trade union for female power loom weavers established in Glasgow in the 1830s. The finishing trades employed a higher proportion of men and boys, with the calico printers being regarded as a highly paid and male-dominated elite.

The cotton industry also reflected the changes in society in the west of Scotland as a result of growing immigration from Ireland, the Scottish Highlands and the Lowlands and the sectarian divide that began to develop between Catholic and Protestant. Migrant labour was a distinctive feature of the Scottish cotton industry, which enabled wages to be kept low in Glasgow and the west of Scotland. A significant proportion of the workforce was made up of Irish immigrants, both Catholic and Protestant, often with little formal education and low levels of literacy. Witnesses giving evidence to the Parliamentary Commissioners on the State of the Irish Poor testified that the Scottish cotton industry could not have developed without supplies of cheap labour from Ireland, partly because of the prejudices of native Scots against factory work.

Employers are the subject of Chapter 6. The Scottish cotton masters have been less well studied than the workers. The 'Tobacco Lords' were the subject of a classic study[38] but there has been less work on their successors, the cotton masters.[39] The cotton masters of Glasgow and Paisley shared a similar, well-established mercantile background with their Lancashire counterparts. Many of the wealthier ones had highly diversified interests and their wills and probate inventories describe them as merchants rather than cotton spinners or manufacturers. In addition to this, multiple partnerships in business were commoner in Scotland than in England.

The chapter examines the origins, education, religious background, political affiliations, business networks, wealth and landownership of the cotton masters, who played a seminal role in Scotland's early industrialisation. For most of this period, the family firm was the dominant form of business organisation, but towards the end of the nineteenth century limited liability companies began to emerge in cotton manufacturing, as in other sectors of Scottish business. The late nineteenth century was also marked by mergers and amalgamations, as firms sought to develop semi-monopolistic positions in products such as Turkey red dyeing, calico printing or cotton thread.[40]

The Conclusion sums up the contribution made by the cotton industry to the Scottish economy as a whole, its role as a 'secret spring' in putting in motion the early industrialisation of the country and the reasons for its premature decline.

Notes

1. Sir J. Sinclair (ed.) *[Old] Statistical Account of Scotland* (OSA) (Wakefield, 1973), VII, 828.

2. Mitchell Library, Glasgow (ML), Glasgow Chamber of Commerce Correspondence (GCC), William Sandeman to Gilbert Hamilton, 24 November 1784.
3. E. Hobsbawm, *Industry and Empire: From 1750 to the Present Day* (London, 1969), 56.
4. See N. F. R. Crafts, 'The Industrial Revolution', in R. Floud and D. McCloskey (eds), *The Economic History of Britain since 1700. Volume I, 1700–1860*, 2nd edition (Cambridge, 1994); S. D. Chapman, *The Cotton Industry in the Industrial Revolution*, 2nd edition (London, 1987); and W. W. Knox, *Industrial Nation: Work, Culture and Society in Scotland, 1800–Present* (Edinburgh, 1999).
5. P. Hudson (ed.), *Regions and Industries: A Perspective on the Industrial Revolution in Britain* (Cambridge, 1989); P. Hudson, *The Industrial Revolution* (London, 1992); and E. Richards, 'Margins of the Industrial Revolution', in P. O'Brien and R. Quinalt (eds), *The Industrial Revolution and British Society* (Cambridge, 1993).
6. M. B. Rose (ed.), *The Lancashire Cotton Industry: A History since 1700* (Preston, 1996).
7. W. W. Knox, *Hanging by a Thread: The Scottish Cotton Industry, c. 1850–1914* (Preston, 1995).
8. T. M. Devine, *The Scottish Nation* (London, 1999), 249 and 108, and the same author's, 'Industrialisation', in T. M. Devine, C. H. Lee and G. C. Peden (eds), *The Transformation of Scotland* (Edinburgh, 2005), 34.
9. C. A. Whatley, *Scottish Society, 1707–1830: Beyond Jacobitism, Towards Industrialisation* (Manchester, 2000), 223. See also the same author's, *The Industrial Revolution in Scotland* (Cambridge, 1997).
10. Knox, *Hanging by a Thread*.
11. I. Donnachie and G. Hewitt, *Historic New Lanark: The Dale and Owen Industrial Community since 1785* (Edinburgh, 1993).
12. A. J. Cooke, *Stanley: From Arkwright Village to Commuter Suburb, 1784–2003* (Perth, 2003).
13. I. Donnachie, *Robert Owen: Owen of New Lanark and New Harmony* (East Linton, 2000).
14. An extensive literature includes: P. Bolin-Hort, 'Managerial Strategies and Worker Responses: A New Perspective on the Decline of the Scottish Cotton Industry', *Journal of the Scottish Labour History Society*, 1994, XXIX, 63–83; J. Butt, 'The Scottish Cotton Industry during the Industrial Revolution, 1780–1840', in L. M. Cullen and T. C. Smout (eds), *Comparative Aspects of Scottish and Irish Social and Economic History, 1600–1900* (Edinburgh, 1977); J. Butt, 'Labour and Industrial Relations in the Scottish Cotton Industry during the Industrial Revolution', in J. Butt and K. Ponting (eds), *Scottish Textile History* (Aberdeen, 1987); J. Butt, 'The Industries of Glasgow', in W. H. Fraser and I. Maver (eds), *Glasgow. Volume II: 1830–1912* (Manchester, 1996); R. H. Campbell, 'The Making of the Industrial City', in T. M. Devine and G. Jackson (eds), *Glasgow. Volume I: Beginnings to 1830* (Manchester, 1995); S. D. Chapman and J. Butt, 'The Cotton Industry, 1775–1880', in C. H. Feinstein and S. Pollard (eds), *Studies in Capital Formation in the United Kingdom, 1750–1920* (Oxford, 1988); W. H. Fraser, 'The

Glasgow Cotton Spinners, 1837', in J. Butt and J. Ward (eds), *Scottish Themes* (Edinburgh, 1976); E. Gordon, *Women and the Labour Movement in Scotland, 1850–1914* (Oxford, 1991); W. Gordon, *Mill Girls and Strangers: Single Women's Independent Migration in England, Scotland and the United States, 1850–1881* (New York, 2002); N. Murray, *The Scottish Handloom Weavers, 1790–1850: A Social History* (Edinburgh, 1978), A. Slaven, *The Development of the West of Scotland, 1750–1960* (London, 1976); and J. T. Ward, 'Textile Trade Unionism in Nineteenth Century Scotland', in Butt and Ponting, *Scottish Textile History.*

15. See H. Hamilton, *An Economic History of Scotland in the Eighteenth Century* (Oxford, 1963) and *The Industrial Revolution in Scotland*, 2nd edition (London, 1966); T. C. Smout, *A History of the Scottish People, 1560–1830* (London, 1969) and *A Century of the Scottish People, 1830–1950* (London, 1986); R. H. Campbell, *Scotland since 1707: The Rise of an Industrial Society* (Oxford, 1971) and *The Rise and Fall of Scottish Industry, 1707–1939* (Edinburgh, 1980); S. G. E. Lythe and J. Butt, *An Economic History of Scotland, 1100–1939* (Glasgow, 1975); B. Lenman, *An Economic History of Modern Scotland, 1660–1976* (London, 1977); O. Checkland and S. G. Checkland, *Industry and Ethos: Scotland 1832–1914*, 2nd edition (Edinburgh, 1989); A. J. Cooke et al. (eds), *Modern Scottish History, 1707 to the Present*, 5 volumes (East Linton, 1998); Whatley, *Industrial Revolution in Scotland*; Whatley, *Scottish Society*; Devine, *Scottish Nation*; and Devine et al. *Transformation of Scotland.*
16. J. L. Carvel, *The Coltness Iron Company: A Study in Private Enterprise* (Edinburgh, 1948) and C. Brogan, *James Finlay and Company Ltd., 1750–1950* (Glasgow, 1951).
17. A. P. Wadsworth and J. L Mann, *The Cotton Trade and Industrial Lancashire, 1600–1780* (Manchester, 1931), 171.
18. A. Durie, *The Scottish Linen Industry in the Eighteenth Century* (Edinburgh, 1979); I. D. Whyte, *Scotland before the Industrial Revolution, c. 1050–c. 1750* (London, 1994) and *Scotland's Society and Economy in Transition, c. 1500–c. 1760* (London, 1997).
19. D. J. McLaren, *David Dale of New Lanark: A Bright Luminary to Scotland* (Glasgow, 1999); I. Donnachie, 'The Textile Industry in South West Scotland, 1750–1914', in Butt and Ponting, *Scottish Textile History*; and A. J. Cooke, 'Cotton and the Scottish Highland Clearances – Spinningdale, 1791–1806', *Textile History*, 1995, XXVI (1).
20. T. M. Devine, *The Tobacco Lords. A Study of the Tobacco Merchants of Glasgow and their Trading Activities c. 1740–1790* (Edinburgh, 1990), 45.
21. *OSA*, 1976, XIII, 165.
22. *OSA*, 1978, X, 490.
23. G. Penny, *Traditions of Perth* (Perth, 1836), 255–7; and Cooke, *Stanley*, 88.
24. Cooke, 'Spinningdale', 93.
25. Chapman, *Cotton Industry*, 54.
26. Quoted in Butt, 'Labour and Industrial Relations', 139.
27. C. H. Lee, *British Regional Employment Statistics, 1841–1971* (Cambridge, 1979).
28. M. B. Rose, *Firms, Networks and Business Values: The British and American Cotton Industries since 1750* (Cambridge, 2000), 103.

29. C. G. Brown, 'The Sunday School Movement in Scotland', *Records of the Scottish Church History Society*, 1995, XXI; and A. J. Cooke, *From Popular Enlightenment to Lifelong Learning: A History of Adult Education in Scotland, 1707–2005* (Leicester, 2006).
30. Whatley, *Scottish Society*, 222. See also S. M. Nisbet, 'The Rise of the Cotton Factory in Eighteenth Century Renfrewshire' (PhD thesis, Paisley, 2003).
31. ML, GCC Correspondence, 9 July 1784.
32. Brogan, *James Finlay.*
33. F. de Saint Fond, *A Journey through England and Scotland to the Hebrides in 1784* (revised Glasgow, 1907), 183.
34. A. E. Musson and E. Robinson, *Science and Technology in the Industrial Revolution* (Manchester, 1969); and Durie, *Scottish Linen Industry*, 103.
35. G. Macintosh, *Biographical Memoir of the late Charles Macintosh FRS by his son* (Glasgow, 1847); and A. Clow and N. Clow, *The Chemical Revolution: A Contribution to Social Technology* (London, 1952), 169.
36. M. Berg, *The Age of Manufactures, 1700–1820: Industry, Innovation and Work in Britain*, 2nd edition (London, 1994), 140.
37. *Parliamentary Papers* (*PP*), 1816, III, 17–19.
38. Devine, *Tobacco Lords.*
39. A. Slaven and S. G. Checkland (eds), *Dictionary of Scottish Business Biography, Volume I, The Staple Industries* (*DSBB*) (Aberdeen, 1986) only includes those who died after 1860.
40. *DSBB* and P. Payne, *British Entrepreneurship in the Nineteenth Century* (London, 1988).

1

Beginnings: the pre-history of the industry

> As the fertility of the land had given birth to the manufacture, so the progress of the manufacture re-acts upon the land and increases still further its fertility. (Adam Smith, *The Wealth of Nations*, 1776)

Introduction

Proto-industrialisation is a concept developed by historians to help explain the process of early industrialisation. It describes what was essentially a rural and regional phenomenon, where agriculture and industry operated in tandem, usually through family groups combining seasonal employment in agriculture with manufacturing work in the home. Typically, it involved textile manufacturing located in the countryside, often on hand-powered machinery in people's homes, but producing goods for the outside market and usually controlled by urban merchant capital in the form of 'putters out'. The linen industry in eighteenth-century Scotland displayed some of these characteristics but Whyte has argued that the late survival of monopoly privileges in royal burghs and burghs of barony meant that the commercial production of textiles and other commodities in Scotland was more urban in character than in many other European countries.[1] Moreover, more general ideas of 'economic backwardness' do not sit easily with the early development of banking and credit systems in Scotland, or of worldwide trading networks by Scots merchants in the second half of the eighteenth century.

The Scottish linen industry

At the beginning of the eighteenth century, the dominant manufacturing industry in Scotland was linen. It accounted for two-thirds of Scottish exports in 1700 and by the 1750s employed 180,000 women (66% of the adult female population) in preparing and spinning yarn. Although linen manufacture was found all over Scotland, there was a strong geographical concentration in two centres – Lanarkshire and Renfrewshire in the west, and Angus, Fife and Perthshire in the east. Within this distribution pattern, there was a marked degree of specialisation. The west of Scotland specialised in fine linens, the east in larger volumes of coarse fabrics. The linen industry received government support through the activities of the Board of Trustees for Fisheries and Manufactures in Scotland, established in 1727.[2]

Some of this money was used to improve the quality of Scottish linen, to increase its attraction to export markets. Annual premiums of 15s an acre were paid to encourage the sowing of hemp or flax seed. A system of quality control was set up, with local stamp masters being appointed to stamp linen of approved quality and two 'General Riding Officers' or Inspectors appointed, with a system of prosecution for those who broke the rules. Money was set aside 'for encouraging Schools for teaching children from the age of 8 years to that of 14 to spin'. There were prizes for the best models of looms and for the best cloth produced by housewives. There was also financial encouragement for bringing over foreign workmen and women to improve the quality of Scottish linen, and assistance for bleachfields and scutching mills, together with awards for new discoveries and improvements.[3]

In the 1720s, Daniel Defoe described Glasgow as 'the cleanest and beautifullest, and best built city in Britain, London excepted', with an active overseas trade and a thriving linen industry.[4] Glasgow specialised in fine linen muslins for sale to England, the Caribbean and North America:

> Here is a manufacture of muslins and perhaps the only manufacture of its kind in Britain, if not in Europe, and they make them so good and fine that great quantities of them are sent into England and sold there at a good price; they are generally striped and are very much used for aprons by the ladies, and sometimes in head-clothes by the English women of a meaner sort, and many of them are sent to the British plantations.[5]

Table 2 shows how the value of linen per yard produced in Lanarkshire and Renfrewshire consistently exceeded the value of that produced in the east of Scotland. With the arrival of the cotton industry in the 1780s, the fine linen trade in the west of Scotland went into a steep decline and it had virtually disappeared by 1822, whereas the coarse linen trade in Angus and Fife continued to grow to the end of the period. This shows the regional and non-linear character of industrialisation, where an important industry like linen could decline in one part of the country but continue to grow in another region.

Linen manufacture was also important in Lancashire, where in 1713 there were 60,000 people engaged in linen production.[6] Here, there was an obvious connection with the later development of cotton manufacturing, as south Lancashire specialised in the production of fustians, a mixture of cotton and linen yarns.[7] The Scottish connection with Lancashire went back well before the Act of Union. As early as 1621 there is a reference to the manufacture

Table 2 Linen stamped for sale in the leading Scottish producing counties, 1738–1822 (millions of yards)

				Percentage				Percentage	
	Angus	Fife	Perth	by volume	by value	Lanark	Renfrew	by volume	by value
1738	1.4	0.9	0.8	67.4	50.8	0.6	0.3	19.5	25.4
1768	4.4	1.5	1.1	59.8	21.5	1.9	0.7	22.0	39.7
1788	9.4	3.8	2.6	77.0	61.3	1.3	1.6	14.1	26.2
1822	22.6	7.9	1.6	88.6	77.8	0.0226	0.0257	0.1	0.3

Source: A. Warden, *The Linen Trade, Ancient and Modern, 1864*, 477–9.

of fustians in Lancashire from a mixture of cotton wool grown in Turkey and Scottish linen yarn. By 1682, Thomas Marsden of Bolton, Lancashire was dealing in cloth, including fustians, linen and woollen cloth, and in yarn, including deliveries to his agent, Hugh Pickering in Nether Darwin, Lancashire of 'Scotch or English yarn'.[8]

The manufacture of mixed linen and cotton goods in Scotland predated the Union of 1707. In Paisley, 'The manufacture of linen and linen mixed with cotton was begun before the union of the two nations, but at that time, was very inconsiderable.'[9] The *Edinburgh Courant* for September 1706 carried an advert by an Edinburgh shopkeeper, for a 'considerable Quantity of Cotton Yearn ready spun from the Indies, fit for making all sorts of Fustians, either Plain, Stripp'd or Raised, for Bed blankets and severall other Uses'.[10]

The trade in fine linen yarn from Scotland to England and Ireland expanded after the Union. In the 1730s, linen manufacturers in the west of Scotland protested about Irish merchants who 'buy up large quantities of our fine linen yarn in the west, as do the manufacturers of Manchester and Kendal yarn of a coarser staple in other parts which is a great loss to us'.[11] The Board of Trustees reported in 1733 that a good deal of Scottish linen yarn was bought for export to Ireland, which raised yarn prices for Scottish manufacturers but provided employment for 'the poorer sort of people'.[12] Twenty years later, about half of the linen yarn produced in Scotland went to the English market, principally Manchester. In 1755, William Sandeman of Luncarty complained that English demand was keeping the price of Scottish yarn so high that it was threatening the profitability of his cloth manufacture, 'upwards of half or even two thirds goes to the English Mercat'. By the late 1750s, manufacturers in the west of Scotland were mixing cotton with linen to 'ornament' their cloth, and when in 1759 the Irish put a high duty on imported linens with any cotton in them, the Scots complained of losing trade worth £50,000 a year.[13]

In both Lancashire and the west of Scotland the development of the linen industry was a precondition for the later development of cotton. In Scotland, the scutching or preparing of flax by hand had been replaced by a water-powered process, a more modest precursor of what was to happen later in cotton. The first water-powered lint mill in Scotland was built at Paisley in Renfrewshire in 1726.[14] By 1772, there were 252 water-powered lint mills throughout Scotland scutching flax mechanically, 29% of them in Perthshire.[15]

Another mechanical breakthrough came about in the linen thread trade, again in the textile stronghold of Renfrewshire. The manufacture of white thread was introduced by Mrs Millar of Bargarron, 'a gentlewoman', in 1722 on machinery brought from Holland. She had picked up the secrets of thread manufacture there, including the 'construction and management of the twisting and twining machines'. The young women in Bargarron were taught to spin fine linen yarn and Bargarron thread became well known. A Mr Pollock picked up on the secret through apprentices and assistants and founded the thread industry in Paisley.[16] This provided the foundation for the later cotton thread industry, in which Paisley became a world leader.

The process involved twisting several strands of fine linen into a strong thread. The original Dutch machine allowed 12 spindles of linen yarn to be spun simultaneously into thread by turning a crank. Like the later multiplication of spindles in cotton spinning, the number of spindles per thread-twisting machine gradually increased over time, by improved gearing, from 12 to 24 to 48. The machines were worked by girls but were hand powered by unskilled labourers turning cranks. Yet again, Renfrewshire saw the first breakthrough in applying water-power to a thread mill, at Kilbarchan in 1755. However, the process was slow to be adopted in Renfrewshire. Water-powered twist mills in Scotland increased from 200 in 1760 to 500 in the mid 1770s, but only about 20 of these were in Renfrewshire, which persisted with the hand-powered version.[17] In 1772, Thomas Pennant described the traveller walking through Paisley, 'to hear, at all seasons, as he passes along the streets, the industrious and agreeable notice of weavers' looms and twist mills', as well as seeing the fields around the town 'covered with cloths and threads' in the summer.[18] By 1780, Paisley had at least 120 thread mills, hand powered by 'mill drivers' or 'stout Highlanders' in shifts. Each machine spun 48 spindles of yarn and employed 12 people, a total of 1,440 thread workers in Paisley alone.[19]

Scottish linen workers, particularly those producing 'fancy' goods, were developing specialised skills, increasingly in demand in an international market. A contemporary boasted, 'so great is the ingenuity of our Paisley weavers, that nothing in their own branch is too hard for them'.[20] Similarly, Scottish linen merchants, bleachers and textile printers had developed a knowledge of workforce control, quality control, markets and specialised production techniques, which would stand them in good stead if and when they decided to switch to cotton. In the west of Scotland, strong links with Lancashire had developed through the linen trade, which meant that new inventions by Hargreaves, Arkwright and Crompton were relatively easily transferred north of the border.

With the Union of 1707, the rich London and colonial markets were opened up for Scottish goods, particularly textiles. As a contemporary explained:

> A free trade with England being opened . . . several of the traders went up to England to sell their Paisley manufactured goods, which yielded great profits, and turned well to their advantage, both by acquiring a more general knowledge of trade and settling a correspondence there, which was of great use to them afterwards when they came home, they thought of establishing other branches, to which they were the more encouraged, by having got several acquaintances and a correspondence settled in England.[21]

As early as 1710, Robert Lang, a Paisley textile manufacturer, was sending muslins and calicos to London and Europe, the latter through another Paisley merchant, Andrew Storie, based in Rotterdam, a major trading base for Scots merchants in Europe. By the 1760s, Kerr and Pollock of Paisley sold 40% of their goods directly to English customers and 40% to Paisley and Glasgow merchants. Working capital for Paisley textile firms was mainly through English bills of exchange. In 1760, more than 98% of working capital for Kerr, Pollock and Co. was provided by bills of exchange, most drawn on a single London agent, William Wight. Wight effectively provided banking facilities for Kerr and Pollock and also bought large amounts of textiles from them.[22]

Glasgow imported fine linen yarn from France and Holland and in 1761 the Board of Trustees complained that because the local supply of linen yarn was insufficient, Scottish manufacturers had to import large quantities from Hamburg, Flanders and other places abroad. Two years later, the Board reported that the woollen and cotton manufactures were gaining ground slowly and many were deserting the linen trade for these others, 'where by the want of regulations, they have a greater opportunity to employ their ingenuity in fraudulent practices'.[23] In 1768, Glasgow manufacturers 'brought over from France upwards of forty women, who are settled in Anderston, and are to be employed in spinning fine yarns'.[24] By 1773, the Board of Trustees noted the introduction of new kinds of manufacture, such as the making of gauzes and thread at Paisley and the growth in the spinning of silk, wool and cotton.[25]

The Glasgow linen trade was organised on proto-industrial or semi-capitalistic lines long before factory production made an appearance. Modest amounts of capital were required to enter the business. Most Glasgow weavers in industrial suburbs like Anderston operated as 'wee corks' (small linen manufacturers). They purchased linen yarn from families, then put it out for weaving by themselves, their journeymen or apprentices. The Anderston 'corks' couldn't afford to keep a warehouse or counting house in Glasgow and so met up in 'Pinkerton's pub opposite the Tron Steeple in the middle of the city to transact business over a gill and a "farl" of oaten cake'.[26] The typical 'wee cork' lived in some comfort:

> [he] generally had a comfortable house, with a small kail yard attached to it. His six loom shop was reared close to, and formed part of his dwelling house, and there, while he plied the shuttle himself, his journeymen, who occupied the other loomsteads of the shop, paid him a shilling a week rent for them; and if he took an apprentice for instruction, the earnings of such apprentices were equally divided between the master and the said apprentice.[27]

In mid eighteenth-century Glasgow:

> homesteads were so cheaply and easily acquired that every thrifty man by the exercise of ordinary diligence and thrift, might secure the room and kitchen, the six loom shop and the kail yard, the very pinnacle of a weaver's ambition; and thus sitting nominally rent free, he could demand his weekly shilling of rent for every loom occupied by his journeymen, and receive besides a profitable proportion of the earnings won by his active apprentices; and by furnishing them with home bought yarns, his profits enabled him to gradually add loom shop to loom shop, till his little factory had become a thriving business and he himself was on the fair way to independence.[28]

The leader of these Anderston linen weavers or 'wee corks' was James Monteith (born 1734), an active member of Secession churches in both Glasgow and Anderston, who diversified into importing linen yarn and bleaching. He was said to have been the first to 'put out' cotton yarn to be woven into pure cotton muslins in imitation of East India Company fabrics. The yarn came from India and was imported in globular balls like a bird's nest, hence it was known as 'Birds' Nest' yarn.[29] Monteith was one of the deputation who met Richard Arkwright on the latter's triumphal visit to Glasgow in 1784. Others in the group included James Finlay, Alexander M'Alpine, John Brown, David Dale, Robert Thomson, the two M'Ilquhan brothers, William Gillespie and 'a long list of wee Anderston corks'.[30]

James Monteith fathered a dynasty of cotton masters. His eldest son, John, founded a cotton weaving factory in Pollockshaws in 1801, 'the first power loom weaving factory in the west of Scotland', and his second son, also James, bought Blantyre cotton mills from David Dale in 1792. His third son, Henry (1765–1848), became a major player in the Scottish cotton industry, the owner of mills at Barrowfield and at Blantyre after his brother's death in 1802, Lord Provost of Glasgow and Tory MP for the Linlithgow burghs.[31]

The 'new' textiles introduced into Paisley in the early 1700s either used cotton or were imitations of cotton. Checks, a mixed cloth made of cotton and linen, were being manufactured as early as 1702.[32] Bengals were a fine lawn or muslin manufactured in imitation of Indian fabrics, which began to be produced in the Paisley area in 1710 and were well established by 1715.[33]

Another specialised luxury textile product introduced into Paisley was silk gauze weaving, established in 1759 by Humphrey Fulton (1713–1779). Fulton had begun as a packman, buying and selling linen yarn in Scotland and England, including the silk manufacturing quarter of Spitalfields in London. Eventually, he moved back to Scotland and settled down as a linen manufacturer in Beith, Ayrshire. He moved to Maxwelltown, an industrial suburb of Paisley, in 1749 to work as a linen weaver before switching to silk production.[34] By 1782, there were 18 silk manufacturers in Paisley, 6 belonging to London merchants, 12 to Paisley, although 8 of these had their own warehouses in London.[35] By the mid 1790s, the Paisley silk industry had secured considerable investment from London capital, attracted by cheap and skilled Scottish labour:

> The weavers found no difficulty in imitating the Spittalfields fabrics, and the manufacturer found it in his interest to push a business so favourably situated for cheapness of labour, compared with the metropolis of Great Britain. A company from London established a warehouse here for that branch in 1761 and several others soon after, composed of partners, some at Paisley, and others at London. This new manufacture gave sufficient room for the display of taste and genius in contriving new patterns. In this they succeeded beyond all expectation. Paisley silk gauzes became the fashionable wear through all the polite circles in Europe. The Spittalfields manufacturers were fairly outdone and the British gauzes were preferred at Paris, in opposition to the French manufacturers, by whom these fabrics were originally invented.[36]

Silk was a luxury product dependent on female fashion and high-quality design and on good distribution networks to affluent metropolitan markets outside Scotland. Because of this, Paisley silk merchants and manufacturers teamed up with London merchants and 'the gentlemen engaged in it had not only warehouses in London and Dublin, but they had correspondents upon the continent, and shops for vending their commodities even in Paris itself'.[37] For a time, silk manufacture became the dominant industry in Paisley, as shown in Table 3.

In 1784, the total value of manufactures in Paisley was estimated at £579,185, to which the manufacture of silk gauze contributed £350,000 (60%), the rest being made up lawns and thread gauzes (£164,385 or 28%) and thread (£64,800 or 11%). The silk industry employed about 10,000 people in the Paisley area, of whom about 5,000 were weavers. Other parts of the Paisley textile industry, including lawn weavers, spinners (7,384 or 45% of the total), machinery makers and bleachers employed some 16,484 people.[38] By

Table 3 Silk and linen looms in Paisley and its immediate area, 1776–1789

	1776	1781	1789
Silk looms	2,500	4,800	5,000
Linen or lawn looms	1,500	2,000	2,800
Total	4,000	6,800	7,800

Sources: 1776 and 1781 figures from R. Brown, *The History of Paisley*, 1886, Vol. II, 57, 1789 figures from *OSA*, 1973, VII, 835.

1787, linen, thread, silk and cotton were all manufactured in the Paisley area. Muslin weaving was at first wiped out by foreign competition. The trade then tried Bengals, a striped fabric made from a mixture of cotton and linen. This was superseded by check handkerchiefs for the English market and then by plain and figured thread gauze. There was a considerable pedlar trade with England, mainly conducted by Glasgow merchants who bought up Paisley goods to sell south of the border.[39]

The skills of west of Scotland spinners and weavers in fine linen and silks were relatively easily transferred to cotton, particularly the finer end of the trade. The same was true of Scottish linen dealers and merchants, some of whom began to move into the cotton industry. The best-known example is David Dale (1739–1806), who started his working life as a 'herd laddie' in Stewarton, Ayrshire and was then apprenticed as a weaver in Paisley. He became a packman who dealt in linen yarn, like Humphrey Fulton, buying small amounts locally from farmers' wives in Ayrshire and Lanarkshire.[40] It was claimed that 'the object of every packman's ambition ultimately was to become a settled shopkeeper or merchant in some commercial town'.[41]

Dale moved into Glasgow, opened a shop and diversified into importing yarn from the Low Countries. By 1783 he was rich enough to spend £6,000 building an Adam town house in Charlotte Street, Glasgow.[42] He founded the New Lanark mills and his other cotton spinning partnerships included Catrine in Ayrshire with Claude Alexander, Newton Stewart with Douglas and McCall, and Oban, Argyll.[43] At Stanley in Perthshire he was not a partner, but advanced substantial sums of money to the owner, James Craig, a Glasgow muslin manufacturer.[44]

Other Scottish textile merchants who became involved in the cotton industry included the Paisley thread manufacturers the brothers James and Patrick Clark. Like David Dale and Humphrey Fulton, they were migrants from Ayrshire. They began as weavers' wrights or furnishers, supplying silk to the silk weavers in Paisley. In 1806, with the disruption of supplies of silk from Hamburg during the war-time embargo, they began to develop the manufacture of cotton thread. They opened a small factory in Paisley employing 120 people, mainly Highlanders.[45] The founders of many other

Paisley cotton mills, the Carliles, Orrs, Browns and the Coats thread dynasty, all came from a similar background of involvement in existing linen or silk gauze trades. John Freeland was another linen manufacturer, who founded a cotton spinning mill in Houston, Renfrewshire.[46]

The Finlays were linen cloth dealers in Glasgow and Paisley before moving into yarn importing and exporting. They entered cotton in 1798, when Kirkman Finlay bought the Ballindalloch mills. Their relations the Buchanans had been 'English merchants' marketing Scottish linens through a network of pedlars or packmen. They acted as Arkwright's agents in Scotland, and the youthful Archibald Buchanan trained at the Cromford mills before going on to manage cotton mills at Deanston and Catrine.[47] In Glasgow, William Gillespie, linen and calico printer and yarn merchant, founded the North Woodside cotton spinning mills, eventually taken over by Henry Houldsworth, who moved from Manchester to manage them in 1799.[48] Most of Arkwright's Scottish partners, including William Sandeman at Stanley, Perthshire and Patrick Barron of Woodside, Aberdeen, had a background of linen dealing, bleaching or manufacturing.

The role of the Atlantic trade

The other major factor behind the development of the Scottish cotton industry was the role of Glasgow and other Clyde ports in the Atlantic trade with the American colonies, the Caribbean and Latin America. Daniel Defoe observed in the 1720s:

> Glasgow is a city of business, here is the face of trade, as well foreign as home trade; and I may say 'tis the only city in Scotland at this time that apparently increases and improves in both . . . as the Union opened the door to our American colonies, the Glasgow merchants presently fell in with the opportunity . . . I am assured that they send near fifty sail of ships every year to Virginia, New England and other English colonies in America and are every year increasing.[49]

Initially the trade was dominated by tobacco, which provided the wealth to build Glasgow's first merchant city and to purchase country estates for the most successful tobacco merchants. It also provided capital for investment in manufacturing industry in Scotland. At least nine cotton manufacturing concerns in Scotland, from Spinningdale in Sutherland to Balfron in Stirlingshire, Glasgow and Paisley, with a total insurance valuation of £59,100 in 1795, had between a third and a half of their capital provided by Glasgow colonial merchants.[50]

The tobacco trade gave Glasgow merchants access not only to capital but also to the extensive commercial networks, based on kinship and nationality, that Scots had built up in the New World. As early as 1728, James Colhoun and Company of Glasgow was trading in the ship *Neptune* to Boston in the American colonies. The ship's ledger listed mainly linen goods such as 'Brown Linen', 'Stript Holland', 'Bed Tyck' and 'plain fustian' as well as 'Bibles with Psalms' and 'Bibles without Psalms', but also included on 27 May 1728 four dozen cotton handkerchiefs valued at £6.16s and on 19 June two dozen valued at £2.12s.[51] Of course, these could have been manufactured somewhere other than the west of Scotland, possibly in Lancashire.

Another illustration of these networks is provided by John Semple, John Jamieson and James Lawson, Scottish merchants with bases in Glasgow and in Maryland in the American colonies. Between 1770 and 1774 they were dealing in tobacco and cotton goods to North America.[52] John Semple and James Lawson were brothers-in-law.[53] John McKenzie, a Glasgow merchant, traded in cotton and linen goods, including handkerchiefs, with England, Ireland, Philadelphia and Virginia from 1771 to 1776. He also dealt in madders (a red dyestuff) from Amsterdam.[54]

Thanks to the Atlantic trade, by the late eighteenth century Glasgow and the Clyde ports had overtaken Edinburgh and the ports of the Forth valley as the principal shipping centres in Scotland. By 1774, the two Clyde ports of Port Glasgow and Port Greenock owned some 32% of the entire Scottish merchant marine and 38% of ships engaged in foreign trade, compared with Leith/Bo'ness's share of 13% and 12% respectively. In the years 1771–1775, the two Clyde ports accounted for 33% of total shipping tonnage entering Scotland and 39.1% of tonnage clearing the country, compared with 18.9% and 18.3% for the two Forth ports.[55]

Early cotton manufacturing ventures

The earliest textile printing works in Scotland were for linen at Gorgie and Bonnington on the Water of Leith, close to the affluent Edinburgh market, which were operating in the 1720s, probably with English printers.[56] In the west of Scotland, textile printing began in 1732 in Blantyre, 30 years before it was introduced into Lancashire.[57] The Pollockshaws Printfield Company was founded around 1742 on the River Cart in Renfrewshire, on the southern edge of Glasgow. Its founder was Archibald Ingram 'at the head of a number of our American merchants'. The cloth printed was a mixture of cotton and linen yarn and the firm was obliged:

> to become the buyers of the cotton wool, give it out to spin, receive the produce in yarn for the wefts and the linen yarns for the warps were bought from the dealers in that article. The process of weaving came under a manager: the dye-stuffs, it is true, were bought at the first hand. The cloth was sent to the field for whitening by an unskilful bleacher. It was afterwards put under the care of a

> master printer, whose skill was annually acquired by stealth from the working printers in London, where the manager was supposed to resort in the winter and return to work in the spring, as full of information in his art as a London dancing master from Paris, with half a dozen of new lessons in his heels.[58]

Here the link between cotton manufacturing and overseas trade was explicit, as capital for the venture came from the Atlantic tobacco trade, in which Ingram played an important part. Archibald Ingram (1699–1770) served two terms as Lord Provost of Glasgow and was also involved in stocking and inkle (linen tape) manufacture.[59] He and his fellow merchants had easy access to imported raw cotton and to credit through shipping and commercial networks. Their involvement in the Atlantic trade also gave them insider knowledge of the eventual markets for the products of the Pollockshaws Printfield Company, mainly 'printed handkerchiefs for the English market, through the channel of a respectable class of men whose business was buying of Scots goods and selling them in the English markets and above all supplying the demands of our stores in Virginia, Maryland and the West Indies'.[60] Another theme that emerges from this account is the low initial skill levels of the Scottish workforce in bleaching and calico printing and the extent to which they were obliged to resort, often surreptitiously, to expertise only available south of the border.

Printed handkerchiefs were the main product of another early Glasgow printfield, at Dalsholm on the River Kelvin. This was the brainchild of William Stirling, a Glasgow merchant (died 1777) who formed a partnership to build the printfield in 1750. Like Archibald Ingram, William Stirling came from a well-established Glasgow merchant family who had made their fortune in the Atlantic trade.[61] His father, John, was Lord Provost of Glasgow in 1728, and William started out by selling printed cottons made from cloth manufactured in India and printed in London. In the *Glasgow Journal* of 10 May 1756, William advertised for sale in his warehouse, 'A neat parcel of printed Cottons of the newest pattern, lately imported from London, at and below first cost.' By March 1764, Stirling was advertising that at 'Dalehome Printfield near Glasgow there is printed all sorts of work upon linen and cotton cloth for gowns and furniture, by William Stirling and Co., merchants in Glasgow, who have engaged a man of character in the printing business lately in London; from which place he has brought this season a great variety of the newest and most fashionable prints'. The printed cotton was sold in shops all over the central belt of Scotland, including Greenock, Port Glasgow, Kilmarnock, Irvine, Ayr, Hamilton, Edinburgh, Falkirk, Perth, Paisley, and at the Glasgow warehouse.[62] This shows that female fashion played a crucial role in the Scottish cotton industry, that the home market was of great importance and within this, retail networks were of prime significance.[63]

William Stirling and Co. began by printing handkerchiefs, then moved on to printed cloth for garments and furniture. The handkerchiefs, on a blue background with a white spot, were known as 'blunks'. Stirling found labour too expensive so close to Glasgow and moved further out, to the River Leven, where he founded a village with its own church called Renton. Eventually the Vale of Leven became the most important textile-printing centre in Scotland.[64] The industry relied heavily on child labour and raised local living standards:

> The young women were taken from their spinning wheel and employed in pencilling the colours in the prints on the callicoes. The boys and girls were taken from idleness to the services of the printers. The wages of industry, diffused amongst a primitive people in this valley, uncorrupted in their manners, produced an immediate change in their dress, as well as their mode of living, for the better.[65]

Another early venture in cotton manufacturing took place in April 1754, when the Edinburgh manager of the British Linen Company reported to its London manager, William Todd, 'I have bought from Mr Shairp about £50 value of Jamaican cotton . . . Our Osnabrigg warehouse now being empty, I have brought in the cotton spinning mistress and her scholars into it and am setting them to work with the cotton bought from Mr Shairp.'[66] The account again shows the importance of the home market, dominated by female taste, for cotton fabrics, which suggests rising living standards, particularly in growing urban centres like Edinburgh:

> The Directors . . . have also introduced into this place the art of fineing and spinning cotton into yarn in a proper manner, a thing hardly if at all known here formerly. In this way a considerable number of people are kept constantly employed and the yarns made by them have been sold in England to advantage . . . the Directors . . . may themselves commence vizt of printing cottons, gowns and furniture, Checks, Stripes and Dimitys, great quantities whereof are in daily demand for home consumpt [67]

Shortly after this, cotton began to be imported into the Clyde. In January 1755, the Paisley merchant William Lang imported several hundred pounds of raw cotton on his own ship. Another Paisley merchant, Robert Allason, imported 2,000lbs of raw cotton from St Kitts to Port Glasgow in September 1755.[68] The *Glasgow Journal* of 4 December 1758 advertised the sale of 'Leeward Island cotton by the bag or in larger quantities' from Joseph Anigus' cellar in Bell's Wynd, Glasgow. The *Journal* advertised on 24 February 1765 regarding the sale of three bags of cotton, and another advert on 11 September 1766 offered seven bags of cotton for sale at the Carron Warehouse in Glasgow, brought from London in the ship *Glasgow* for the Carron Wharf.[69] By 1775, 503 bags of cotton per annum were coming into the Clyde.[70]

The impact of cotton manufacturing on the linen and silk industries

The decline in fine linen manufacture was closely linked to the rise of the cotton industry. In 1783, in Glasgow, 'Such efforts have been made and such perfection in the spinning of cotton and manufacturing of muslin that the branch now grows on a larger field than the original stem.'[71] In the Barony parish, Glasgow in 1791, there had been an almost complete switch in the past decade from the production of linen or cotton/linen combinations called 'blounks', made of linen warp and cotton weft, to pure cotton muslins. Two years later, the linen trade in Glasgow had declined as a result of the expansion of cotton, but was still important.[72]

At Strathaven in Lanarkshire, formerly a centre for spinning and manufacturing Dutch flax, 'the weavers are almost wholly employed by the Glasgow and Paisley manufacturers and cotton yarn is the principal material'.[73] In Paisley, the production of linen goods peaked in 1783–1784 at nearly two million yards, valued at £164,385. From this high point it fell in 1806–1807 to 660,346 yards, worth £27,771, and by 1809–1810 to 40,503 yards, worth a modest £4,833.[74]

In some places, it was the silk industry that was displaced by cotton manufacturing. In Dalry, Ayrshire, silk weaving had declined by the early 1790s and been supplanted by cotton weaving. There were now only 36 silk weavers and eight women preparing silk yarn, compared with 107 cotton weavers and 127 women and children who prepared the cotton yarn for the loom.[75] At Eaglesham in Renfrewshire, a large cotton spinning mill was built in 1791. There had been 63 silk weavers in Eaglesham but now there were only 33, who were mostly weaving cotton for Glasgow and Paisley manufacturers.[76]

The effects of the expansion of cotton manufacturing were felt far away from the west of Scotland. In Blair Atholl, in Highland Perthshire, in 1791 the linen industry 'has already felt the baleful effects of the cotton manufactures, the materials of which are brought from afar and by which few gain in proportion'.[77] Some years earlier, a memorandum entitled 'Considerations on the Cotton Manufacture', which may have been written by William Sandeman, had been sent to the Duke of Atholl. Although undated, the memorandum refers to the invention of Crompton's spinning mule and so must date from after 1779. It warned:

> I know but two means by which the Linen Manufacturers can escape being ruined by the rapid progress of the cotton Manufacture, one is the Invention of a means of spinning Linen yarn by Machines. Mr. Arkwright is said to have discovered the art of doing so. But he is too old and too rich to prosecute an uncertain and laborious discovery. The other is for the Linen Manufacturers to betake themselves to the Manufacturing of Cotton . . . The more quietly this is undertaken the better chance it has to succeed. Little should be said until we

> are fully possessed of every Machine whether for weaving or spinning that is known and used anywhere else.[78]

These twin themes, of the threat posed to Scotland's traditional textile industries by the 'new' fibre and the response of borrowing heavily (and secretively) from English technology, provide some of the themes for the next chapter.

Notes

1. I. D. Whyte, 'Proto-industrialisation in Scotland', in P. Hudson (ed.), *Regions and Industries: A Perspective on the Industrial Revolution in Britain* (Cambridge, 1989), 234. See also L. A. Clarkson, 'Proto-Industrialisation: The First Phase of Industrialisation?', in L. A. Clarkson (ed.), *The Industrial Revolution: A Compendium* (London, 1990); P. Hudson, *The Industrial Revolution* (London, 1992); M. Berg, *The Age of Manufactures, 1700–1820: Industry, Innovation and Work in Britain*, 2nd edition (London, 1994) and C. A. Whatley, *Scottish Society, 1707–1830: Beyond Jacobitism, Towards Industrialisation* (Manchester, 2000).
2. A. Warden, *The Linen Trade, Ancient and Modern* (London, 1864), 445; and I. D. Whyte, *Scotland before the Industrial Revolution, c. 1050–c. 1750* (London, 1995), 302. See also Whatley, *Scottish Society.*
3. Warden, *Linen Trade* and A. J. Durie, *The Scottish Linen Industry in the Eighteenth Century* (Edinburgh, 1979).
4. D. Defoe, *A Tour through the Whole Island of Great Britain* (reprinted London, 1971), 605.
5. Defoe, *Tour*, 607.
6. G. W. Daniels, *The Early English Cotton Industry with Some Unpublished Letters of Samuel Crompton* (Manchester, 1920), 9.
7. S. D. Chapman, *The Cotton Industry in the Industrial Revolution*, 2nd edition (London, 1987), 11.
8. A. P. Wadsworth and J. L. Mann, *The Cotton Trade and Industrial Lancashire, 1600–1780* (Manchester, 1931), 15 and 83.
9. W. Carlile, *A New Description of Paisley* (Paisley, 1787), 34.
10. *Edinburgh Courant*, 6–9 September 1706. My thanks to an anonymous referee for this reference.
11. Durie, *Scottish Linen Industry*, 39.
12. Warden, *Linen Trade*, 450.
13. Durie, *Scottish Linen Industry*, 155–7 and 67.
14. R. Brown, *The History of Paisley* (Paisley, 1886), Vol. II, 398.
15. Warden, *Linen Trade*, 455 and N. E. McLain, 'Scottish Lint Mills, 1729–1770', *Textile History*, 1970, I.
16. *OSA*, 1973, VII, 676–7 and 825–5 and W. Carlile, 'Sketches of Paisley', *Scots Magazine and Edinburgh Literary Miscellany* (Edinburgh, July 1806), 35.
17. S. M. Nisbet, 'The Rise of the Cotton Factory in Eighteenth Century Renfrewshire' (Paisley, PhD, 2003), 68–9.

18. T. Pennant, *A Tour in Scotland and Voyage to the Hebrides, 1772* (reprinted Edinburgh, 1998).
19. Nisbet, 'Cotton Factory'.
20. G. Crawford (rev. Semple), *History of the Shire of Renfrewshire* (Paisley, 1772), 313.
21. *Ibid.*, 311.
22. Nisbet, 'Cotton Factory', 42 and 51–5.
23. Warden, *Linen Trade*, 453–4.
24. R. Reid (Senex), *Glasgow Past and Present* (Glasgow, 1858), 343.
25. Warden, *Linen Trade*, 455.
26. G. Stewart, *Curiosities of Glasgow Citizenship* (Glasgow, 1881), 101.
27. Reid, *Glasgow Past and Present* (1858), 316.
28. Stewart, *Curiosities*, 96.
29. R. Reid (Senex), *Glasgow Past and Present* (Glasgow, 1884), Vol. III, 374.
30. Reid, *Glasgow Past and Present* (1858), 302.
31. Stewart, *Curiosities*, 111–15.
32. J. Gibson, *The History of Glasgow* (Glasgow, 1777), 239.
33. G. Crawford (rev. Semple), *Renfrewshire*, 311 and J. Wilson, *A General View of the Agriculture of Renfrewshire* (Paisley, 1812), 329.
34. A. Brown, *A History of Glasgow and of Paisley, Greenock and Port Glasgow* (Glasgow, 1795), Vol. II, 245–6 and Brown, *History of Paisley*, Vol. II, 56.
35. G. Crawford (rev. Semple), *Renfrewshire*, 313.
36. Brown, *History of Glasgow*, Vol. II, 245–6.
37. *OSA*, 1973, VII, 826–7.
38. Brown, *History of Glasgow*, Vol. II, 247.
39. *OSA*, 1973, VII, 825–6.
40. D. McLaren, *David Dale of New Lanark, A Bright Luminary to Scotland* (Glasgow, 1999).
41. T. Clarke and T. Dickson, 'Class and Class Consciousness in Early Industrial Capitalism, Paisley, 1770–1850', in T. Dickson (ed.), *Capital and Class in Scotland* (Edinburgh, 1982), 30.
42. A. Slaven, *The Development of the West of Scotland, 1750–1960* (London, 1976), 89.
43. McLaren, *David Dale*.
44. A. J. Cooke, *Stanley: From Arkwright Village to Commuter Suburb, 1784-2003* (Perth, 2003), 74.
45. M. McCarthy, *A Social Geography of Paisley* (Paisley, 1969), 65–6.
46. Slaven, *West of Scotland*, 90.
47. *Ibid.*
48. H. Hamilton, *The Industrial Revolution in Scotland* (2nd edition, London, 1966), 128–9.
49. Defoe, *Tour*, 606.
50. T. M. Devine, *The Tobacco Lords. A Study of the Tobacco Merchants of Glasgow and their Trading Activities c. 1740–1790* (Edinburgh, 1990), 45.
51. National Archives of Scotland, Edinburgh (NAS), Court of Session Papers (CS) 96/3814.

52. NAS, CS 96/1203.
53. Devine, *Tobacco Lords*, 181.
54. NAS, CS 96/3176, fos 1–2.
55. G. Jackson, 'Scottish Shipping, 1775–1805', in P. L. Cottrell and D. H. Aldcroft (eds), *Shipping, Trade and Commerce. Essays in Memory of Ralph Davis* (Leicester, 1981), 124–5.
56. J. Shaw, *Water Power in Scotland, 1550–1830* (Edinburgh, 1984), 343.
57. G. Turnbull, *A History of the Calico Printing Industry of Great Britain* (Altrincham, 1951), 23 and 90.
58. Brown, *History of Glasgow*, II, 212–13.
59. Devine, *Tobacco Lords*, 181.
60. Brown, *History of Glasgow*, II, 213–14.
61. Devine, *Tobacco Lords*, 39.
62. Reid, *Glasgow Past and Present* (1884), III, 374.
63. See S. Nenadic, 'The Rise of the Urban Middle Classes', in T. M. Devine and N. Mitchison (eds), *People and Society in Scotland. Volume I, 1760–1830* (Edinburgh, 1988); B. Lemire, *Fashion's Favourite: The Cotton Trade and the Consumer in Britain, 1660–1800* (Oxford, 1991); and S. Levitt, 'Clothing', in M. B. Rose (ed.), *The Lancashire Cotton Industry: A History since 1700* (Preston, 1996).
64. J. Hume, *Industrial Archaeology of Glasgow* (Glasgow, 1974), 43.
65. Brown, *History of Glasgow*, II, 215.
66. A. J. Durie (ed.), *The British Linen Company, 1745–1775* (Edinburgh, 1996), 60.
67. *Ibid.*, 88.
68. Nisbet, 'Cotton Factory', 58.
69. Reid, *Glasgow Past and Present* (1884), III, 370–1.
70. *OSA*, 1973, VII, 293.
71. Brown, *History of Glasgow*, II, 53.
72. *OSA*, 1973, VII, 341 and 296.
73. *OSA*, 1973, VII, 6.
74. Wilson, *Renfrewshire*, 74.
75. *OSA*, 1982, VI, 157–8.
76. *OSA*, 1973, VII, 640–1.
77. *OSA*, 1977, XII, 103.
78. Blair Castle, Perthshire, Atholl Mss. 25/XI, 1, Memorandum on the Cotton Industry, undated.

2

The expansion of the industry, 1778–1830

> The minds of men were excited to new enterprises; a new genius, as it were, had descended upon the earth, and there was an erect and outlooking spirit abroad that was not to be satisfied with the taciturn regularity of ancient affairs. (John Galt, *Annals of the Parish*, 1821)

Introduction

One of the earliest studies of industrialisation in Scotland emphasised that 'the study of the Industrial Revolution in Scotland must be regional in character.[1] Increasingly, historians have recognised that 'a regional perspective is more important for studying the Industrial Revolution than, perhaps, almost any other period in British history' and have stressed the importance of regional specialisation.[2] The Scottish cotton industry was always heavily regionalised and became increasingly concentrated in the west of Scotland – particularly Glasgow, Renfrewshire and Paisley. The area enjoyed a number of advantages – a skilled workforce, plentiful supplies of cheap labour from Ireland and the Highlands, good resources of water power and later of coal, easy access to raw cotton imports from the New World via the Clyde ports, and a prosperous merchant class in Glasgow and Paisley with worldwide trading links.

Founders and proprietors – the role of the state and the English connection

The earliest water-powered cotton spinning mills in Scotland developed on rural sites outside the major urban centres. In 1786, Glasgow Chamber of Commerce claimed that the industry had arisen 'without public aid', in contrast to the linen industry, which was supported and regulated by the Board of Trustees for Manufactures, as outlined in Chapter 1.[3] However, this was misleading, as in 1774 the Board had set up a committee to investigate carding and spinning machines for cotton. This was in response to Peter Brotherstone, an Englishman who had written to the Board with details of a carding machine which he had invented. In 1774, the Board appointed Brotherstone to manage a new cotton spinning school in Edinburgh with 12 spinning machines, and asked him to make carding and spinning machines. Brotherstone's spinning machine was advertised in the Scottish press in 1780 and displayed by the Board in Edinburgh.[4]

Peter Brotherstone and the Board were both involved in the first water-powered spinning mill to be established in Scotland, at Penicuik in Midlothian. In 1776, Brotherstone formed a partnership with the Edinburgh bankers Bertram, Gardner and Company and feued land from Sir James Clerk of Penicuik.[5] The site was below the waulk (fulling) mill of Penicuik and by July 1778 the Company had set up a cotton mill with water-powered carding, roving (twisting) and spinning machinery. Arkwright tried to have the Penicuik mill shut down for infringing his patent, but the Board of Trustees supported Brotherstone and took legal advice from the Lord Advocate, who ruled that the patent did not extend to Scotland.[6] The mill was built 'under the inspection and direction' of James Hackett, a former employee of Arkwright and an acquaintance of James Hargreaves.[7] It was this mill that the Duke of Atholl visited when the Stanley mills were being planned on his estates. In December 1784, one of the Stanley partners, George Dempster, MP, wrote to another partner, Robert Graham of Fintry, 'I hope his Grace [Atholl] will find leisure to take a look at the Cotton Mill at Penny-Cook, Bertram and Co. would wait on his Grace there.' The ducal visit evidently took place, as a week later Dempster wrote, 'I am also happy you and the D of A have seen with your own Eyes the wonder of Art at the Cotton Mill.'[8] By 1793, the Penicuik mill was employing 500 people.[9]

The second cotton spinning mill to be built in Scotland, at Rothesay on Bute, was also promoted by someone with close links with the Board of Trustees and with their financial support. Robert Oliphant, a Commissioner for the Board and for the Earl of Bute, offered the Rothesay site to a group of Sheffield entrepreneurs who were looking for a water-powered site in Scotland.[10] The land at Rothesay was leased 'on very liberal terms' from the Earl of Bute. In 1778, an English engineer had planned 'the buildings, water courses, dams and machinery for a large spinning manufactory to be erected above the town, where the mills for beating lint formerly stood'.[11] However, the site was poorly chosen, being too remote, too sparsely populated and with unreliable water supplies:

> The situation of this mill had been injudiciously chosen by the original company . . . in a place where there was neither access to a sufficiently plentiful supply of water, nor to a sufficiently populous neighbourhood, where young persons could be had, at small wages, to perform the numerous inferior operations of the manufacturer. The company were also obliged to carry all the mechanics, of whom a great many are necessary, from Glasgow and to prevail on them by exorbitant wages to settle in Bute.[12]

In December 1778, two of the partners withdrew from the mills, whereupon the remaining partner, James Kenyon, had 'the address to buy off from about Arkwright's works some men who were known to understand the construction and making of machinery'.[13] Kenyon carried out trials on water frames in the old lint mill at Rothesay before building his spinning mill. Like Brotherstone at Penicuik, he was threatened with patent infringement by Arkwright, but had the benefit of the Lord Advocate's ruling and received a premium of 20 guineas from the Board.[14] Kenyon entered into partnership with a group of Glasgow merchants in 1781, but the mills struggled to survive and were offered for sale in 1785, reaching a knock-down price of £1,500 from the original asking price of £4,500.[15] The involvement of people like Brotherstone, Hackett and Kenyon with the two earliest spinning mills in Scotland formed part of a more general 'English invasion', as at least 14 individuals active in the Scottish cotton industry between 1779 and 1795 'were associated directly or indirectly with English practice'.[16]

The industry grew with astonishing rapidity. Whatley has argued that the speed of industrial transformation was faster in Scotland than in England, so that 'whatever doubts there may be about the applicability of the term "Industrial Revolution" in England, arguably, there are fewer in Scotland's case'.[17] The history of the cotton industry supports this view. The Penicuik and Rothesay mills were followed by a rash of mill building in Renfrewshire, mostly in the Cart Basin, which had rich water-power resources. In 1778, mills were built at Barrhead in Neilston and at Busby on the Water of Cart.[18] The founder of the Busby mill was William Ferguson, a linen draper with a 'Scotch cloth shop' at Glasgow Green. Another Renfrewshire mill was at Dovecotehall on the River Levern, the result of a partnership of three Glasgow merchants and three Lancastrians, including John Churdsley, a merchant from Preston, and two brothers, Jonathan and William Haugh. It was alleged that the manager, Jonathan Haugh, had acquired his technical knowledge by spying on an English water frame mill.[19]

In 1782, a large mill of six stories was built at Johnstone in Renfrewshire. It was rescued from failure by Robert Burns, a native of Paisley.[20] Burns was a significant figure. In 1812, some years after his death, he was named in the Court of Session as the man who, 'as every cotton spinner in the West of Scotland knows', introduced cotton spinning into the west of Scotland, 'according to Sir Richard Arkwright's methods'.[21]

The Arkwright connection

Against this background, the involvement of Richard Arkwright in the Scottish cotton industry appears rather more complex than the 'razor to shave Manchester' explanation given by contemporaries[22] and looks more like a defensive operation to stop Scottish infringement of his patent. In a number of early Scottish cotton mills, the technical expertise came from Arkwright's former workmen, with or without his knowledge and consent. Inevitably, some turned out to be charlatans. A Glasgow cotton spinner, in the 1830s, claimed: 'Many of those who had been employed in the works of Arkwright, left his service, pretending to a knowledge of the business which they did not possess; and those men were eagerly sought after by new adventurers in the manufacture in both the kingdoms.'[23]

In October 1784, celebrations took place in Glasgow in which key roles were played by Arkwright and George Dempster, MP for the Perth burghs. They were entertained by the Lord Provost at his house in Kelvingrove, and Arkwright received the freedom of the city. The *Glasgow Mercury* described the scene:

> The manufacturers of Anderston, through which they had to pass, in order to testify their gratitude to Mr. Dempster, the patron of manufactures in Scotland, and their esteem for Mr. Arkwright, assembled their workmen to receive them. On their arrival, the workmen wanted to unyoke the horses from Mr. Dempster's carriage in order to draw him to Kelvin Grove. This honour he declined, as it has been his uniform wish and practice to lead his countrymen to freedom, rather than put them under the yoke. Mr. Arkwright however was forced to comply with their offer and the cavalcade proceeded in a triumphant fashion to the Lord Provost's country seat.[24]

This was the highlight of a triumphant Scottish tour for Richard Arkwright. At Paisley, on 29 September 1784, he was created a Free Burgess, 'for his good deeds done and to be done for the utility of the Burgh'. On 4 October, he was presented with a Lanark burgess ticket for his involvement at New Lanark. Finally, on 27 October, he arrived in Perth, where the magistrates presented him with the freedom of the burgh for his part in the planning of Stanley mills.[25]

Why was Arkwright interested in Scotland and why were the Scots so eager to secure his involvement in the local cotton industry? The answers lie in two areas – firstly Arkwright's hostility towards his English competitors, who were challenging his patent rights in the English courts, and secondly, the fear of Scottish linen merchants and manufacturers of being left behind by the rapidly expanding English cotton industry. Baines explained Arkwright's involvement in Scotland:

> The Lancashire spinners were indeed Arkwright's great enemies. Owing partly perhaps to his humble origin and partly to the doubt whether he was the author of the inventions, 'he had no honour in his own country' . . . He therefore favoured the Scotch spinners as much as possible and formed a partnership with David Dale Esq of Lanark mills; in allusion of which and probably by way

of retorting the unworthy taunts of his opponents, relative to his former occupation, he said that 'he would find a razor in Scotland to shave Manchester'.[26]

This is confirmed by the Perthshire bleacher, William Sandeman, who travelled south in 1784 to 'look into the Cotton Manufactures in Lancashire'. Writing from Nottingham to Gilbert Hamilton, of Glasgow Chamber of Commerce, in November 1784, Sandeman regretted: 'Mr. Arkwright does not stand so high in esteem with many in his own Country as his Merit deserves I have had access to See both Sides.' Sandeman also thought that the recent junkets and honours in Scotland had created envy and unease amongst Arkwright's English competitors.[27]

The link between Arkwright and Scotland was provided by George Dempster, MP, who came across Cromford mills whilst stopping to take the waters at Matlock Bath, Derbyshire on his way home from Parliament. Dempster described how Arkwright:

offered to assist me in establishing a cotton mill in Scotland, by holding a share of one and instructing the people. Private business carried him the following summer to Scotland, where he visited Perth, Glasgow and Lanark and I believe Stanley, for I was not then in Scotland. Mr Dale and I became partners in mills to be erected in Lanark. A company of five or six Perth gentlemen, he and I, entered into partnership in mills to be built at Stanley in Perthshire . . . Sir Richard instructed Mr Dale's artists and young children gratis, as he did those sent from Stanley.[28]

Once Arkwright had been introduced to Scotland, he was careful, in choosing partners for his cotton spinning ventures, to include someone with proven expertise in textile manufacture. David Dale supplied this expertise in the west of Scotland, along with merchants and manufacturers such as James Monteith of Anderston and James Finlay.[29] In the east, expertise was provided by William Sandeman, who had founded Luncarty bleachfield, Perthshire as early as 1752.[30] Sandeman, with the Duke of Atholl and a weaver called George Penny, who had pioneered the manufacture of cotton muslins in Perth, met Arkwright in the King's Arms Inn, Perth to plan Stanley.[31] Further north, on Donside on the edge of Aberdeen, Patrick Barron, an Aberdeen merchant and the local landowner, entered into partnership with other Aberdeen merchants in 1775 for a printfield and bleachfield for linen. One of the partners, Alexander Milne, became friendly with Arkwright and in 1785 they agreed to build a cotton mill at Woodside and for Arkwright to train the Aberdeen workers at Cromford.[32]

Industrial training for Scottish workers at Cromford was a crucial part of the 'Arkwright invasion' of Scotland. At New Lanark, 11 men and 15 boys dressed in 'complete dresses of brown cloth, with red collars to their coats' were sent to Cromford in 1785 to learn cotton spinning.[33] The Contract of

Co Partnership for Stanley Mills, Perthshire referred to 'Sundry Indentures with different persons to be sent to the said Richard Arkwright at Cromford aforesaid to be taught the construction and making of the Machinery used by him in preparing and Spining of the said [cotton] wool itself.'[34] The arrival of the Perthshire trainees, 'with bagpipes and other music playing', in Cromford in May 1785 caused a stir and they celebrated with 'a dance in the evening to congratulate each other on the performance of so long a journey'.[35]

Arkwright also provided training at Cromford for managers. Andrew Keay, the first manager at Stanley, spent time there and wrote to William Sandeman in June 1785 that the boys who had left Perth 'Monday sennight' had not yet arrived and that the Stanley Company would have to wait until Arkwright's return from London to finalise water power arrangements.[36] Keay died at Stanley on 28 October 1787.[37] He was succeeded by David MacVicar, another Perth merchant, and in November 1789 Arkwright offered instruction at Cromford for MacVicar.[38]

More significant for the Scottish cotton industry as a whole was the management and technical training provided at Cromford for the teenage Archibald Buchanan. He was one of five brothers, the sons of James Buchanan, a small farmer from Carston, Stirlingshire. Archibald's older brothers, George and John, were Arkwright's first agents for the sale of his cotton twist in Scotland, having been involved (somewhat unsuccessfully) in cotton spinning in Glasgow since 1776. Archibald himself was apprenticed as a wright to Bogle, Edmiston and Young in Glasgow and was only 15 when he met Arkwright during his triumphal visit to Glasgow in October 1784. He spent 18 months at Cromford and stayed with the Arkwright family in their house, The Rock. When he returned from Cromford in 1787, Archibald, at the age of 18, was made manager of the Deanston mills in Perthshire built by his brother John.[39] Over a career spanning almost 50 years, Archibald Buchanan managed cotton mills at Deanston, Ballindalloch in Stirlingshire and Catrine in Ayrshire, where he became resident and managing partner He also trained James Smith, who became resident partner at Deanston.[40]

Arkwright was also involved with the mills at Catrine, Ayrshire. They were founded in 1786 by David Dale and Claude Alexander, who had returned from the service of the East India Company to take over the Ballochmyle estate.[41] Arkwright's millwright, Thomas Lowe, installed four large water wheels at Catrine and Arkwright was also involved in supplying spinning machinery to the mills. On 7 April 1788, a letter from Glasgow to Claude Alexander advised: 'I have received a letter from Sir Richard Arkwright advising me that he had sent off 2 Boxes containing Plates wheels and rollers for 2 spinning frames 48 spindles directed for me at Mauchline by Dumfries. You will please to send to the house in Mauchline where the Carlile Carrier puts up and desire them to leave the Boxes that have this direction lest they carry them to Glasgow.'[42]

Aristocratic and landed involvement

Another key element in the expansion of the Scottish cotton industry was the active support of the landed classes. This was vital, as Scottish landowners not only had access to the necessary land for industrial development, including water rights on rivers such as the Ayr, the Cart, the Clyde, the Don, the Tay and the Teith, but also were key opinion formers and controlled most of the machinery of government. Some contemporaries thought this support took place at the expense of the traditional creator of wealth – agriculture. The Rev. Mr John Monteith, minister of Neilston in Renfrewshire, complained in 1791:

> it appears at present to be the wish of the landholders, in the western districts of Scotland, to give every possible encouragement to all types of manufactures, nay, such is the rage for them in this parish, that corn mills are despised or forgotten, even by their proprietors.[43]

Aristocratic and landed support for the cotton industry was found over most areas of Scotland amongst large and small landowners, both rich and impoverished. Geographically, this ranged widely from south-west Scotland, including places like Gatehouse of Fleet in Kirkcudbrightshire, where James Murray let land to the Yorkshire cotton firm of Birtwhistle, to Spinningdale on the Dornoch Firth in Sutherland, on the Highland estate of George Dempster, MP, a shareholder in Stanley mills, Perthshire.[44] Significantly, the Earl of Selkirk refused permission for a cotton mill on his estate at Kirkcudbright for fear that 'his mansion might be disgraced by the vicinity of an establishment of manufacturing industry'. However, another local landowner, James Murray at Gatehouse of Fleet, had no such qualms. He not only granted the Birtwhistles a lease of land on the River Fleet but even held shares in their joint stock company.[45]

Most of the large water-powered spinning mills in Scotland were built with landed support, whether of Sir James Clerk of Penicuik at Scotland's first cotton mill, the Earl of Bute at Rothesay, Robert Macqueen, Lord Braxfield (who became Lord Justice Clerk) at New Lanark, Claude Alexander (a former paymaster in the East India Company) at Catrine, Ayrshire, or John, the fourth Duke of Atholl at Stanley, Perthshire. Unlike the Earl of Selkirk, Lord Braxfield was said to have no fears that 'the privacy of his demesnes would be invaded' by the construction of New Lanark.[46] Stanley Mills, Perthshire lay at the far southern edge of the extensive Atholl estates, so there was little chance that the mills here would intrude on the Duke's privacy in faraway Blair Atholl.

In Stirlingshire, the cotton mills at Ballindalloch were promoted by the Glasgow tobacco merchant and landowner Robert Dunmore, 'in whom were united the activity of the country gentleman and the liberality of the merchant'. Dunmore introduced a colony of cotton weavers into the area in 1789 and built a cotton mill on the Water of Endrick the next year. By 1792, there were 105 substantial new houses, built of stone and roofed with slate, in the village of Balfron.[47] Dunmore was a partner in numerous business enterprises, including Ballindalloch Cotton Company, Endrick Printfield Company, Pollockshaws Printfield Company, Spinningdale Cotton Company, Port Glasgow Sugar House, Dalnottar Iron Company and Muirkirk Iron Company. He went bankrupt in 1797.[48] In Kirkintilloch, Dunbartonshire, the local minister reported in 1790 that 'Mr Stirling, Younger of Glovat, a gentleman of distinguished public spirit, lately erected a small cotton mill. Hand machines, for spinning cotton were at the same time introduced.' The owner of the cotton mills was Gloria Folsom, Stirling's wife.[49]

Village planning was fashionable amongst Scottish landowners, reflecting an Enlightenment-inspired desire to impose their will on the landscape. It implied a rejection of the past and a desire for rational improvement and profit. Planned villages were associated particularly with agricultural improvement but were also founded as 'new' fishing villages, villages to encourage rural industries and factory villages.[50] Between 1770 and 1799, 164 planned villages were built in Scotland, followed by another 119 in the next two decades.[51] One of the earliest was at Ormiston, East Lothian, where the landowner John Cockburn laid down strict building regulations.[52]. Laurencekirk in Kincardineshire was planned by Lord Gardenstone along similar lines, to encourage rural industries such as 'bleachfields, a printfield, linen workers, stocking knitters, cabinet makers, smiths and other sorts of country tradesmen'.[53]

Other village planners included the Angus laird George Dempster, MP. In 1788, he laid out a planned village at Letham on his Dunnichen estate, which began to acquire numbers of small tradesmen and hand loom linen weavers.[54] Dempster was involved in cotton mills at Spinningdale on his Skibo estate in Sutherland, where in 1794, 'the weavers instructed at the cotton works begin to remove to their parents' houses with their looms and a little beginning is actually made towards converting Sutherland into a Lancashire'.[55] He was also a partner in Stanley Mills, Perthshire, where John, fourth Duke of Atholl, kept strict control over village planning. All houses in Stanley had to be of the same height and no dung or rubbish was to be left in the street.[56]

Similar aristocratic intervention took place in the west of Scotland at Eaglesham, Renfrewshire, where the Earl of Eglinton demolished the old village in 1769 and rebuilt on 999-year feus. By 1782, Eaglesham had 68 houses and 50 looms, and a cotton spinning mill was built in 1791.[57] The Earl laid down specifications for the development, which resulted in:

> two rows of elegantly built houses, all of freestone, with a large space between, laid out in fine green fields, interspersed with trees, with a fine gurgling streamlet running down the middle . . . Towards the higher end and on the rivulet, the cotton mill stands.[58]

Elsewhere in Renfrewshire, George Houston of Johnstone feued off land for a new town at Johnstone in the early 1780s. This ambitious scheme involved a main street running east to west, 40 feet wide and 750 yards long. By October 1782, nine houses had been built, two more were being completed and a further 42 sites had been feued off.[59] This became the setting for one of the largest cotton mills in Scotland, in which George Houston, a landowner with a Glasgow merchant background, was one of three partners.[60] A contemporary remarked:

> it may well be considered that this town will be of very great service to the workmen at the cotton mill, especially in lodgings, vegetables etc., on the other hand, the mill will be of great service to the said town by employing a number of their boys and girls who must otherwise be idle for some time.[61]

Paternalism and the factory village

Some of these aristocratic and paternalistic attitudes were adopted by some of the middle-class merchants and manufacturers who began to emerge as the dominant players in the Scottish cotton industry. David Dale at New Lanark was praised as 'the benevolent father of a numerous family and a bright luminary to Scotland'.[62] Dale's religious beliefs seem to have been the main inspiration for his paternalism. His son-in-law, Robert Owen, testified that Dale was 'the pastor of upwards of forty churches or congregations, dissenters from the Church of Scotland'.[63] This type of religious belief also heavily influenced paternalistic management approaches by some English cotton manufacturers, particularly in the rural factory villages of Cheshire and Derbyshire. Arkwright's partner at Cromford, Jedediah Strutt (1726–1797) came from a dissenting, probably Presbyterian, family from Alfreton, Derbyshire, whilst Samuel Greg of Quarrybank Mill, Cheshire was a prominent Nonconformist born in Belfast.[64]

At Catrine in Ayrshire, in partnership with Claude Alexander, Dale was concerned with the quality of workers' housing and keen to learn from the example of Stanley, Perthshire. He wrote to Alexander in February 1787, 'The Stanley Company have no plans of their houses they have sent the dimensions of some of them but we shall be very little wiser thereby but there will be no difficultie getting proper plans.'[65] Alexander was praised for providing

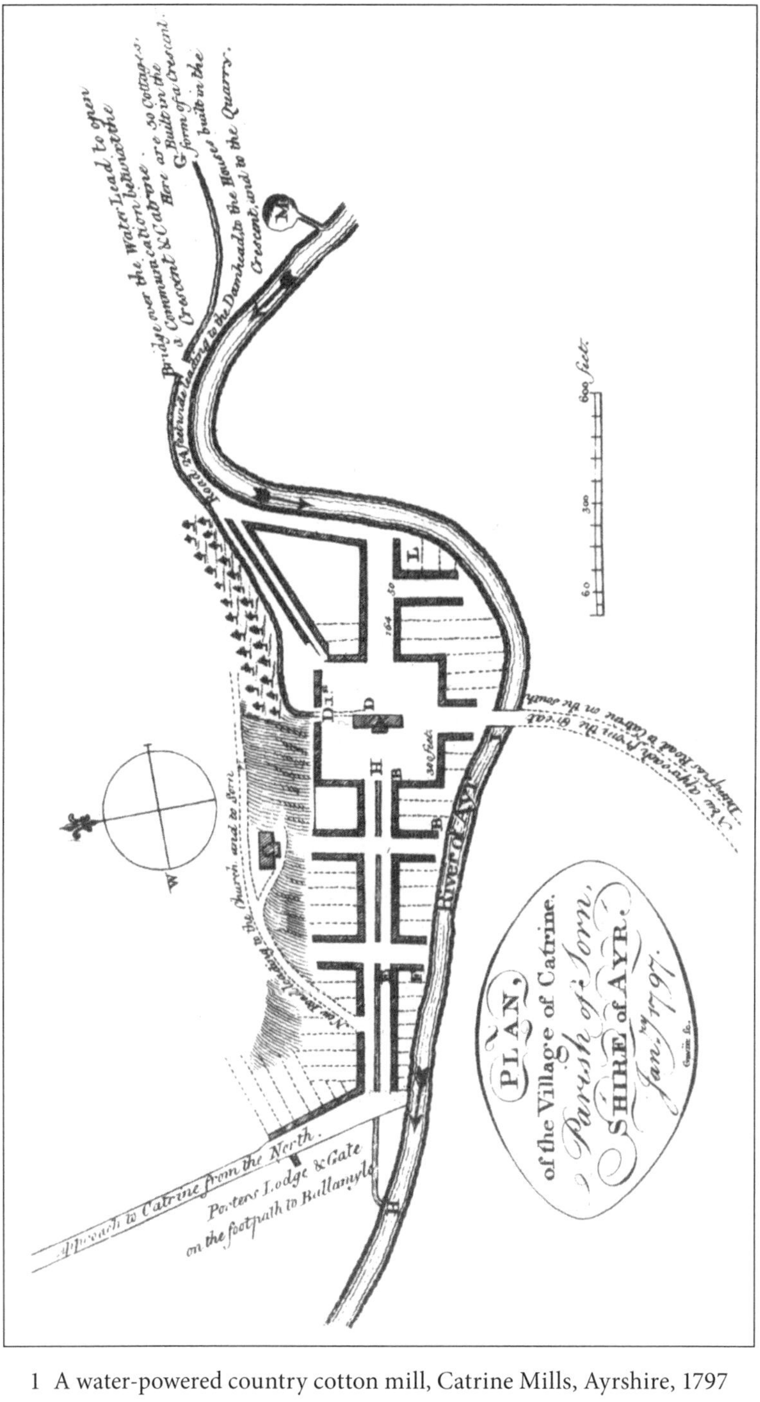

1 A water-powered country cotton mill, Catrine Mills, Ayrshire, 1797

15 to 25 acres of ground for gardens for the workers at Catrine, where people could grow potatoes, and for encouraging villagers to keep their own milking cows.[66]

As Scotland was a Calvinist country, there was a commitment to educate all children to read the Bible, and some embarrassment about lower levels of literacy amongst young factory workers. In 1816, at Catrine, Ayrshire, the Company employed a schoolmaster at a salary of £36 a year plus a house. This teacher taught an evening school and a Sunday-school. All the Scottish children could read before they were 10, but the Irish children were recommended to attend school.[67] Robert Owen criticised his father-in-law's educational provision at New Lanark, saying that long working hours under Dale's ownership were detrimental to the health and development of the factory children, particularly if they had begun work at an early age, 'their limbs were very generally deformed, their growth was stunted and . . . in general they made but a very slow progress, even in learning the common alphabet'. Owen claimed to have reconciled the humane treatment of his workforce with economic efficiency. As a result of the excellent schooling provided for their children at New Lanark, parents were willing 'to work at much lower wages'.[68]

Mill owners were also concerned about easy access to alcohol by workers, and its effects on morale and productivity. Claude Alexander was praised for his efforts to reduce whisky consumption at Catrine by founding a brewery in the village. The local minister reported:

> A brewery was built in the year 1793, by the proprietor of the village and let to a very respectable gentleman in Kilmarnock, with a view to introduce malt liquor in place of whisky, which has so baneful effect on the morals of the people. It gives me great pleasure to add that this benevolent scheme has, in a great degree, answered its purpose; for nearly 500 bolls of malt are brewed annually.[69]

In 1793, 'a great proportion' of the New Lanark population were Highlanders, who were 'naturally generous, hospitable and fond of strangers, which induces them sometimes to make free with the bottle; but drunkenness, among the better class of inhabitants, is of late rather unusual. It is less so among the other inhabitants; but on the whole, they are a decent and orderly people.'[70] This was due to management strategies at New Lanark, where 'pot and public houses were gradually removed from the immediate vicinity of their dwellings'.[71] Similar employer attitudes existed at Blantyre, Lanarkshire, where Henry Monteith, Bogle and Co. controlled the sale of liquor by buying taverns and closing them down. Only one public house had survived and that was strictly regulated by being closed at 11.00 p.m. every night and all day on Sundays. No sales of liquor were allowed during working hours.[72]

These paternalistic attitudes were characteristic of the early water-powered country mills but began to change rapidly with the growth of the cotton industry in larger and more anonymous urban centres such as Paisley and, above all, Glasgow. It was impossible to impose restrictions on alcohol sales in Paisley or Glasgow, where the cotton industry came to be concentrated. In 1792, in Govan parish, where a steam-powered cotton mill had recently been built, some 1,500 gallons of whisky were consumed in the village (total parish population 5,800) in a single quarter of the year.[73] Similarly, educational provision by cotton firms, widespread in the rural factory villages, was much less common in the large urban mills of Paisley and Glasgow. Henry Houldsworth, who owned spinning mills at Anderston and Woodside, Glasgow, was challenged by the Parliamentary Select Committee on the State of Children Employed in Manufactures to explain why 28% of 250 children in his mills couldn't read. Houldsworth replied that these illiterate children were mainly recent recruits from Ireland.[74]

One way of providing basic education for the children and young people who were flooding into Glasgow and Paisley seeking work was through the Sunday-school movement, which began to take off in Glasgow from November 1787, when Glasgow town council, in cooperation with the General Session and private citizens, set up eight Sunday-schools for 400 boys.[75] Paisley also had Sunday-schools, from 1797 onwards, 'to counteract the baneful effects arising from want of education', and by 1805, 30 were in existence under the auspices of the Paisley Sunday School Society. In the same year, there were 1,200 pupils attending three evening schools in the burgh.[76] Sunday-schools were seen as vital in meeting the challenge of irreligion, illiteracy and worse amongst a rapidly growing, young and rootless population: 'an antidote must be provided against the violation of the day of rest . . . vice must be discountenanced and open profanity discouraged'.[77]

Expansion and its effects

Contemporaries quickly began to grasp the significance of the rapid expansion of cotton manufacturing in Scotland. Galt's *Annals of the Parish*, published in 1821, described the impact of a water-powered cotton mill built in 1788 in the fictional Ayrshire parish of Dalmailing. The fictional mill (modelled on Catrine Mills) was built on the Brawl Burn and financed by 'Mr. Cayenne', a Virginia planter. The quotation at the head of this chapter suggests that it was seen as a destabilising influence, its impact as much social and cultural as economic.

The upheaval of industrialisation in Britain was accompanied by the impact of political revolutions in America and France. The Paisley radical, Arthur Sneddon, who had started as a 10-year-old piecer in the Underwood cotton mills and became a cotton hand loom weaver, remembered this period with affection: 'The minds of men were everywhere at this period under a strong excitement, and enquiry and investigation and novelty were the order of the day.'[78]

Elsewhere in the west of Scotland, at Neilston, Renfrewshire in 1791, 'There is great speculation in the cotton business at present', whilst, 'Paisley Port Glasgow and Greenock are daily increasing; new villages, cotton and spinning mills constantly building'. In Glasgow, in 1793, 'cotton mills, bleachfields and printfields have been erected on almost all the streams in the neighbourhood', although even then the industry couldn't keep up with the local demand for cotton yarn, so that 'a considerable quantity is still daily brought from England'.[79] George Penny, a Perth weaver, journalist and local historian, remembered the excitement of the 1780s, when he was a young man and his father was a muslin weaver in Perth:

> Various fabrics were by times introduced in the cotton line. As the trade was at first very prosperous, a manufacturing mania seemed to pervade society. Every gentleman who had a second son of the requisite age, put him apprentice to the loom . . . Such was the demand that not a herd boy could be found in the country, all flew to the loom.[80]

The growth of the cotton industry benefited other sectors of the economy, particularly agriculture. At Blantyre, Lanarkshire in 1791, the cotton mills created a market for agricultural products, particularly potatoes, whilst in Carmichael parish, 'The establishment of cotton works at Lanark and Douglas has brought ready markets for butter, cheese and grain', which formerly had to go over 30 miles to market in Edinburgh and Glasgow. The mills had also increased the demand for local coal.[81] Similarly in Ayrshire, the mills at Catrine benefited local farmers, who, 'instead of being obliged, as formerly to carry the product of their farms to Kilmarnock or Ayr at the distance of 12 or 14 miles, find a ready and an equally advantageous market for it at their own doors . . . Butter-milk and whey, which were before the commencement of the cotton trade here of little use now bring ready money to the farmer. In this view, manufactures must prove highly beneficial to the public and to the husbandman in particular.'[82] In Killearn parish in Stirlingshire, the growth of neighbouring Balfron, where there was a newly built cotton mill, provided an important market for local farmers.[83] This suggests rising living standards brought about by industrialisation.

Markets

Rising living standards also created a robust and expanding domestic market for cotton goods. The expansion of the cotton industry at the expense of fine linen manufacture was due to changing fashions and consumer tastes, as the price of cotton goods fell and cotton displaced linen and wool as the clothing of the masses. In the Borders woollen town of Melrose, 'cotton is found both more cleanly and more profitable than either woollen or linen'.[84] At Mains of Fintry, a parish with nine bleachfields on the edge of Dundee, there had been a shift in fashion by 1790 from wool and linen to cotton, 'cotton vests are common' and 'cotton and thread stockings are worn by both sexes, masters and servants' in place of the former woollen stockings.[85] This suggests rising living standards amongst all classes. As Berg has argued, 'We must seek for the origins of the Industrial Revolution not just in women's labour, but in women's wants and desires.'[86]

As well as the domestic market, another major market for Scottish cotton goods was England, where by 1785 there had been a major shift in taste and fashion, driven by female consumers from lower down the social scale:

> A handsome cotton gown was not attainable by women in humble circumstances and thence the cottons were mixed with linen yarns to make reduce their price. But now cotton yarn is cheaper than linen yarn and cotton goods are very much used in place of cambrics, lawns and other expensive fabrics of flax: and they have almost totally superseded the silks. Women of all ranks, from the highest to the lowest, are clothed in British manufactures of cotton, from the muslin cap on the crown of the head to cotton stockings under the sole of the foot. The ingenuity of the calico printers has kept pace with the ingenuity of the weavers and others concerned in the preceding stages of the manufacture, and produced patterns of printed goods which for elegance of drawing, far exceed anything that was imported; and for durability of colour, generally stand the washing so well as to appear fresh and new every time they are washed, and give an air of neatness and cleanliness to the wearer beyond the elegance of silk in the first freshness of its transitory lustre. But even the most elegant prints are excelled by the superior beauty and virgin quality of the muslins, the growth and manufacture of the British dominions.[87]

The dominant role of the London market, and the way in which it was driven by female fashion, were noted by a Scottish muslin weaver, writing in 1788: 'As the muslin trade depends principally on fancy goods, it is absolutely necessary that the manufacturers go to London to see Fashions and to get new patterns. It is necessary that they be on the spot themselves to see which way the whims of the moment point, and be enabled to form new things that will hit the varying taste of the times.'[88] Twenty years later, a Paisley weaver remarked ruefully, 'The fancy trade is not a monopoly. It shifts with every wind of fashion.'[89] The truth of his remarks was brutally confirmed in the Paisley depression of the early 1840s and in the later history of the Scottish cotton industry.

Table 4 Andrew Brown's valuation of the cotton industry in Scotland, 1791

Description	Capital	Costs	Employ-ment	Output
39 Water-powered mills @ £10,000	£390,000			
1,200 Jennies @ £6	£7,200			
600 Mules @ £30	£18,000			
Housing for last two	£75,000			
Total capital in buildings/ machinery	£490,200			
Employment of men, women and children in above			25,000	
Total annual wages bill for above		£500,000		
Raw cotton (4,629,043 lbs @ 2s a lb.)		£462,904		
Value of Scottish yarn				£1,256,412
Value of English yarn into Scotland		£520,000		
Weaving and all charges		£592,137		
Weavers			38,815	
Women for winding warp and weft			12,938	
Printing and King's duty, tambouring and needlework		£840,000		
Tambourers and needle decoration for muslin, women and children			105,000	
Total employment in cotton (excluding bleaching and finishing)			181,753	

Source: A. Brown, *History of Glasgow and of Paisley, Greenock and Port Glasgow, 1795*, III, 239–244.

Mills, workers and capital

By 1791, only 13 years after the first mill at Penicuik, there were 39 water-powered cotton mills in Scotland valued on average at £10,000 each, a total of £390,000 (Table 4). These mills housed 124,800 spindles on water frames, averaging 3,200 per mill. There were also 1,200 jennies with an average of 84 spindles each and 600 mules with an average 144 spindles each, making an

Table 5 Sun Fire Office insurance valuations of Scottish cotton mills, c. 1795, grouped by region

Region	Number of firms	Total valuation	Average valuation
Glasgow	11	£35,500	£3,227
Lanarkshire	6	£30,850	£5,140
Paisley	11	£44,300	£4,027
Renfrewshire	12	£53,550	£4,462
Fife	5	£28,180	£5,636
Perthshire	3	£26,200	£8,730
Aberdeenshire	2	£15,600	£7,800
Others	17	£97,050	£5,708
Total	67	£331,230	£4,943

Source: Adapted from S. G. E. Lythe and J. Butt, *An Economic History of Scotland, 1100–1939*, 1975, 187.

additional 187,200 spindles, an overall total of 312,000 spindles. Although about 75% of spindles were producing finer yarn, the value of coarse yarn in Scotland was higher, because three times as much coarse yarn was produced as fine. The total value of coarser cotton warp and weft (counts averaging No. 25) in Scotland was £710,411 and of fine yarn (counts averaging No. 75) £546,000.[90]

Table 4 is revealing of the composition of the workforce and the balance between factory workers and outworkers. In 1791, only 14% of the Scottish workforce in cotton worked in factories (spinning mills) – 25,000 men, women and children, out of a total of 181,753. They were greatly outnumbered by those who worked outside factories, either in their homes or in small workshops. Outworkers such as weavers, women winding warp and weft, and women and girls embroidering muslins (tambouring) made up 86% of the workforce. Indeed, the scattered female workforce in tambouring made up 58% of the cotton workforce, although many only worked part time.

Brown's figures on the amount of capital in the Scottish cotton industry have been challenged by modern scholars, using insurance valuations. According to one calculation, by 1795 there were 55 water-powered cotton spinning mills in Scotland, with an average valuation of £5,300, rather than the £10,000 quoted by Brown. Only three Scottish mills were valued over £10,000 for insurance purposes in 1795. New Lanark was easily the largest, with an insurance valuation of £24,400, followed by Stanley at £10,500 and Ballindalloch at £10,300.[91] A later calculation, reproduced in Table 5, examined the number of cotton firms in Scotland, grouped by region, together with their insurance valuations.

Chapman constructed a typology of early cotton spinning mills in Britain based on evidence from insurance valuations, and found three main types. The most basic were small factories housing carding machines, spinning jennies and mules, driven by hand or horse power. Many were probably too small to trouble the insurance companies. Their valuation could be as little as £1,000 if they were horse driven but could rise to around £2,000 for later, steam-powered examples (Type A). Most of the cotton mills featuring in Scottish insurance valuations in the mid 1790s were of the second type, the water-powered preparing and spinning mill three or four stories high, housing about 1,000 spindles. The mill was typically 70 to 80 feet long and 25 to 30 feet wide and was valued at around £3,000 for insurance (Type B1). A later and larger variant might be twice the length and twice the productive capacity and be valued in the region of £5,000 (Type B2). Finally, towards the end of the eighteenth century came the taller and typically steam-powered mills valued in the region of £10,000 for insurance purposes (Type C).[92]

The reality in Scotland and the rest of the UK was more complicated than this. Many cotton manufactories took over existing buildings, such as water-powered corn or flax mills or even houses. In Kilwinning parish in Ayrshire in 1792, two houses had been filled with 12 mules and 16 jennies, and in Dalry, one house contained 15 mules and there was 'a small carding mill, which goes by water'. In Dundonald, Ayrshire, there was a cotton mill employing 30 people and 'The carding machines are turned by a horse'.[93] In East Kilbride, Lanarkshire, a cotton mill was built in 1783 employing about 60 people, where the yarn was 'all spun on plain or rolling jeanies', whilst in 1791 in Douglas parish, Lanarkshire, a Glasgow company had built a small cotton spinning and weaving work where 'The carding is performed by horses and the spinning by hand jeanies.' In Cambuslang, Lanarkshire, a cotton mill had been built in Flemington in 1787. It contained water-powered carding machines and 17 jennies and employed 'some 50 people, old and young'.[94]

Many hand looms were housed in homes or in hand loom workshops housing six or eight looms. Even when the power loom made its appearance, technical arrangements could appear somewhat primitive. The first power looms in Glasgow were introduced in 1793 by James Lewis Robertson of Dunblane, 'who bought a couple of looms from the [convict] hulks and brought them to Glasgow, when they were fitted up and wrought in a cellar in Argyle Street. He removed the driving bar and employed a large Newfoundland dog, walking in a drum or cylinder, to drive the looms.'[95] Given that the workshop was situated in Argyle Street, this may have been more of a marketing device than a realistic technical solution.

The use of insurance valuations also raises the question of how accurate they were. For example, the New Lanark valuation of £24,400 in 1795 should be compared to the price of £60,000 paid for the mills in 1800 by Robert

Table 6 Raw cotton imported into Great Britain in 1789

Area of origin	Weight in pounds
British settlements (West Indies)	9,998,986
French settlements	6,143,623
Brazil	4,755,635
Turkey	4,668,231
East Indies	2,101,104
Other countries	4,542,316
Total	32,209,895

Source: R. Reid (Senex), *Glasgow Past and Present*, 1884 edition, Volume III, 369–370.

Owen.[96] At Stanley, the 1796 valuation of £10,500 seems more accurate, considering the price of £4,600 paid by James Craig in 1801 after one of the two mills had burnt down.[97] The Rothesay cotton mills on Bute cost £4,892 to build in 1778 but only realised £1,500 when they were sold seven years later, despite being valued at £4,475. By 1795 they were valued for insurance purposes at £4,800.[98] Because the cotton industry was both cyclical and speculative, much depended on the state of trade when mills were put up for sale. It was claimed in 1800 that 'nine out of ten of the cotton mills that have come to a public sale in this country, have not brought above one fourth of their cost'.[99]

One estimate for Scotland as a whole was that the insurance figures represented an undervaluation 'at a rate which varied widely, but usually amounted to less than half the true value'.[100] This would suggest that the figures supplied by Brown were reasonably accurate. Certainly, his estimates include the costs of spinning by jennies and mules, which are not included in the insurance figures, which apply only to water frames. They also include an estimate of weaving costs and labour and of the costs of printing and tambouring. They do not include the (considerable) capital costs of bleaching and printing, which a modern estimate has put at £80,000 in 1790 and £160,000 in 1795. Capital investment in Turkey red dyeing and other yarn and thread dyeing in the same period has been estimated at £40,000.[101]

Raw cotton supplies and yarn markets

The expansion of the industry required much greater supplies of raw cotton, which were increasingly supplied by new growing countries. By 1789, imports of raw cotton into Britain had risen to 32,209,895lbs (Table 6). The West Indies and South America dominated cotton imports, with the British West Indies providing some 31% of total cotton imports into Britain. In the same year

Table 7 Bags of cotton held in British ports, December 1791

Port	Bags
Liverpool	29,500
London	29,000
Manchester	10,000
Glasgow	3,000
Bristol	2,000
Lancaster	1,200

Source: M. E. Edwards, *The Growth of the British Cotton Trade, 1780–1815*, 1967, 109

Scotland imported 1,700,000 lbs of raw cotton from the British West Indies.[102] The West Indies and North America also provided an important export market for Scottish manufactured cotton cloth. In the last decade of the eighteenth century, Scottish exports to the West Indies and North America increased nearly ten times, from 4,800 yards to 4,500,000 yards of cloth.[103]

Scottish business records are very fragmentary for the late eighteenth century, but in December 1791 the Adelphi Cotton Works at Deanston in Perthshire was supplied with raw cotton from the Company's Glasgow warehouse, including two bales of Indian cotton valued at £178 15s 8d and two bales of Pernambuco (Brazilian) cotton valued at £35 5s 8d.[104] A weigh book for an anonymous cotton merchant dated 1791–3 revealed that cotton from the East Indies, Bourbon, Brazil and Pernambuco was received from Liverpool, Manchester and London.[105]

The Scottish cotton industry was smaller in scale than the industry in Lancashire. This is revealed by figures for the import of raw cotton into Scottish and English ports. However, these figures underestimate the size of the Scottish industry, as raw cotton was often bought in both Liverpool and London by Scottish manufacturers, and Lancashire yarn was routinely brought in for Scottish weavers. In 1791, some 29% of cotton yarn used in Scotland was brought in from England.[106] Because of this and because the Lancashire industry was much larger than the Scottish cotton industry, the yarn market in Scotland was heavily influenced by Manchester prices. The dominance of the English industry over that in Scotland is shown in Table 7, which shows import figures for raw cotton held by each port in Britain in December 1791, calculated by an anonymous Liverpool merchant.

The two largest cotton spinning firms in Manchester were M'Connel and Kennedy, and Adam and George Murray. Both these firms were founded by Kirkcudbright-born Scots – James M'Connel and John Kennedy, Adam and George Murray – who had been apprenticed in machine making, at Leigh in Lancashire, to William Cannan, another Kirkcudbright-born man. Both firms retained strong Scottish connections and M'Connel and Kennedy in particular specialised in the finer counts of yarn, from 100 upwards, which they sold principally to the Glasgow and Paisley markets. From 1795, they employed John Sinclair as an agent in Glasgow, selling yarn at a commission of 5%, for which he had to take the risk for the payment of all debts. On their behalf Sinclair sold Mule and India Twist, as well as Dutch Twist and Weft. In 1796, he sold 1,220lbs of yarn for £693 0s 9d net. In the same year, Robert Kennedy, the brother of John Kennedy, was selling yarn for M'Connel and Kennedy in Glasgow.[107]

The Scottish yarn market was sufficiently important to some Lancashire spinning firms for it to be worthwhile for them to attempt to fix prices there. In 1803, two of the largest cotton spinners in Lancashire, Benjamin Gray and Adam and George Murray, agreed to sell yarns at a uniform price in the Scottish market. This was followed by an agreement in November 1807 between the two Manchester firms M'Connel and Kennedy and John Houldsworth to sell at agreed minimum prices in Glasgow and Paisley, although each firm remained nervous of the other. However, the market was very price sensitive both ways, and M'Connel and Kennedy kept a close eye on the yarn prices of their Scottish competitors. When yarn prices in Manchester went up and those in Glasgow stayed the same they wrote to their Glasgow agent, Robert Kennedy, in July 1809, 'If things continue in this way a few days longer and you don't raise your prices, we are certain that some of our Manchester weavers and exporters will go to Glasgow to get what they want.'[108]

By the early 1790s, American cotton had begun to feature in British import figures. Robert Owen was the first manufacturer in Britain to spin American Sea Island cotton, in Peter Drinkwater's Bank Top Mill in Manchester in 1792–1794. One of the first customers for Owen's fine Sea Island yarn was James Craig, a Glasgow muslin merchant, who later owned Stanley mills, Perthshire.[109] There was a huge expansion of cotton production in the southern United States from the mid 1790s onwards, reflecting increasing demand from British and European manufacturers, the vast acreage of cheap land available for cotton growing, the invention of the cotton gin by Eli Whitney in 1793, and the growth of slave labour to pick and process the cotton.[110] Table 8 shows the growth of cotton exports from the USA in the period 1791–1806

By the early nineteenth century, supplies of raw cotton were coming into Scotland from a wider variety of sources. At New Lanark, in 1802–1803, Owen was using raw cotton from places such as Georgia, New Orleans, Trinidad, Jamaica, Granada and Guadeloupe. He kept meticulous records to measure the input of raw cotton into each mill against the output of yarn and the associated costs of labour, storage, repairs etc.[111] Between 1801 and 1811, Owen also bought raw cotton for Stanley Mills, Perthshire on the Glasgow markets,

Table 8 Exports of raw cotton (in lbs) from the USA, 1791–1806

Year	Quantity	Year	Quantity
1791	189,316	1799	9,532,268
1792	138,328	1800	17,789,603
1793	487,600	1801	20,911,201
1794	1,601,700	1802	27,501,075
1795	6,276,300	1803	41,105,623
1796	6,106,729	1804	38,118,041
1797	3,788,429	1805	40,383,491
1798	9,360,005	1806	37,491,282

Source: E. Baines, *History of the Cotton Manufacture in Great Britain*, 1835, 302.

Table 9 Imports of raw cotton into the Clyde, 1775–1810

Year	Bags	lbs
1775	503	137,160
1790	6,509	1,757,504
1804–1810[a]	31,364	8,468,832

(*Note:* [a] Annual average)

Source: J. Wilson, *General View of the Agriculture of Renfrewshire*, 1812, 251.

including Georgia, New Orleans, Brazils, Pernambuco, Orinoco, Demerara, Trinidad and Carriacou (British West Indies).[112] The French Wars meant that cotton supplies and the demand for manufactured cotton goods were subject to unpredictable fluctuations. In December 1803, Owen wrote to James Craig at Stanley, 'There is never any Brasils and no Demerara in the Market, the Island is the most plentiful and cheapest. Demeraras and Americas are expected in about two months, and the price of cotton is likely to rise till then. If War continues, we cannot expect lower prices. The spinning trade was never worse and many are losing money.' [113] In the years 1807–1809, James Eadie, a Glasgow cotton spinner, was also using cotton from a wide variety of sources, including Berbice, Brazil, Demerara, Georgia and Narenham.[114]

The finer and more expensive type of cotton brought into Scotland was the long stapled, which included American Sea Island, Brazilian, Demerara, West Indian and Egyptian. The cheaper, shorter-stapled cotton included that grown in the US interior, such as Upland or Bowed Georgia, New Orleans and Alabama, and East Indian cotton such as Bengal, Madras and Surat.[115] Table 9 shows the growth of raw cotton imports into the Clyde:

Table 10 shows the increasing importance of American raw cotton imports into the Clyde in the years 1810 and 1811. In 1810, American cotton amounted to 41% of total Clyde cotton imports and in 1811 to 46%.

Table 10 Origins of raw cotton imports into the Clyde, 1810–1811

	Bags	
Origin	**1810**	**1811**
America	21,828	19,868
Brazil	1,827	3,170
Demerara	10,255	5,136
West Indies	14,445	10,581
	48,323	38,755
Coastwise	5,040	3,994
Total	53,368	42,749

Source: Glasgow Herald, 10 January 1812.

In 1812, cotton stocks in Glasgow amounted to only 5% of UK totals, with London accounting for 63% of stocks and Liverpool 31%.[116] By 1833, Liverpool had overtaken London as the largest cotton port, accounting for an overwhelming 90.4% of cotton imports by volume (bags of raw cotton), with Glasgow at 5.3% and London a mere 4.3%.[117]

Cotton was a highly speculative business and imports were subject to widely varying standards of quality and the vagaries of war and trade depression. This theme emerges strongly in the letters of George Yuille, a Glasgow cotton merchant. In October 1817, in the difficult period after the end of the Napoleonic Wars, he wrote to James Wallace in New York, who had been speculating in tobacco, 'your prices are by far too high for all the European markets. It would have been much better if you had speculated in Cotton either in Virginia Charlestown or New Orleans.' A month later Yuille complained: 'Cotton has been very dull of late and prices lower', whilst in January 1818 he advised another correspondent: 'The prices of Cotton with you have got up out of all bounds and in whatever way Shipments may turn out is nevertheless a most dangerous speculation.'[118]

Finance and credit

These fluctuations in the world market meant that finance and credit were ongoing problems for Scottish cotton manufacturers, and even more for their bankers, creditors and suppliers. The Glasgow agency of the Royal Bank of Scotland made large advances to Glasgow mill owners and from the late 1790s was giving cash credits to a range of cotton manufacturers of £500, £800 and £1,000. David Dale's son-in-law, Robert Owen of New Lanark, had a cash credit of £1,000.[119] In 1789, the Ship Bank in Glasgow under the management of Robert Carrick was advancing cash credits totalling £43,800 to 80 accounts in the west of Scotland. Most of the accounts belonged to

Glasgow merchants, but they also included Thomas Sheddon, manufacturer, Anderston (£300), William Gillespie, linen and calico printer, Anderston (£400), Charles Kemp, manufacturer, Anderston (£300), Walter Weir, manufacturer, Paisley (£200), and James and John Macilwham, manufacturers, Anderston (£200).[120]

Having a privileged access to banking and credit facilities could be of considerable benefit to cotton manufacturers. David Dale manufactured cotton fabrics for printing and sold many of them to William Stirling and Sons at a credit of 12 month bills, 'which bills he discounted at his pleasure in the Royal Bank, being manager at the said bank in Glasgow, this in fact made it a CASH business for Mr Dale and the long credit secured a valuable customer'.[121]

The crisis of 1793

The first major setback to the virtually unchecked expansion of the cotton industry in Scotland was the outbreak of the French Wars in 1793, which precipitated a series of failures by Scottish banks. In Glasgow, the Glasgow Arms Bank and Thompson's Bank failed and the Merchant Bank closed, although it eventually re-opened, with knock-on effects on the cotton industry.[122] The Edinburgh banking firm of Bertram, Gardner and Co., a partner in the Penicuik cotton mills, Midlothian, stopped payment in April 1793.[123] The price of cotton yarn fell by 45% and James Monteith, who had bought Blantyre from David Dale in the previous year, panicked and appealed to Dale to buy the mills back from him. Dale refused and Monteith was reduced to manufacturing the unwanted yarn into cloth, which he then sent for sale at auction in Glasgow. This strategy proved highly successful, netting a profit of £80,000 over the next five years.[124]

The *Statistical Accounts* are full of tales of cotton projects scaled down or abandoned because of the economic crisis brought on by the outbreak of the French Wars. Linwood in Renfrewshire boasted 'the most splendid establishment in the cotton spinning business, perhaps in Britain'. This giant mill was still being built in 1791, planned to contain 25,000 spindles and 1,800 workers. However, due to the 'dullness of trade' it had only 600 spindles working and employed 75 workers.[125] This may have been simply a matter of a firm over-extending itself and running out of capital and credit. However, other cotton firms were directly affected by the 1793 crisis. In Luss parish, Dunbartonshire, a cotton mill was built in 1790 which employed '30 to 40 hands, young and old'. However, in 1793, 'of late owing to the general stagnation of trade, little work had been carried on in it'.[126] In Perth, in 1794, 'The cotton manufacture was rapidly extending but met with a severe shock last summer, by a reduction of the goods manufactured, and has not yet recovered its former vigour. The shock did not affect the linen manufactures in a similar degree.'[127]

In Killearn, Stirlingshire, the Endrick Printfield began in 1792 with the latest technology, including washing wheels 'which are not surpassed by any in Europe'. In spite of this investment, the business was struggling, 'an entire stop was almost put to the work by the present stagnation of trade, which has communicated its baleful influence through all this country. The whole work at present [September 1793] employs no more than 250 persons most of whom reside in Balfron.' [128] In Kinghorn, Fife, four spinning mills for cotton and flax had been built by the early 1790s. In 1793, 'the largest of them which was built last season, owing to the shock which has lately been given to public credit, and the consequent stagnation of all business, have not as yet been completely fitted up, and filled with machinery by the proprietors'.[129] However, none of these mills lasted long and the area reverted to linen production.

Promise and penury – profit and loss in cotton manufacturing

In the early days cotton spinning could be very profitable for those who were capable of spinning the finest yarns. In 1792, when Robert Owen was managing Peter Drinkwater's Bank Top Mill in Manchester, raw cotton at 5s a pound was sold at £9 8s 6d when made into fine thread for muslins. Owen sold this particular yarn to Alexander Speirs of Kilbarchan, Renfrewshire, who used it to make muslins as a present for Queen Charlotte. After the outbreak of the French Wars in 1793, prices for fine cottons were never as high again. These exceptional profits were largely due to the fine yarns that Owen manufactured, which commanded a premium of 50% over the going rate. His only rival was Archibald Buchanan of Catrine, Ayrshire, whose fine yarn fetched 10% above the list price.[130]

Owen's management of the New Lanark mills from 1799 onwards likewise proved very profitable. He made a gross profit of £90,000 between 1799 and 1810, an annual average return of 15% on capital. His second partnership at New Lanark, from 1811 to 1814, showed a gross profit of £109,871 (including the capital gain of the mills), representing an annual return of nearly 46%. The third partnership at New Lanark, from 1814 to 1825, allowing for capital depreciation and a loss at Stanley mills in 1814, produced a gross profit of £192,915 or an annual return of just over 15%. Altogether, the gross gain at New Lanark over the period 1799 to 1828 amounted to a cool £399,345. Owen's share of this was a handsome £128,500.[131]

However, cotton spinning could be an unforgiving business for those who didn't know what they were doing. The impoverished Angus laird George Dempster, MP, a partner in Stanley mills, Perthshire, wrote with misplaced optimism to another partner, the equally impoverished Robert Graham of Fintry, in May 1785 that 'while we are spinning cotton we may play upon velvet'. Four years later, he had completely lost his optimism and was worried that 'I signed this last Bond for a large sum tho it was not as usual accompanied by a single Line from Mr MacVicar [the Stanley manager] acquainting me as to what purpose this money is to be applied . . . Now I am really afraid that this Mill is a losing concern and if so, I fear the losses will not be on a small scale.' In June 1790, Dempster complained to Graham, 'It is hard to be borrowing when all the cotton spinners in Great Britain are making fortunes.' Disaster struck the company in September 1799, when the flax mill at Stanley burned down. Dempster asked bitterly: 'Where are our Dukes of Athols? Our Arkwrights? & Sandemans originally engaged to partake in this Adventure? Some have escaped by their Strength, others by our weakness, and nothing remains but a few of us poor mice to be crushed under the immense ruin, It has not only crushed me, but my Poor Wife.'[132] A year later, Dempster explained that 'The war surprised us just as we were beginning to reap the profit of our labours. The price of cotton rose, the value of cotton yarn fell and considerable loss was incurred.'[133] In 1803, Dempster claimed to have lost £8,000 on the Stanley venture.[134]

Cotton spinning was a speculative and risky business. At Rothesay Mills on Bute, the company regulations of M'Alpine, Fleming and Co. provided for a review if the company did not make a 10% profit. However, the company not only failed to make 10% profit but was dissolved in February 1785, having made, 'no profit at all or any prospect of it improving'.[135] At Penicuik Mills, Midlothian, the Brotherstone Trustees reported in July 1789: 'we are not only satisfied that the concern has been a losing one, but that the debts due by the Company do so much exceed the value of the mills, machinery, lands and others . . . that we as trustees foresaid cannot undertake to carry on the said business, or pay the debts of the Company'.[136] The energetic Robert Burns, Managing Partner of Cartside Mills, Renfrewshire, retired on health grounds and accused another partner, George Houston of Johnstone, of drawing £20,000 of unauthorised money on the company for the use of himself and his friends.[137]

The Glasgow muslin merchant James Craig, who bought Stanley Mills, Perthshire in January 1801, lost large sums of money, in spite of financial support from David Dale and the Dale trustees and the efforts of Robert Owen to guide him towards profitability.[138] In March 1811, Owen warned Craig: 'I must candidly tell you I think you will never make a penny by cotton spinning it is not your forte', and in May, Owen insisted: 'It becomes absolutely necessary that you cease all connections with the mills', as the Dale Trustees had already lost over £40,000, due to Craig's mismanagement. Owen continued: 'You may truly believe me when I tell you that were you to continue to manage the Stanley Mills you would ruin the richest Man in the Kingdom if they were connected with it.'[139] Later, Owen was accused of concealing these debts from the other Dale trustees, and the affair ended in an acrimonious court case between the Royal Bank of Scotland and the Stanley Company, precipitated by the bankruptcy of John More, successor to David Dale at the Royal Bank. On 13 January 1817, the Royal Bank claimed £87,285 from More's estate, of which £33,186 was in discounted bills granted on behalf of the Dale trustees in connection with Stanley, plus £8,096 in interest. The Dale trustees lost over £41,000 because of Craig's mismanagement of Stanley.[140]

Others also found the cotton industry to be not as profitable as they had hoped or expected. James Dunlop (1741–1816), a Glasgow colonial merchant, who had investments in the Duntocher Cotton Company and in coal companies, went bankrupt in the depression year of 1793. Another Glasgow colonial merchant, Robert Dunmore (born 1773), who had interests in printfields and iron works in the west of Scotland and in the Ballindalloch cotton mills, went bankrupt four years later.[141] In 1803, James Paterson, a Glasgow cotton manufacturer and friend of Robert Scott Moncrieff of the Glasgow agency of the Royal Bank, failed. In the same year Scott Moncrieff estimated that J. A. Monteith was worth £46,000 'all made by our mills and [bleach and print] fields which he took from us at about one third the cost – yet I believe nobody else would have given us so much'. As a result, Scott Moncrieff held a low opinion of 'that vile manufacturing trade'.[142]

War and trade depression, 1801–1819

Because it was an international commodity, in terms both of the raw material supply and of the sale of the finished product, cotton was extremely vulnerable to disruption by war and trade depression. In March 1801, Andrew Campbell, a Glasgow yarn dealer, wrote to M'Connel and Kennedy in Manchester: 'We hold just now in this market about 1,000 bales of the best Sea Island quality upon the sale of which we shall commence as soon as soon as [*sic*] we can ascertain with certainty the footing we shall be upon with the Northern powers, especially that with the King of Prussia.'[143] These fluctuations are reflected in letters from Robert Owen to James Craig at Stanley, Perthshire to try to improve the profitability of the Stanley concern. In January 1803, Owen reported that sales of cotton yarn were currently very brisk, but by August of that year he complained that the price of raw cotton was rising and that 'If War continues we cannot expect lower prices. The spinning trade was never worse and many are losing money.'[144] In spite of the expansion of the Atlantic markets, Europe remained the main export market for Scottish cotton goods, and by 1801 Germany was importing plain cloth from Scotland worth £421,796, muslins worth £200,194 and yarn worth £47,446. Exports to Europe showed a steady increase, except for 1810–1811 and the post-war depression of 1816, rising from £9,534,465 in 1805 to £22,289,645 in 1815.[145]

Two events that had a major impact on the British cotton industry during the French Wars were the Napoleonic Blockade of 1805–1806 and the American Embargo of 1807–1809. Cotton firms had to keep an eye open for fluctuating supplies and see-sawing prices for raw cotton, yarn and cloth, and there was a search for alternative markets in South America and the West Indies. In March 1806, the Manchester spinning firm of M'Connel and Kennedy wrote to the Glasgow dealer William Whyte: 'It is the general opinion here that cotton will not maintain the present price, therefore we shall only buy small quantities at one time just now, but you may frequently send samples with the price.' On 15 November 1806, they wrote to Stow and Pollack, another Glasgow firm, that 'Spinning numbers below 80 at present price is really such a threadbare trade that there is scarcely any room to give way in price.' By November of the following year they were writing to another Glasgow dealer, William Kelly, that 'Sea Islands and other cottons looking down in price here, but there is very little good either here or in Liverpool. Last week some considerable lots of Boweds [Georgia cotton] were sold in Liverpool to some London speculators.'[146]

Kirkman Finlay, who owned cotton mills at Ballindalloch, Catrine and Deanston, was shrewd enough to find a way round the 1805–1806 blockade by establishing a trading house at Dusseldorf in 1806 to beat the Berlin Decrees. He also set up a house (John Thomson and Co.) in Heligoland in 1807 to supply northern Germany, and one on Malta (Struthers, Kennedy and Co.) to supply southern Europe. Finlay's business interests were extraordinarily wide. By 1812, he had a merchant house in London, 'a considerable connection on the continent of Europe, one in Malta, in New Orleans and in New Providence, one of the Bahamas islands'.[147]

During the American Embargo of 1807–1809, Robert Owen's solution to the problem of escalating prices for raw cotton at New Lanark was 'to stop all the machinery, retain the people, and continue to pay their full wages for only keeping the machinery clean and in good working condition', which he did for four months, at a cost of £7,000. However, this expensive gesture paid off, as it 'won the confidence and hearts of the whole population and henceforward I had no obstructions from them in my progress of reform'.[148] The American Embargo hit the Scottish cotton industry particularly hard, as it was heavily dependent on fine Sea Island cotton from Georgia and South Carolina. On 21 November 1808, Owen wrote to James Craig at Stanley Mills, Perthshire that it was extremely hazardous to hold stocks of either raw cotton or yarn; the price of raw cotton was so high that it was better to pay the workers full wages than spin such expensive cotton. A few days later, he wrote to Craig again to advise him to keep stocks low until the embargo was either lifted or confirmed.[149] Unlike Craig, Owen kept a keen eye open for political developments across Europe and beyond, and how they might affect the cotton industry. Writing from Glasgow in March 1809, Owen noted: 'The continental politics remain in a very uncertain state though it is generally expected that Austria will declare war against France and strong hopes are entertained that Russia and Prussia will join her.'[150]

In July 1810, 'a hurricane of bankruptcies . . . swept over England and Scotland'.[151] In Perth:

> During the war, the fluctuation in business had been so great that commerce had assumed more of the hazardous character of gambling than of fair trade, often overwhelming merchants in the most inextricable difficulties. It was emphatically remarked that business was driven at the point of the bayonet. The news of a victory or a defeat, or political convulsion, were alike the harbingers of ruin to many, by the fall in the price of goods on the one hand, or the entire loss of them on the other. The regular channels to the markets were often shut up by the exclusion of British goods from the continent; and the general chances of the war, had an irresistible tendency to involve in difficulties those engaged in trade. But in spite of these difficulties, a class of men got into business on the credit of others, who obtained material on long credit and sold their goods on short bills, often sacrificing largely to obtain cash to keep moving.[152]

The 1810 crash amongst Perth textile firms was precipitated by the loss of £100,000 of goods owned by the London branch of the Cromwellpark cotton mills in a fire in Cadiz. As a result, 'about sixty of the small manufacturers were driven out of business, leaving only about eight firms who were able to carry on business. The weavers were now obliged to apply for work from Glasgow, in which quarter an endless variety of cotton fabrics had been introduced.'[153]

The end of the French Wars brought little respite to the cotton industry. From 1 February to 16 March 1816, 43 west of Scotland commercial and manufacturing firms went bankrupt, including 4 calico printers, 2 calico manufacturers, 4 muslin manufacturers, 1 power loom manufacturer, 10 manufacturers (unspecified) and 6 West India merchants.[154] As a result of the depression, 'the liabilities of bankrupt firms in Glasgow alone amounted to two millions sterling'.[155] There were further crises leading to a spate of bankruptcies in 1819, when there were 175 failures in Scotland.[156] This trade crisis was the background to the Radical War of 1819–1820, which will be discussed more fully in Chapter 5.

Changing markets and the growth of steam power

Despite these crises, the cotton industry continued to expand. By 1812, there were 41 cotton mills in Renfrewshire, 19 of them driven by water power from the rivers Levern, White Cart, Black Cart, Calder and Gryfe, the others by steam.[157] However, the arrival of steam power meant that the cotton industry in

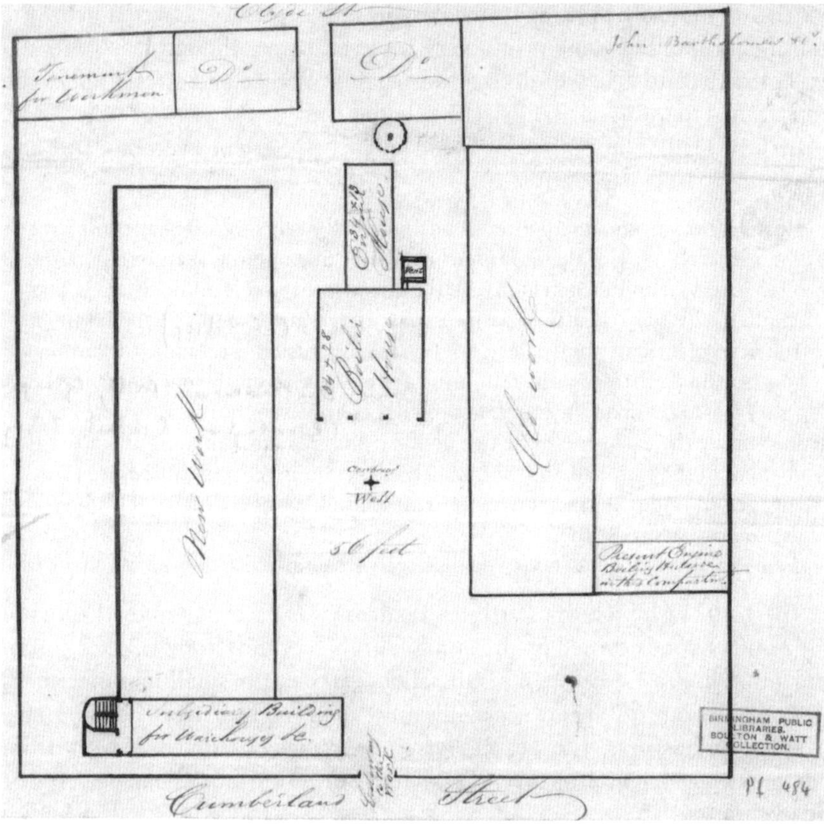

2 A steam-powered urban cotton mill, John Bartholomew's Mill, Clyde Street, Glasgow, showing 1823 extension

Glasgow began to overtake its country rivals from 1800 onwards. By 1819, there were 52 cotton mills in Glasgow, containing 511,200 spindles and accounting for capital of £1 million invested in buildings and machinery. The city produced 105 million yards of cloth, worth about £5.2 million. Glasgow had 16 power loom factories in 1819 containing 2,380 looms, producing 8,200 pieces of cloth weekly. The city also had 18 calico printing works and 14 calendar houses. In the same year, there were 18,537 handlooms in Glasgow, of which 13,281 were currently occupied. There were a further 13,463 weavers outside Glasgow who worked for Glasgow manufacturers.[158] However, the nature of the cotton industry in Scotland had changed. Initially, the Scottish industry had produced fine yarns and fabrics. By 1818, some 85% of Scottish cotton cloth exports consisted of cheaper, coarser fabrics, plain calicoes and heavier fabrics.[159] Because of the lack of water power in Glasgow, most factories there had to be powered by steam engines, and in April 1825 there were 310 steam engines in the city with a combined horse power of 6,406. Of these, 176 were in manufacturing with a total of 2,970 hp, a modest average of 16.87 hp.[160]

Those active in the industry devised ways to get round shortages of capital. It was commonplace to rent mill buildings and machinery. In December 1822, William Ewing, a Glasgow yarn merchant, was building a steam-powered weaving mill at Bothwell Street, Anderston to rent to Archibald Duncan and Ninian Strang, co-partners in Archibald Duncan and Co. The new mill consisted of 'four flats and garrets presently erecting by the said William Ewing' and 'a warehouse and accommodation for starching, winding, warping and drawing'. Ewing was responsible for the maintenance and repair of the steam engine, used for driving 250 power looms along the lines used by William Corbett in his factory in Hutchesontown. The looms worked at 80 to 85 shots of the shuttle a minute and the tenants were allowed to use the steam engine boiler to heat the mill. A yearly rent of £3 14s was established for each of the 250 looms, making a total annual rent of £925 for the looms, payable in two instalments a year. Initially only 100 power looms were to be installed. The arbitrators in any dispute were to be Robert Humphries, a Glasgow cotton spinner and Robert Owen's former manager at New Lanark, and William Corbett, a Glasgow manufacturer.[161]

Another financial crisis in July 1825 followed a boom earlier in the year. Speculators used their funds to hold large stocks of cotton and raise prices, whilst mill owners in Glasgow and Paisley found themselves facing industrial action by the spinners. The mill owners' reaction was to go over to half-time working. As well as facing volatile trading conditions, cotton manufacturing was highly speculative and firms frequently overextended their credit and exaggerated their assets. In 1826, the Royal Bank believed that amongst the cotton manufacturers of Glasgow and the west of Scotland, the real capital of most Scottish bills did not amount to a third of the sum discounted.[162]

A year earlier, total employment in textile manufacturing in Scotland was 257,900, of which cotton employed 154,000 (60%), linen 30% and wool 10%. Sir John Sinclair described the cotton industry as 'by far the most important in the kingdom, in regard both to the number of persons employed and to the value of their labour'. Sinclair believed that it was much more profitable to carry on cotton manufacturing with a large capital rather than relying on credit. He argued that 'proportionately, more money is made with a capital of £30,000 than with one of £3,000. Money, in the hands of a merchant or manufacturer, may be said to be power.' This provides one explanation for the small numbers of self-made men in the cotton industry. Sinclair also believed that power loom weaving was currently more profitable than cotton spinning, 'because being newer, it is not so much run down with competition; besides, more business is done on the same capital employed in machinery'.[163]

Cotton manufacturing in Scotland was highly export orientated. In 1825,

Sinclair estimated that out of a total workforce of 154,000 in cotton, no fewer than 133,180 (86%) were producing goods for export. Another 13,600 (9%) were manufacturing goods for the English market and only 7,220 (4.6%) were producing goods for the domestic market.[164] Sinclair viewed this export dependency with grave concern. Writing about the manufactures of Scotland as a whole, he lamented: 'It is impossible to see without alarm, that 189,420 souls, or nearly one tenth of the population of Scotland, depend for their subsistence upon the sale of goods in foreign markets, over which we have little or no control, and of which we may be suddenly be [*sic*] deprived. In what a hazardous state is a nation placed, whose prosperity and internal quiet depend on so precarious a basis?' He believed Great Britain should 'dread the rivalship of foreign nations, many of who are aiming, not only to supply themselves, but to supplant us in other markets'.[165] This prescient warning forms one of the main themes of the next chapter.

Notes

1. G. M. Mitchell, 'The English and Scottish Cotton Industries', *Scottish Historical Review*, 1925, XXII.
2. P. Hudson, *The Industrial Revolution* (London, 1992), 101. See also M. Berg, *The Age of Manufactures, 1700–1820: Industry, Innovation and Work in Britain*, 2nd edition (London, 1994).
3. Mitchell Library, Glasgow (ML), Glasgow Chamber of Commerce (GCC), Minutes, Vol. I, 170, 24 January 1786.
4. J. Shaw, *Water Power in Scotland, 1550–1830* (Edinburgh, 1984), 318; and S. M. Nisbet, 'The Rise of the Cotton Factory in Eighteenth Century Renfrewshire' (PhD thesis, Paisley, 2003), 133.
5. Signet Library, Edinburgh (SL), Court of Session Papers (CS), 449/23, 1803. Under the Scottish system of landowning, feued land was land leased from a feudal superior.
6. Shaw, *Water Power*, 318.
7. R. S. Fitton, *The Arkwrights, Spinners of Fortune* (Manchester, 1989), 70.
8. National Archives of Scotland, Edinburgh (NAS), Graham of Fintry Papers, GD, 151/11/8, fols 22–3.
9. Sir J. Sinclair (ed.) *[Old] Statistical Account of Scotland* (*OSA*) (Wakefield, 1973), 1975, II, 371.
10. Nisbet, 'Cotton Factory', 134.
11. Shaw, *Water Power*, 318.
12. SL, CS, 411/62, 1800.
13. Fitton, *The Arkwrights*, 70–1.
14. Shaw, *Water Power*, 318.
15. SL, CS, 290/34.
16. S. G. E. Lythe and J. Butt, *An Economic History of Scotland, 1100–1939* (Glasgow, 1975), 186.

17. C. A. Whatley, *The Industrial Revolution in Scotland* (Cambridge, 1997), 6.
18. *OSA*, 1973, VII, 795.
19. Shaw, *Water Power*, 332; and Nisbet, 'Cotton Factory', 136–40.
20. J. Montgomery, *The Theory and Practice of Cotton Spinning* (Glasgow, 1832), 242–3.
21. SL, CS, 264/2.
22. E. Baines, *History of the Cotton Manufacture* (1835, reprinted London, 1966), 193.
23. Montgomery, *Cotton Spinning*, 241–2.
24. *Glasgow Mercury*, 7 October 1784.
25. A. J. Cooke, 'Richard Arkwright and the Scottish Cotton Industry', *Textile History*, 1979, X; and Fitton, *The Arkwrights*, 72–4.
26. Baines, *Cotton Manufacture*, 193.
27. ML, GCC, 1783–4, Box II, William Sandeman to Gilbert Hamilton, 15 November 1784.
28. NAS, RH, 449, 2 Vol. III, 266–8.
29. R. Reid (Senex), *Glasgow Past and Present* (Glasgow, 1858), 317.
30. A. J. Cooke, *Stanley. From Arkwright Village to Commuter Suburb, 1784–2003* (Perth, 2003), 59.
31. G. Penny, *Traditions of Perth* (Perth, 1836), 251.
32. P. Morgan, *Annals of Woodside and Newhills* (Aberdeen, 1886), 19–21.
33. I. Donnachie and G. Hewitt, *Historic New Lanark. The Dale and Owen Industrial Community since 1785* (Edinburgh, 1993), 35.
34. NAS, Sheriff Court of Perthshire, SC 49/48/104, Contract of Co-Partnership, 1 January 1787.
35. *Derby Mercury*, 12 May 1785.
36. NAS, GD 151/12/21.
37. NAS, CC 8/8/127/1187.
38. NAS, GD 151/11/8/65 and Cooke, 'Richard Arkwright'.
39. Fitton, *The Arkwrights*, 79.
40. *Parliamentary Papers*, 1834, Vol. XX, A1, 93.
41. Fitton, *The Arkwrights*, 80.
42. ML, Dale/Alexander Correspondence, MS 63/3, 1787–97.
43. *OSA*, 1973, VII, 823.
44. I. Donnachie, 'The Textile Industry in South West Scotland, 1750–1914', in J. Butt and K. Ponting (eds), *Scottish Textile History* (Aberdeen, 1987), 19–36, and A. J Cooke, 'Cotton and the Scottish Highland Clearances – Spinningdale, 1791–1806', *Textile History*, 1995, XXVI (1).
45. R. Heron, *Scotland Delineated* (Edinburgh, 1799), Vol. II, 217–18. I am grateful to Ian Donnachie for this reference.
46. Donnachie and Hewitt, *New Lanark*, 25.
47. *OSA*, 1978, IX, 177–8.
48. T. M. Devine, *The Tobacco Lords. A Study of the Tobacco Merchants of Glasgow and their Trading Activities c. 1740–1790* (Edinburgh, 1990), 180.
49. *OSA*, 1978, IX, 77 and NAS, CS 96/1371.

50. See T. C. Smout, 'Scottish Landowners and Economic Growth, 1650–1850', *Scottish Journal of Political Economy*, 1964, XI; and T. C. Smout, 'The Landowner and the Planned Village in Scotland 1730–1830', in N. T. Phillipson and R. Mitchison (eds), *Scotland in the Age of Improvement* (Edinburgh, 1970).
51. D. G. Lockhart, 'Planned Village Development in Scotland and Ireland', in T. M. Devine and D. Dickson (eds), *Ireland and Scotland, 1600–1850: Parallels and Contrasts in Economic and Social Development* (Edinburgh, 1983).
52. J. Colville (ed.), *Letters of John Cockburn of Ormiston to his Gardener, 1727–1744* (Edinburgh, 1904), 79–80.
53. Smout, 'Landowner and the Planned Village', 94.
54. *OSA*, 1976, XIII, 201.
55. J. Fergusson (ed.), *Letters of George Dempster to Sir Adam Fergusson, 1756–1813* (London, 1934), 252.
56. Blair Castle, Perthshire, Atholl Mss. Box 25/IX, I.
57. Shaw, *Water Power*, 331, and *OSA*, 1973, VII, 640–1.
58. *New Statistical Account of Scotland* (*NSA*) (Edinburgh, 1845), VII, 402.
59. Shaw, *Water Power*, 331.
60. ML, Houston of Johnstone Papers, TD 263/194, Contract of Co-Partnery, 1788.
61. G. Crawford (rev. Semple), *History of the Shire of Renfrewshire* (Paisley, 1772), 257.
62. *OSA*, 1977, XX, 89.
63. J. Butt (ed.), *The Life of Robert Owen Written by Himself* (London, 1971), 71.
64. Fitton, *The Arkwrights*, 34–46; and M. B. Rose, *The Gregs of Quarry Bank Mill. The Rise and Decline of a Family Firm, 1750–1914* (Cambridge, 1986), 13–16.
65. ML, Dale/Alexander Correspondence, 63/1, Dale to Alexander, 14 February 1787.
66. *OSA*, 1982, VI, 563–4.
67. Select Committee on the State of Children Employed in Factories, *Parliamentary Papers* (*PP*), 1816, III, 10–11.
68. *PP*, 1816, III, 20–2.
69. *OSA*, 1982, VI, 564. A boll was a measure of grain, in Scotland usually equivalent to six imperal bushels.
70. *OSA*, 1973, VII, 467.
71. Smout, 'Landowner and the Planned Village', 96.
72. *PP*, 1816, III, 164.
73. *OSA*, 1973, VII, 370.
74. *PP*, 1816, III, 247.
75. For Sunday-schools see C. G. Brown, 'The Sunday School Movement in Scotland', *Records of the Scottish Church History Society*, 1981, XXI; and A. J. Cooke, *From Popular Enlightenment to Lifelong Learning. A History of Adult Education in Scotland, 1707–2005* (Leicester, 2006).
76. W. Carlile, 'Sketches of Paisley', *Scots Magazine and Edinburgh Literary Miscellany*, July 1806.
77. J. Cleland, *Annals of Glasgow* (Glasgow, 1816), I, 265.

78. J. Parkhill (ed.), *The Life and Opinions of Arthur Sneddon, An Autobiography* (Paisley, 1860), 34.
79. *OSA*, 1973, VII, 812, 729 and 296.
80. Penny, *Traditions*, 251–6.
81. *OSA*, 1973, VII, 26 and 150.
82. *OSA*, 1982, VI, 569.
83. *OSA*, 1978, IX, 393.
84. H. Hamilton, *The Industrial Revolution in Scotland* (2nd edition, Oxford, 1966), 124.
85. *OSA*, 1976, XIII, 489–90.
86. Berg, *Age of Manufactures*, 135.
87. Quoted in D. Bremner, *The Industries of Scotland. Their Rise, Progress and Present Condition* (Edinburgh, 1869), 282.
88. M. M. Edwards, *The Growth of the British Cotton Trade, 1780–1815* (Manchester), 1967, 149.
89. W. Taylor, *An Answer to Mr Carlile's Sketches of Paisley* (Paisley, 1809), 19.
90. A. Brown, *A History of Glasgow and of Paisley, Greenock and Port Glasgow* (Glasgow, 1795), III, 240.
91. S. D. Chapman, 'Fixed Capital Formation in the British Cotton Manufacturing Industry', in J. P. P. Higgins and S. D. Chapman (eds), *Aspects of Capital Formation in Great Britain, 1750–1850* (London, 1971), 102–3.
92. *Ibid.*, 61–2.
93. *OSA*, 1982, VI, 356–6, 158 and 177.
94. *OSA*, 1973, VII, 411, 265 and 99.
95. *NSA*, VI, 152.
96. Donnachie and Hewitt, *New Lanark*, 62.
97. Cooke, *Stanley*, 73.
98. SL CS 209/34 and Chapman, 'Fixed Capital', 89 and 102.
99. SL, CS 411/62.
100. Chapman, 'Fixed Capital', 115.
101. S. D. Chapman and J. Butt, 'The Cotton Industry, 1775–1880', in C. H. Feinstein and S. Pollard (eds), *Studies in Capital Formation in the United Kingdom, 1750–1920* (Oxford, 1988), 108.
102. R. Reid (Senex), *Glasgow Past and Present* (Glasgow, 1884), III, 369–70.
103. C. H. Lee, *A Cotton Enterprise, 1795–1840: A History of M'Connel and Kennedy, Fine Cotton Spinners* (Manchester, 1972), 24.
104. Glasgow University Archives (GUA), UGD, 91/1/5/3/21.
105. NAS, CS 96, 1593.
106. Brown, *History of Glasgow*, III, 242.
107. Lee, *Cotton Enterprise*, 10–12 and 25.
108. Edwards, *Cotton Trade*, 138–40.
109. Butt (ed.), *Life of Robert Owen*, 33; and Cooke, *Stanley*, 73–4.
110. E. Baines, *History of the Cotton Manufacture* (1835, reprinted London, 1966), 301.
111. I. Donnachie, *Robert Owen. Owen of New Lanark and Harmony* (East Linton, 2000), 97–8.

112. A. J. Cooke, 'Robert Owen and the Stanley Mills, 1802–1811', *Business History*, 1979, XXXI (1); and Cooke, *Stanley*, 2003.
113. Atholl Mss, Box 25, XI, 3.
114. NAS, CS 96, 4039.
115. Baines, *Cotton Manufacture*, 311.
116. S. D. Chapman, *Merchant Enterprise in Britain* (Cambridge, 1992), 83.
117. Baines, *Cotton Manufacture*, 318.
118. NAS, CS 96/2233, fols. 114, 140 and 184.
119. S. G. Checkland, *Scottish Banking. A History, 1695–1973* (Glasgow, 1975), 230–1.
120. Reid, *Glasgow Past and Present*, 1884, II, 505–10.
121. *Ibid.*, III, 372–3 and 494–5.
122. C. W. Munn, *The Scottish Provincial Banking Companies, 1747–1864* (Edinburgh, 1981), 49.
123. SL, CS 449/23.
124. R. Reid (Senex), *Glasgow Past and Present* (Glasgow, 1858), 301.
125. *OSA*, 1973, VII, 74.
126. *OSA*, 1978, IX, 109.
127. *OSA*, 1976, XI, 492–4.
128. *OSA*, 1978, IX, 394.
129. *OSA*, 1978, X, 490.
130. Butt (ed.), *Life of Robert Owen*, 35.
131. J. Butt, 'Robert Owen as a Businessman', in J. Butt (ed.), *Robert Owen, Prince of Cotton Spinners* (Newton Abbot, 1971), 199–200 and 211–13.
132. NAS, Graham of Fintry Papers, GD 151/11/8/8, fols 30, 55, 82 and 141.
133. NAS, Sinclair of Ulbster Mss., RH 449, 2, Vol. 3, 266–8.
134. A. M. Lang, *A Life of George Dempster, Scottish Member of Parliament of Dunnichen, 1732–1818* (Lampeter, 1998), 253.
135. SL, CS 411/62.
136. SL, CS 449/23.
137. SL, CS 264/2.
138. Cooke, *Stanley*, 72–98.
139. Atholl Mss, Box 25, XI (3), fols 172–6.
140. See A. J. Robertson, 'Robert Owen and the Campbell Debt, 1810–1822', *Business History*, 1969, XI (1), 23–30; Butt, 'Owen as a Businessman'; and Cooke, 'Owen and the Stanley Mills'.
141. Devine, *Tobacco Lords*, 180.
142. Checkland, *Scottish Banking*, 404–7.
143. Edwards, *Cotton Trade*, 116.
144. Atholl Mss, Box 25, XI, 3, fols 24–7 and 32–6.
145. Lee, *Cotton Enterprise*, 24.
146. Edwards, *Cotton Trade*, 116, 127 and 109.
147. C. Brogan, *James Finlay and Company Ltd., 1750–1950* (Glasgow, 1951), 15 and 18.
148. Butt (ed.), *Life of Robert Owen*, 64.

149. Atholl Mss, Box 25, XI, 3 fols 109–12.
150. Atholl Mss, Box 25, XI, 3, fol. 121.
151. Checkland, *Scottish Banking*, 404–7.
152. Penny, *Traditions*, 255.
153. *Ibid.*, 257.
154. Lee, *Cotton Enterprise*, 34.
155. G. Stewart, *Curiosities of Glasgow Citizenship* (Glasgow, 1881), 127.
156. Lee, *Cotton Enterprise*, 41.
157. J. Wilson, *A General View of the Agriculture of Renfrewshire* (Paisley, 1812), 249.
158. Sir J. Sinclair, *Analysis of the Statistical Account of Scotland* (Edinburgh, 1825), Vol. I, 62–3.
159. A. J. Robertson, 'The Decline of the Scottish Cotton Industry, 1860–1914', *Business History*, 1970, XII (2), 116–28.
160. Sinclair, *Statistical Analysis of Scotland.*
161. GUA, UGD 189/4/3, Lancaster, Duncan and Co., Tack dated 14 December 1822.
162. Checkland, *Scottish Banking*, 418.
163. Sinclair, *Statistical Analysis of Scotland*, 44.
164. *Ibid.*, 321.
165. *Ibid.*, 207, 333 and 336.

3

Foreign competition, diversification and decline, 1830–1914

> Great Britain no longer possesses the monopoly of cotton spinning; the Americans, French, Swiss and other nations already tread closely on the British Merchant, and in some instances compete with him in markets where he was formerly without a rival. (A. E. Speirs, Fintry cotton mills, Stirlingshire, evidence to the Select Committee on the Employment of Children in Factories, *Parliamentary Papers*, 1834)

Introduction

By the mid nineteenth century, Britain was beginning to lose its dominant position as the 'Workshop of the World' and to face increasing competition from countries such as Germany and the USA as they industrialised. Traditionally, historians have sought an explanation for this decline in the failure of British entrepreneurs, particularly those in family firms, to adapt to new circumstances and compete in world markets. Research in the late 1980s questioned this view, stressing the diverse experience of British entrepreneurs in this period and placing them in a more favourable light.[1] The Scottish cotton industry provides an early example of industrial decline, although even here, the picture is an uneven one. Whilst cotton spinning in Scotland went into steep decline, specialised weaving firms survived and even prospered, as did some dyeing and textile-related chemical firms. The greatest success story was that of the Paisley cotton thread industry, which operated factories in Europe and the USA and eventually enjoyed a virtual monopoly of world markets.[2]

Foreign competition

In 1833, Kirkman Finlay gave evidence to the Select Committee on Manufactures, Commerce and Shipping. Looking back over nearly 50 years he claimed:

> When I first knew the cotton manufactures in this country, which was in the year 1787 and when I first entered into business extensively, which was in 1792,

> there was no manufacture of cotton of any importance in any part of Great Britain . . . In those times there was no cotton manufacture in France at all; none in Switzerland worth speaking of; none in any part of Germany . . . now there is not a single country in which there is not a great manufacture of cotton carried on.[3]

This was exaggerating the situation, as Glasgow Chamber of Commerce had warned about foreign competition as early as 1784[4] and by 1791 there were already 39 water-powered cotton mills in Scotland, plus buildings for spinning jennies and mules with a total capital of £490,000[5]. However, there was growing pessimism amongst cotton manufacturers. In 1834, A. E. Speirs of Fintry cotton mills, Stirlingshire voiced his fears about foreign competition and warned: 'I may add, several of the latest improvements in cotton spinning are of American invention.'[6]

The fear of foreign competition runs like a Minoan thread through the evidence given in the early 1830s to the Parliamentary Commissioners on the Employment of Children in Factories. It was used by cotton manufacturers to try to frighten Parliament away from overly strict legislation to regulate working conditions in textile mills. They argued that restricting the use of child labour in British textile mills would benefit foreign competitors, who had no such punitive legislation. The Commissioners were anxious to question witnesses about any experience of conditions in the textile industry in other countries, or of foreign competition. Robert Dick, of John Dennistoun and Co., Bridgeton, Glasgow, believed that competition from Europe and the USA would ruin the cotton industry if working hours were reduced. John Buchanan of Fulton, Buchanan and Co., Lochwinnoch, Renfrewshire, also expressed his fears of American competition.[7] John Orr, Provost of Paisley, a partner in cotton spinning works at Underwood, Renfrewshire, quoted a colleague, James Cochrane, a yarn agent in Glasgow, who had recently visited Germany and Switzerland. Cochrane had found 'that the wages of spinners were, compared with the wages of spinners in this country, very low, one half lower than in this country'. The average weekly wages of spinners in France were 5s 8d, in Switzerland 4s 5d, whilst in Britain they were 8s 4d.[8]

However, Robert Thomson, a Glasgow mill owner, was dismissive of foreign competition. Thomson had 'seen spinning mills in Saxony and other parts of Germany; never in Switzerland, France or Austria. Thinks the danger of competition from those he has seen not great. Machinery inferior and workers not so steady or in such discipline as in this country. Thinks the workpeople more industrious in this country than anywhere else; meaning they will stick to their work more steadily than foreigners, in the prospect of making better wages. Has always found that when he offered a workman a slight advance of wages to leave a comparatively easy situation to take one of more labour and less ease, the offer was accepted.'[9] Archibald Buchanan, 'sixty years old and upwards', Managing Partner at Catrine, Ayrshire, was reluctant to answer the question as to 'whether it is his opinion that if a ten hours' act be passed, foreign nations will be able to compete successfully with the British manufacturer with respect to cotton goods'. Buchanan fudged by saying 'that general question he declines to enter, but that foreign nations will evidently in that case be more able to compete with us than at present'.[10]

Other witnesses were operative cotton spinners from a trade union background and active in the Short Time Association. They highlighted better working conditions and wages amongst overseas competitors. William Smith, a Glasgow cotton spinner, who was sponsored by the Cotton Spinners' Association and gave evidence on behalf of the Short Time Association, had worked in cotton mills in Rouen, St Quentin, Lisle (Lille) and Paris. He testified that French workers would not come in to work on Mondays, unlike the English, and would not be summoned by a bell, as in England. Smith described how 'they threw stones at him and at the bell and he was obliged to leave the place'. He also reported that there had been much emigration from Glasgow to America, where spinners' wages were a third higher than in the UK. Another member of the Spinners' Association, the Glasgow 'operative spinner' James McNeish, gave evidence that cotton mills in the USA were not allowed to use physical punishment on children, as happened in Great Britain.[11]

Another activist in the Short Time Association was Patrick M'Gowan, a cotton spinner who had been dismissed from Charles Todd's works in Glasgow shortly after chairing a meeting in September 1832 in the Universalists' Chapel, Glasgow to campaign for shorter working hours. M'Gowan believed that shorter hours would benefit the industry, which was suffering from overproduction. He claimed that whereas the volume of cotton goods exported had more than doubled between 1803 and 1830, the real value of these goods had fallen from around £45 million in 1803 to £35 million in 1830. M'Gowan was complacent about foreign competition, being 'convinced that the British manufacturer has nothing to fear from the competition with foreign nations, because on the continent of Europe, although a worker receives lower wages than here for the time he is employed, yet he actually receives more for the same quantity of yarn produced; that for example a spinner produces nine or ten hanks per spindle per week in France, while from the British spinner a quantity of from eighteen to twenty two hanks per week of the same number of cotton must be had; that with respect to America, he is satisfied that anything like competition is at present out of the question'.[12]

More evidence about overseas conditions came from two male cotton spinners at William Hussey and Son's mill in Bridgeton, Glasgow. This was a large steam-powered operation employing 500 workers and containing 43,000 spindles, which claimed to spin 'the finest cotton in Scotland . . . generally from

No 90 to 180'. The two men – John Adams and Patrick Boyes – had worked in the USA for 15 months, returning to Scotland in October 1832. Adams worked for three weeks as a spinner in Paterson, New Jersey and afterwards for nine months at a cotton factory in Great Barrington, Yorkshire County, Massachusetts. He returned to Glasgow because conditions in America were little better than in Scotland, he preferred fine spinning and considered 'the machinery in all the works he saw, and he visited above a dozen of cotton factories, to be quite inferior to ours – a hundred years behind us, that he saw no part of their work to be compared with ours, and the carding and spinning to be alike defective . . . that he came back because he preferred fine work, and his wages or earnings were about as good'. Adams was unimpressed by the US cotton industry and concluded 'that the Americans will never in his time compete with our cotton goods in the market'. Patrick Boyes had worked in New York for a year as a hand loom weaver and then 'for a few days at a factory in Pennsylvania', but had been unable to get regular employment. Like Adams he thought 'very little of their machinery wherever he was, and as for wages, he thinks himself as well off here as he would be there'. Both these men were highly paid spinners of fine yarn, earning from 27s to 28s a week on average.[13]

Another witness with American work experience was Hugh Shanks, who had gone to the USA in February 1832 to 'better his condition as a spinner' and had worked at Pleasant Valley, Duchess County on the River Hudson about 100 miles from New York. Shanks testified that he had been better paid in the USA and that prices for cotton goods were higher there than in Britain. He received 6s 2d for 1,000 hanks of common twenties in the USA, as compared to 4s 2d for the same amount in Bartholomew's mill, Glasgow. A cotton neckcloth which cost 3s in the USA could be purchased for 10d in Glasgow, whilst a pair of short stockings costing 18d in the USA cost only 8d in Glasgow.[14]

Expansion, geographical concentration and diversification

In spite of competition from Lancashire and overseas, the Scottish cotton industry continued to expand. Expansion was accompanied by increasing geographical concentration in the Glasgow/Renfrewshire/Paisley area. In 1833, there were 134 cotton mills in Scotland – 74 in Lanarkshire and 41 in Renfrewshire. Lanarkshire and Renfrewshire accounted for 1,353,860 (78%) of Scotland's total 1,728,628 spindles and consumed 78% of raw cotton supplies in Scotland. The average number of spindles per mill had risen from 8,000 in 1793 to 12,000, 40 years later. The rapid expansion of factory production was matched by the expansion of outwork, particularly hand loom weaving. In the 1780s, there were some 20,000 hand loom weavers in

G	=	Glasgow and its suburbs had 78 cotton spinning mills and power loom factories in 1831, driven by 91 steam engines. (**Source:** J. Cleland, *Enumeration of the Inhabitants of the City of Glasgow and County of Lanark.* (Glasgow, 1831)
P	=	Paisley had 12 steam powered spinning mills in 1833-4. (**Source:** Factory Inquiry Commission Reports, *Parliamentary Papers,* 1833, XX and 1834, XX)

3 Distribution of cotton mills, Scotland 1778–1834

Scotland, many of whom had begun to make the transition from linen to cotton. They were concentrated in the west of Scotland, with an estimated 4,000 in Glasgow alone. By 1831, there were 40,000 hand loom weavers in the west of Scotland – 20,000 in Glasgow, 6,000 in Paisley, 7,000 in Lanarkshire excluding Glasgow, and 7,000 in Ayrshire. This expansion accompanied the growth of power loom weaving. By 1831, there were 15,000 power looms in 60 power weaving factories in Scotland, an average of 250 looms per factory. Some Scottish weaving factories were considerably larger than average. Monteith at Blantyre, Todd at Hutchesontown and Finlay at Catrine each had some 500 power looms or more in their factories.[15]

Increasingly, firms specialised in the types of fabric they produced. William Dunn of Duntocher, 'the most extensive and successful spinner in Scotland', had 600 looms producing 'very beautiful plain fabrics'. In the early 1830s, Sommerville and Sons built 'new and splendid works' in Hutchesontown, Glasgow, where they produced 'a very superior manufacture of furniture stripes and checks, and an infinite variety of similar goods for women's dresses, shirtings etc'. Steam-powered looms were increasingly seen as the future, although the number of hand looms expanded because many specialised types of cloth with complex patterns could only be woven on hand looms. By August 1831, the Lancefield Spinning Company had 635 looms and Messrs Johnston and Galbraith, James Finlay and Company and William Dunn between them had 2,405 power looms. These four large companies produced an estimated 10 million yards of cloth a year, valued at £189,393.[16]

The industry was heavily dependent on credit. Lancaster, Duncan and Co. owned power loom factories in Anderston, Glasgow and a printfield and dyeworks in Dalmarnock, Glasgow. The firm was sequestrated in 1834, owing debts of £18,428 to 138 creditors. Some 25% of the debts were owed to Scottish banks, including Bank of Scotland (£1,282), Paisley Union Bank (£811), Commercial Bank (£798), Glasgow Bank (£557) and other banks (£1,272).[17] In 1834, John Orr, a Paisley cotton spinner, calculated that raw materials amounted to 54% of costs in cotton spinning and 'wages, accounts, interest on capital etc'. were 46% of costs of yarn manufactured.[18] At J. and P. Coats of Paisley, cotton yarn was the largest item in costs, rising from 40% of costs in the late 1840s to a peak of nearly 70% in 1864. After the Cotton Famine was over, yarn costs fell back to 43%. Wages costs were relatively stable at around 13%.[19]

Table 11 compares the size of the Scottish cotton industry with that of the North of England in 1835. The dominant form of motive power in the North of England was steam, accounting for 81% of total horse power in cotton mills. In Scotland, steam power was much less dominant, accounting for only 56% of total horse power. Another difference was that the average size of workforce per mill was larger in Scotland than in the North of England.

Table 11 Comparison of cotton mills in Scotland and the North of England by number of mills, horse power and size of workforce, 1835

Country/ region	No. of mills	Steam horse power	Water horse power	Total workforce	Average workforce per mill
Scotland	125	3,200	2,480	31,099	249
N. of England[a]	934	26,513	6,093	175,268	188

(*Note:* [a] Includes Lancashire, Yorkshire, Cheshire, Derbyshire, N. Staffordshire, Flintshire and Denbighshire.)

Source: E. Baines, *History of the Cotton Industry*, 1835, 389–390.

Paternalism and the Scottish factory villages

The continuing importance of water power in Scotland as compared to the North of England reflected greater water-power resources in Scotland and the survival of large and relatively prosperous manufacturing units in factory villages such as Catrine, Deanston, New Lanark or Stanley. Paternalistic management practices were a long-standing feature of these villages, modelled on aristocratic, landed and even Highland relationships between employer and employed. In Scotland, paternalism in the larger urban centres came slightly later than in the Lancashire cotton towns, where a 'new paternalism' emerged from the 1840s onwards.[20]

However, there were significant differences between Scotland and the North of England. The paternalism of some of the Lancashire mill towns owed a good deal to Anglican and Tory ideals, which exerted a heavy influence on the employer class.[21] Similarly, because paternalism was not a one-way street and demanded a reciprocal deference from its working-class recipients, some of the Lancashire cotton towns, such as Blackburn and Bolton, were also strongholds of working-class Toryism.[22] By contrast, the employer ethos in Scotland was overwhelmingly Calvinist and Presbyterian. The Scottish cotton masters were largely Whig, and later Liberal and then Liberal Unionist, in their politics, with a strong attachment to laissez-faire ideas in their social and economic outlook, but also to ideas of moral, educational and social improvement. In a Calvinist country like Scotland, particular importance was attached to education and the ability to read the Bible. Conversely, there was some degree of embarrassment amongst employers and ministers of religion about illiteracy amongst child factory workers, usually dismissed by the explanation that these were first-generation Irish immigrants and therefore not a product of the Scottish education system.

These attitudes are displayed in the evidence given to the Parliamentary

Commissioners in the early 1830s by Scottish cotton masters, many of whom were anxious to advertise their educational and philanthropic activities. The degree of paternalism displayed by cotton firms depended on geographical location, on the religious beliefs of employers and on their views of what constituted efficient management. At Gordon, Barron and Co. in Woodside, Aberdeen, the company provided, 'a free school house, fire and light' for a week-day school and religious instruction on Sunday. As a result, 'all of those who have been employed from infancy can read, several can write and know the simple rules of arithmetic, but occasionally some of them who come to the work at a later period of life cannot even read'.[23] Another Aberdeen mill owner, Thomas Bannerman, described how 'a small library is in the works, formed lately by the contributions of the work people who choose to subscribe; managed also by themselves . . . A desire for instruction and improvement is thus communicated and kept alive among them, better than by any direct superintendence on our part.' This was part of a strategy for workforce management whereby 'the bad have been weeded out'.[24]

Similar attitudes prevailed in the cotton mills of Rothesay, Isle of Bute, where 'the children are taught reading, writing and arithmetic in an evening school in the mill and at the expense of the proprietors, and no bad character is taken into or allowed to remain in the works'.[25] In Busby in Renfrewshire, William Kelly Junior, a partner in a cotton spinning and weaving company, boasted of his workers: 'their moral improvement is cared for by the establishment of Sabbath and weekly evening school, by the regular attendance of a clergyman who makes regular visitations to their houses and who preaches to them twice every Sunday'. Similarly, at Neilston in Renfrewshire, Charles Dunlop described how 140 cotton workers lived in company houses and, 'For their moral and social improvement, the proprietors afford gratuitously elementary education to all their workers.'[26] This emphasis on character, on 'respectability', on moral and social improvement, and the desire to eradicate disruptive influences and dispense with 'bad characters' in the factory community was characteristic of a Calvinistic approach to life, with its rigid demarcation between the 'elect' and the 'others'.

This degree of social control was much more difficult for mill owners to exercise in the larger and more anonymous urban centres such as Paisley or, particularly, Glasgow. The Glasgow and Paisley/Johnstone cotton masters rarely mentioned educational, philanthropic and religious provision by their firms. Table 12 shows that only 3 firms (8%) out of 37 in the Glasgow/Paisley/Johnstone triangle mentioned company housing, as compared with 10 (37%) out of 28 firms elsewhere in Scotland. Alexander Allen, of John Miller and Company, Hutchesontown, Glasgow testified: 'There are some houses belonging to the proprietor but the inhabitants are at the same liberty as in any other property.' Similarly, Henry Houldsworth of the Anderston

Table 12 Educational, philanthropic and religious provision by Scottish cotton firms, 1833–1834

City/county	No. of firms	Company school	Sunday school	Company housing	Church/ religious instruction	Other
Aberdeen	3	1			1	1[a]
Glasgow	19			2		
Lanarkshire	2	1		1	2	1[b]
Paisley/Johnstone	18	1		1	1	
Renfrewshire	16	6	2	6	1	
Elsewhere	7	4	2	3	1	2[c]
Total	65	13	4	13	6	4

(*Note:* 'Other' includes: [a] canteen, [b] street sweeping and [c] street sweeping and restricting number of public houses.)

Source: Factory Inquiry Commission Supplementary Report. Employment of Children in Factories, Part II, *BPP*, 1834, XX, A1.

mills, Glasgow described how the firm had houses for workers but they were not required to live in them.[27] In Paisley, John Orr of John Orr Junior and Co. reported that the company owned 'one large dwelling house occupied by thirty five families' but that most of their workers lived in the town.[28] In Scotland, my survey of 65 cotton firms, summarised in Table 12, shows that in 1833 only 20% provided housing for workers. In Britain in 1833, out of 881 large firms, 19% provided housing, although most of them made only a few houses available.[29]

A similar picture applied to education, where Table 12 shows that only one out of 37 cotton firms in the Glasgow/Johnstone/Paisley triangle mentioned a company school, compared with 11 schools mentioned by the 28 firms located elsewhere in Scotland. The exception was the Paisley firm of Brown, Malloch and Company, who paid a teacher 'for the instruction of the destitute and deserving of our factory children'.[30] However, in earlier evidence, the firm of James Oswald and Co. in Barrowfield, Glasgow, a large steam-powered spinning mill, was said to have 'an excellent and successful school attached to it'.[31]

Glasgow cotton manufacturers provided education for their young workers indirectly by supporting local evening schools and the thriving Sunday-school movement. In 1833 William Wyper had taught for seven years at 'the Calton education school' in Glasgow, where the children 'have been principally drawn from the cotton factories'. Wyper gave damning evidence that the factory children 'are in the evening so worn out with the fatigues of the day, that they are fitter for sleep than receiving instruction'. He complained about irregular attendance and testified that 'the greater number of factory women under eighteen years cannot, it consists with the deponent's knowledge, write'. The children attending the evening school were so exhausted by their day-time work that, 'instead of being fit for entering a school and deriving any thing like [a] rational proportion of improvement from it, they would rather require to be taking exercise in the open air, and invigorating their emaciated frames to fit them for the duties of a new day.' Wyper concluded sadly: 'Indeed, I consider the factory system detrimental to the intellectual and moral condition of the rising generation.'[32]

However, in many of the larger urban areas the poorest children escaped the net of evening and Sabbath schools altogether. In the Aberdeen area, there were 33 Sabbath evening schools in 1833, with an enrolment of 2,000 children. Only one, at the cotton mills of Gordon, Barron and Co. at Woodside, was directly connected with a manufacturing firm. However, in Aberdeen:

> A very large number of the poorest children, who suffer most from labouring in these [manufacturing] establishments, are not able, from want of clothes, debility and fatigue, to attend Sabbath Schools . . . they really have no time left for acquiring elementary education. Their strength and spirits are quite exhausted by the quantity of daily labour and confinement, which they undergo. Hence many females, who have been at work in factories from a very early age, cannot read distinctly a single word of the Bible when at thirty years of age and have children of their own . . . We know families who would send their children to our schools to receive religious and moral instruction, but they affirm that they cannot, as they must from necessity allow their children a large portion of the Lord's Day for rest and sleep.[33]

The anonymity of a large city such as Glasgow was similar to conditions in the Manchester cotton industry, where James Kennedy, a partner in the firm of James Kennedy and Co., ruefully conceded that its workers 'can and frequently do, leave us on a Saturday night without any notice, and without us ever knowing more of them'.[34] No such anonymity was possible in the tightly run factory villages, where the company controlled employment, often housing, and frequently schooling and religious provision. A rural cotton spinning company such as Robert M'Gregor and Co. of New Kilpatrick, Stirlingshire drew up strict and detailed rules for its tenants. Household behaviour was monitored, as was subletting to lodgers: 'You are strictly prohibited from harbouring beggars, idle or disorderly persons about your house, and are enjoined to observe orderly conduct in your own family.' The sale or consumption of alcohol was discouraged: 'No tenant in these houses allowed to sell spirits or malt liquors of any description.'[35]

The apogee of employer paternalism was reached in the large factory villages of Catrine, Deanston, New Lanark and Stanley. At Catrine in Ayrshire, the company employed between 800 and 900 workers, 'all occupying houses originally built by the company of a very different and superior description from those generally occupied by persons of the same situation in life in this country'.[36] At Deanston in Perthshire in 1833, there was a day school supported by fees from scholars, attended by 109 children, who paid school fees of 2s 6d a quarter for reading and 2s for writing. Deanston also had an evening school, attended by an average of 162 workers under 16 who were 'obliged to attend unless a reasonable excuse can be given'. In addition, there was a Sabbath evening school, attended by an average of 60 children and young adults.[37]

At New Lanark, James Stuart, the factory inspector, reported in 1833 that 'the school and apartments attached to it are magnificent'. This was another large concern, employing 930 workers in three mills. The mills supported a day school and an evening school, which met during the week and on Sunday evenings. Stuart claimed that 'the workers are instructed at the school and have medical assistance even on ordinary occasions, altogether at the expense of the company'. In fact the sick fund was supported by worker contributions of a penny out of every 5s wages. This produced an income of £20 to £25 a month, and any shortfall was made up by the company. Enough money was generated to support those who had grown old in the service of the company and those injured at work.[38]

Stanley, in Perthshire, supported a school, evening school and Sabbath school. Children were sent to day-school from 4 years old to 9, when they entered the mills, which employed nearly 1,000 people. School fees were kept low at 2s a quarter. Paupers and orphans were educated by their respective parishes and 'the children of the more destitute by a society lately instituted to provide instruction and bibles for all within the place who cannot afford to pay for them'. The Sabbath school attracted some 300 to 400 young people and boasted a library of 'several hundred volumes, chiefly religious and moral'. The Stanley Benevolent Society was designed for 'those who have been distinguished for Christian principles, frugality, and industry shall be regarded as particularly entitled to the society's assistance; and it is understood that the subscribers to this society shall always have a preferential claim'. Members subscribed a penny a fortnight and a committee managed its affairs. Other societies included a Gardeners Society and a Funeral Society, and the total impact of these organisations was 'to provide for the sick, the aged and the destitute and by means of which much suffering and misery have been relieved and prevented'.[39]

Paternalistic employers were also found in the finishing trades. The Crums of Thornliebank Printworks in Renfrewshire provided free schools for the children, a church, a park, sports grounds, swimming baths and the 'Halls', which housed the Thornliebank Club.[40] In the Vale of Leven, the Ewing family left money to churches and community projects. James Ewing, who died in 1854 with an estate of £281,296, left £18,000 to the Free Church both nationally and locally, including £500 'for the purpose of building and maintaining a free church in the village of Bonhill'.[41]

The changing economy of the west of Scotland

The apparent certainties and unchanging nature of the factory villages were being challenged by the 1830s, when some industrialists were already beginning to be concerned for the future of the cotton industry in Scotland because of its low profitability. A. E. Speirs, of Fintry cotton mills, Stirlingshire complained in 1834 that 'at the present time, cotton spinning is not a beneficial mode of employing capital'.[42] Henry Houldsworth, who ran spinning mills in Bishopton and Anderston, Glasgow, believed there was a very low rate of return on capital on power loom weaving and claimed in 1835: 'power loom weaving is a very lean trade for the capitalist, a profit of a penny on twenty five yards of calico, is not in my opinion, much below the average'.[43] This might be dismissed as a case of special pleading were it not for the fact that only a year later Houldsworth bought the Coltness estate in Lanarkshire and began to set up the Coltness Ironworks. Kirkman Finlay also complained in 1836 that 'the business of weaving by power has been a losing one'.[44]

Others were also diversifying into coal and iron. William Dunn, 'the most successful and extensive spinner in Scotland', owned a country estate at Duntocher, Dumbartonshire. Dunn died on 13 March 1849 and left an estate of £88,004, of which the value of cotton and other goods and cotton spinning machinery in his mills at Milton, Duntocher, Hardgate and Paisley, and machinery in his coal works at Duntocher was estimated at £32,166 (36% of the total). However, his business interests in the iron trade were more valuable than those in cotton, as his Machine Works and Iron Foundry at John Street, Glasgow were valued at £43,678 (49% of the total estate).[45]

The second half of the 1830s saw a significant shift in the economic climate of the west of Scotland. Writing in January 1836 to his son in Bombay, Kirkman Finlay noted wistfully: 'The whole trade of the country is in a state of the greatest activity, especially the iron trade, in the manufacture of which the profit is immense . . . From being a few years since in a state of great depression it is now the most profitable manufacture in the Kingdom and many persons are making immense fortunes.' Finlay added that Colin Dunlop (of Larkhall, Lanarkshire) was making an extra £60,000 a year. Between 1832 and Kirkman Finlay's death in 1842, Deanston cotton mills showed a modest average annual profit of 3.75%, Catrine profits being slightly higher.[46] However, the Finlays had diverse business interests and were cushioned from a modest performance in the cotton industry by their profits on overseas trading. From 1830 to 1839, the Paisley thread firm of J. and P. Coats made an annual average return on capital of 7.5%.[47]

The year 1837 was a difficult one for the Scottish cotton industry, with overproduction leading to falling prices for manufactured cotton goods. The long-established Glasgow cotton firm of James Oswald and Co., founded in 1783, failed in 1837. The company, with an annual wages bill of from £40,000 to £60,000 and a capital value of £128,837, had overextended, investing too much in plant and machinery. Many cotton mills in the west of Scotland reacted to the crisis by paying off workers or closing down their mills completely. James Finlay and Co. had a more paternalistic attitude and kept its mills at Ballindalloch, Catrine and Deanston going through the depression, paying wages to the workforce and meeting the cost of holding stocks, for which it obtained finance of £50,000 from the Royal Bank of Scotland.[48] Attempts by Scottish cotton firms to cut wages and substitute cheaper female labour for male mule spinners led to the Glasgow Cotton Spinners' Strike of 1837 in the west of Scotland, and there were similar acrimonious disputes in the Lancashire industry in the same period.[49] This will be discussed at more length in Chapter 5.

The late 1830s and early 1840s saw a significant shift in the markets for Scottish cotton yarn exports. In 1835, exports of Scottish yarn amounted to just under three million pounds, of which 56% went to India and China and 37% to Germany and Holland. By 1842, this had increased slightly to over three million pounds, of which 83% went to India and China, 10% to Russia and a mere 0.5% to Germany and Holland.[50] This shift in exports reflected the rise of European competition, resulting in increasing concentration by the Scottish cotton industry on 'softer' colonial and Far Eastern markets. This trend, reflected in the British cotton industry as a whole, continued through the second half of the nineteenth century, in exports of yarn and cloth.[51]

The bitter industrial conflict of the Cotton Spinners' Strike in 1837 accelerated the trend by Scottish employers to replace men by cheaper and allegedly more docile female labour. The 1840s saw the beginnings of the long decline of hand loom weaving, largely dominated by men, and the rise of large-scale power loom weaving factories, staffed largely by women. The number of hand loom weavers in Scotland fell from 84,560 in 1840 to 25,000 in 1850.[52] This was matched by a rise in the number of power looms, from 14,970 in 1833 to 30,110 in 1861, and the increasing feminisation of the Scottish workforce.[53]

The Paisley crisis of 1841

The 1837 strike was followed by a crisis in the Paisley shawl trade. By the 1840s, Paisley had gone through a number of industrial crises, from the decline of the silk gauze trade and the fine linen trade in the late eighteenth century to that of the Paisley shawl, which became a victim of changing fashions and the depression of the 1840s. The staple trade of the town was the manufacture of fine, hand-woven textiles, particularly shawls made in imitation of Kashmir shawls. It was carried on by numerous small capitalists, who relied heavily on credit, and by some larger manufacturers, who usually lived elsewhere, often in Glasgow, but used Paisley as a reservoir of skilled, relatively cheap labour. After the depression of 1841–1843, 'the shawl ceased to be the town's staple industry', although shawls continued to be produced in large numbers down to 1870.[54] The decline was blamed on changing female fashions: 'the decay of the shawl trade was not due to any deficiency or fault of the manufacturers. The fashion changed and the demand ceased.'[55]

By July 1841, the collapse in the shawl industry had led to mass unemployment, with 2,000 people dependent on the financial support of a relief committee, following a spate of bankruptcies in May. Later that month, James Kerr, a partner in the cotton thread firm of J. and J. Clark, wrote: 'Last week has been a most disastrous week for Paisley, we have had failures to the amount of £300,000.' However, Clarks continued to prosper, 'as yet we have stood almost clear and continued as thriving as ever, working day and night'.[56] Numbers on poor relief grew to 11,000 by Christmas 1841 and 15,000 by February 1843. The town went bankrupt in 1842, with a debt of £60,000, losing some £20,000 of savings bank money.[57] This was followed by another spate of bankruptcies and by spring 1843, 67 out of 112 businesses in the town had gone bankrupt. At the height of the depression, 25% of the population were on charity, probably the worst economic crisis to affect a British city in the nineteenth century. The crisis was so extreme that Sir Robert Peel's cabinet donated nearly £2,000 out of their own pockets, and Queen Victoria launched an appeal to channel charity donations into the burgh.[58]

The early 1840s were a difficult time for other parts of the Scottish cotton industry, although not on the same scale as Paisley. From 1840 to the outbreak of the American Civil War, the industry 'entered into a period of stagnation'. The average weekly consumption of raw cotton in Scotland rose to 2,364 bales in 1840 and remained fairly stable, with some fluctuations until 1861. Between 1838 and 1843, several large Glasgow cotton mills were destroyed by fire and not rebuilt. One of those affected, William Graham of Lancefield spinning mills, Glasgow, moved into overseas trade.[59] In 1838, Henry Houldsworth reported that more self-acting mules were coming into the industry and that men were leaving cotton manufacturing for better-paid work in heavy industry. This was reflected in the changing ratios of women to men in the industry. The ratio of women to men in cotton spinning in Scotland increased from about 3:1 in 1835 to 4.25:1 in 1856, when large numbers of women and girls replaced boys as piecers in spinning.[60] Similar far-reaching changes were taking place on the weaving side of the cotton industry, as hand loom weaving went into a long and painful decline. The number of hand loom weavers in the West of Scotland fell from 45,000 in 1840 to 10,000 in 1860.[61]

In 1844, James Finlay and Co. put its cotton mills at Ballindalloch, Catrine, and Deanston up for sale, but only sold Ballindalloch. This attempted sale was connected with the depression of the early 1840s. For the first time since their profit and loss records began in 1802, Catrine Mills recorded a loss of £5,500 in 1841, and the firm cut working hours from 69 hours a week in 1841 to 46 hours in 1842. Earnings for hand loom weavers employed by Catrine declined from 7s a week in 1837 to 5s 3d a week in 1842.[62]

Alexander Crum and Co. abandoned its spinning and weaving mills at Thornliebank near Glasgow in 1850 to concentrate on calico printing.[63] At New Lanark, the Walkers tried unsuccessfully to sell the mills and village in 1851–2.[64] Between 1850 and 1856, 24 new mills and 22 extensions to existing mills were built in Scotland, but 38 mills closed down in the same period.[65]

Expansion in the weaving and finishing trades

However, for other Scottish cotton firms the picture was one of expansion. Weaving expanded during most of the nineteenth century. In Glasgow, there were 37 weaving factories in 1854, with a further 16 firms combining spinning and weaving. In 1875, there were 17,500 power looms in the city and by 1891 there were 46 weaving factories.[66] The expansion was driven by specialist weaving firms such as David and John Anderson of Atlantic Mills, Bridgeton, Glasgow, which began as manufacturers of pullicates (a type of cotton cloth used for men's ties and cravats) and ginghams, trading with London and the East and West Indies in handkerchiefs or pullicates for men's neckware. Ginghams were manufactured for women's and children's dresses for both Britain and the USA. In 1844, David's son John joined the firm and he and his brother James built it up 'as one of the greatest cotton firms in the world'. Anderson's gingham became a household word in the USA and the firm farmed out its weaving to hand loom weavers all over Scotland, developing a fine-quality gingham cloth known as 'Zephyr'.[67]

Another Glasgow weaving firm, the muslin manufacturers John Lean and Sons, was founded in June 1840 by a father and son team from Lanark, who had been drapers and general merchants. They began modestly, buying cloth from hand loom weavers in outlying districts and recording a profit of £159 on a capital of £2,279 in 1848, a 7% return on capital. In 1845, the Leans began to employ hand loom weavers directly from their warehouse, and four years later took on a specialist hand loom weaver foreman. In 1841, home sales were 100% of turnover, but from 1846 onwards consignments were sent out to India on a regular basis. The retirement of John Lean Senior in 1847 and his replacement by his two sons marked a more aggressive attitude to overseas sales and production. Some 200 to 250 hand loom weavers were employed in Bridgeton, Calton and Parkhead in Glasgow, together with others in Larkhall for deep dhoties, Darvel for harness lappets and scarves, Eaglesham for books and Lisburn in Northern Ireland for mulls and jaconets.[68]

By 1853, the Leans found 'great difficulty in procuring labour as work is abundant for the now diminished numbers of hand loom weavers'. The firm solved this problem by opening a power loom factory in an old mill in Tobago Street, Glasgow in June 1854, renting out two floors and buying 152 second-hand lappet looms. In 1857 they built a new weaving factory in Reid Street, Bridgeton at a cost of £13,440. Turnover rose from £21,672 in 1855 (73% overseas sales) to £51,851 in 1870 (100% overseas sales). Sales were concentrated on the Indian market, particularly Calcutta, and from 1856 to 1870 Calcutta's share of total turnover was never less than 61%, and usually more than 70%.[69]

The finishing trades in Scotland also expanded in this period. The main centres for bleaching in Scotland were the Vale of Leven, the Cart Valley in Renfrewshire and around Perth on the rivers Almond and Tay. The major centre for calico printing and dyeing was the Vale of Leven in Dunbartonshire. The area was close to the textile centres of Glasgow and Paisley, had plentiful supplies of lime-free water from the River Leven, which drained Loch Lomond, and cheaper labour than the cities. Scotland was a major centre for calico printing within Britain. In 1840, Scotland had 70 printworks (42%) out of a British total of 166, and 10 years later, 81 (40%) out of 202. Lancashire was the major centre of textile printing in Britain by 1840.[70]

Renton in the Vale of Leven was the setting for two large finishing firms belonging to William Stirling and Co. of Glasgow – Cordale Printfield and Dalquharn Dyeworks. The cotton cloth and yarn dyed and printed in both places came mainly from Glasgow and Manchester. In 1868, Dalquharn employed between 900 and 1,000 people, of whom two-thirds were women and 'a considerable proportion are Irish'. The works dyed 18,450,000 yards of cloth and between 600,000 and 800,000lbs of yarn annually. The processes used huge amounts of water, equivalent to supplying every citizen of Edinburgh with 10 gallons of water a day. Madder was used to give the red colour to the cotton and was fixed by a mordant, usually salt of alumina. In the production of Turkey red the madder was mixed with bullocks' blood, of which the works used an astonishing 130,000 gallons annually.[71]

Stirling's Cordale Printworks and Dalquharn Dyeworks produced cotton yarn and cloth aimed at colonial markets, particularly India. In 1868, 'all the yarn and more than half of the cloth dyed at Dalquharn are exported in a plain red state'. The rest of the cloth was taken to the Cordale Printworks to be printed. The cloth produced was in bright colours and exotic patterns – 'as most of the goods are for the Indian market, the colours are somewhat "loud" and the designs peculiar'. Patterns varied according to the nature of the market in different parts of the Indian subcontinent. Dress pieces for Hindus sported a naturalistic peacock design round the border, whereas those for Muslims had an abstract mosaic design loosely based on the peacock (see Plate 2). As Bremner rather patronisingly explained, 'None of the designs of these Indian garments would find admirers in this country; and as the artists are bound by certain conventional rules, they have no scope for the creation of original patterns.' The same considerations applied to the production of cloth for turbans.[72]

Another speciality was the production of bandanna handkerchiefs for the Indian market. Previously these had been hand made in India, of silk with white spots on a dyed background. Monteith and Co. of the Barrowfield Dyeworks, near Glasgow made a breakthrough with the mechanical production of bandanna handkerchiefs; other Scottish firms followed suit, 'and Glasgow now has almost a monopoly of the trade'.[73] The Vale of Leven firms exported all over the world, the main markets being 'India, the Far East, certain Pacific islands, West Africa and South America'. There was some trade with Europe and Australia, but little with North America. Although some changes took place from the mid nineteenth century, India remained the major market.[74] Milton Printworks, near Dumbarton targeted mainly Asian markets. In 1861, it received orders for the Borneo Company, Batavia worth £395 and for R. Smith and Co. of Singapore worth £5,659.[75]

The chemicals industry grew out of the textile finishing trades. One of the largest chemical works in Europe was that of Tennants in St Rollox, Glasgow. Charles Tennant (1768–1838) developed a patent for dry bleaching powder in 1799 and about the same time the firm moved from Darnley to St Rollox. By 1830, the St Rollox works covered 10 acres and produced bleaching powder, sulphuric acid, soda and soap. As production increased, the price of bleaching powder fell dramatically. In 1799–1800, the works produced 52 tons of bleaching powder at £140 a ton. By 1870, it was producing 9,231 tons at £8 10s a ton.[76] Eleven years later, the works covered 180 acres of ground and paid out £120,000 a year in wages.[77]

The crisis of 1857

Cotton was an industry subject to rapidly changing fashions and the swings of international trade. Whilst the 1850s saw steady expansion in the finishing trades and in certain branches of the weaving trade, the embroidered muslins industry, one of the staples of the west of Scotland, was collapsing. In the 1840s, the Glasgow warehouse of the Campbell Brothers employed girls in embroidering muslin (Moravian print) along machine-printed patterns. The

1 Emblem (metal tray) of the Friendly Association of Cotton Spinners showing spinning mule with male spinner and girl piecer, c. 1825 (People's Palace, Glasgow)

2 Turkey Red dyeing for the Indian market. Peacock design for a sari border or shawl, c. 1860 (National Museums of Scotland, Edinburgh)

main market for Campbell's goods was London.[78] However, the dominant firm in the business was D. and J. McDonald and Co., another Glasgow firm. This company built 'a palatial warehouse' in Glasgow where its employed 1,500 men and 500 women, who were greatly outnumbered by large numbers of outworkers, between 20,000 and 30,000 needlewomen in the west of Scotland and Ulster. The value of the sewed muslin produced by the firm was £500,000 a year. In 1857 there was a commercial crisis, starting in America, the major market for sewed muslin. McDonalds and another large Glasgow muslin firm, Henry Monteith and Company, together with several smaller firms, went bankrupt, bringing down with them Glasgow's Western Bank, which had loaned them large sums of money.[79] The City of Glasgow Bank was also badly affected by the crisis but managed to survive until 1878. This crisis ended the attempts of the new Glasgow joint stock banks to challenge the dominance of Edinburgh.[80]

The crisis of 1857 was precipitated by overproduction in home and overseas markets, leading to ruinous price competition, so that 'Sewed muslin was thus placed within the reach of purchasers of the poorest class and the result was that the article ceased to be fashionable in the upper and middle ranges of society.'[81] This was similar to the crisis in the Paisley shawl industry in the previous decade. An important contributing factor to the demise of the sewed muslin industry in Scotland was foreign competition, with the rise of the Swiss machine embroidery industry from around 1840, which targeted the American market.[82] The outbreak of the American Civil War in the early 1860s, and the consequent interruption of raw cotton supplies into Glasgow, compounded these problems for the sewed muslin industry, as well as disrupting cotton manufacturing as a whole in Scotland.

The Cotton Famine and the impact of the American Civil War

The crisis of 1857 was followed by another and more devasting one, the Cotton Famine produced by the outbreak of the American Civil War. A number of historians have seen this as heralding the beginning of the end for the industry in Scotland, although the figures showing the recovery of the industry afterwards do not support this. In the years immediately after 1861, imports of raw cotton into Scotland fell dramatically, although production, represented by exports of cotton goods and yarn, increased in volume and value, as shown in Table 13.

With the outbreak of the American Civil War in 1861, British imports of raw cotton, of which 80% came from the southern states of the USA, fell from a total of 1,261 million pounds in 1861 to 533 million pounds in the following year and did not recover until 1865. The value of English cotton exports fell from £40 million in 1860 to £28.5 million in 1862, but recovered steadily

Table 13 Cotton imports and exports into and out of Scotland, 1861–1867

	Imports		Exports			
	Raw cotton	Cotton manufactures	Cotton manufactures		Cotton yarn	
Years	cwt	value	yards	value	lbs	value
1861	172,055	£19,009	150,754.031	£2,644,419	6,550,401	£467,612
1862	10,794	£63,105	120,119,627	£2,538,076	5,516,094	£504,045
1864	7,216	£30,027	94,766,371	£2,693,731	5,827,611	£831,395
1865	10,063	£18,411	126,912,955	£3,154,183	5,787,075	£653,155
1866	19,736	£24,711	164,194,915	£4,346,157	7,733,268	£847,833
1867	26,320	£12,745	206,394,756	£5,002,158	9,495,469	£842,326

Source: D. Bremner, *The Industries of Scotland*, 1869, 288.

to reach £58 million in 1866. The Cotton Famine caused huge distress in the cotton manufacturing districts of Britain. By November 1861, 49 mills in Lancashire had stopped and 119 were on short time. Out of 500,000 cotton workers in Lancashire, over 250,000 were receiving poor relief in November 1862. Manchester bankruptcies totalled 1,193 in 1861–1864, 338 cotton mills closed between 1861 and 1868, and the workforce fell by 50,505. The crisis led to a 'speculation mania' in cotton futures and a general banking crisis in the spring of 1866, when the London bank Overend, Gurney and Co. Ltd, stopped payment with liabilities of nearly £19 million.[83]

The Cotton Famine hit Scotland equally hard. In 1861, there were 161 factories in Scotland with nearly 2 million spindles and 30,000 power looms, employing over 40,000 people. Table 13 shows that raw cotton imports into Scotland fell from 172,055 cwt in 1861 to a low of 7,216 cwt in 1864 and exports from 150 million yards of cloth in 1861 to 94 million yards in 1864, although the value of cloth exports remained the same. Scottish cotton workers were in a worse state than in Lancashire, where able-bodied but unemployed workers received outdoor relief or workhouse relief. In Scotland, the Royal Commission on the Relief of the Poor ruled 'relief to able-bodied persons from funds raised by assessment is neither necessary nor expedient' and 'nothing herein contained shall be held to confer a right to demand relief by able-bodied persons out of employment.'[84]

An earlier generation of historians believed that the Cotton Famine dealt a fatal blow to the industry in Scotland and 'marked a stage in the permanent decline of the industry which had already begun with the financial crisis of 1857.'[85] However, Table 13 shows that cotton yarn exports from Scotland, which amounted to 6.5 million pounds in 1861, declined to 5.5 million

Table 14 Amounts and origins of raw cotton used at Catrine Works, Ayrshire, 1856–1864 (lbs)

Year	Total	Orleans (US)	Surat (E. India)	Other[a]
1856	1,000,773	436,128	291,948	272,697
1857	1,005,480	387,562	397,649	220,269
1858	1,000,040	300,980	503,446	195,614
1859	1,097,678	734,307	123,630	239,741
1860	1,120,103	381,715	481,183	257,205
1861	1,167,212	430,428	596,163	140,621
1862	728,501	102,010	582,746	43,745
1863	66,730	–	66,730	–
1864	659,951	80,459	572,552	6,940

(*Note:* [a] Other types of cotton included Mobile (Alabama), Upland (Georgia) and in 1857 Texan.)

Source: GUA, James Finlay and Co., UGD 91/1/5/2/1/2/2, Catrine Works, Ayrshire, Annual Statements, 1857–1864.

pounds in 1862 but recovered to 9.5 million pounds by 1867, while the value of yarn exports increased from £468,000 in 1861 to £842,000 in 1867. However, the industry gradually ceased to be a major employer of labour in Lanarkshire. In 1861, the cotton industry employed 23.6% of the total female workforce in Lanarkshire but by 1901 this had declined to a mere 4.7%.[86] Employment figures in Renfrewshire held up rather better, because of the success of the cotton thread trade.

One of the few surviving sets of records for a Scottish cotton mill in this period is from Catrine in Ayrshire, owned by James Finlay and Co. These show that supplies of cotton from different parts of the world fluctuated from year to year, according to harvests, prices and world trading conditions (Table 14). From 1856 to 1861, between 49% and 89% of the firm's raw cotton supplies came from the USA, but American cotton imports collapsed in 1862 and completely dried up in 1863. A year later, 87% of the firm's raw cotton came from Surat in India. However, the overall consumption of raw cotton at Catrine had fallen by about two-thirds from the boom years of 1856–1861.

The main costs at Catrine were accounted for by raw cotton rather than by wages. In 1857, the total costs of water spinning were £19,435, of which raw cotton amounted to 75% and wages 10%. In the same year, mule spinning costs were £19,185, of which raw cotton amounted to 72% and wages 9%.[87] This pattern of raw material costs dominating overall costs is similar to that in the 1830s for both Finlays and J. and P. Coats.

Responses to the Cotton Famine were mixed. A paternalistic firm like James

Finlay closed the mills at Catrine and Deanston for lack of cotton but paid its workers half wages and extended school hours, so that young workers had five hours' schooling a day. The cost of paying half wages was estimated at £13,000 a year.[88] At Stanley in Perthshire, the owner, Samuel Howard of Burnley, Lancashire, ensured himself a place in local demonology by stockpiling supplies of raw cotton to sell on to Lancashire at a profit, in the meantime closing down the mills for five years, from 1862 to 1867, and throwing almost the whole population out of work. The population of Stanley fell from 1,272 in 1861 to 932 in 1871.[89] New Lanark saw a more dramatic decline, from 1,399 in 1861 to 973 in 1871, part of a longer-term decrease from 2,300 in 1821 to 672 in 1891.[90]

The growth of specialised niche markets

The number of cotton spinning firms in Scotland, excluding thread makers, fell from over 100 in 1861 to 15 in 1889 and only 9 in 1910.[91] However, it was still possible to buck the trend. Often the recipe for survival took the form of entering specialised 'niche markets', such as cotton thread in the case of Paisley or, on a much smaller scale, fishing nets at New Lanark or Scandinavian cotton belting at Stanley Mills, Perthshire. At Stanley, the Perthshire-born William Fenton leased part of the mills in 1881 to produce Scandinavian cotton belting, with which he had become familiar during 18 years of managing textile mills in Jonsorod, Sweden. Weaving of belt to drive steam engines was eventually taken over by F. S. Sandeman and became a staple of production at Stanley for many years.[92]

Another long-established factory village, New Lanark, was taken over in 1881 by Henry Birkmyre and his brother-in-law, Robert Sommerville. They continued cotton spinning but introduced the manufacture of fishing nets. As at Stanley, the new management installed Jonval turbines to supplement and eventually replace the water wheels. The first one at New Lanark was installed in March 1884, three years after Stanley, and generated power via rope and belt drives. A second was installed in 1898 and the two turbines generated 827 horse power between them.[93] Birkmyre's main business interest was the Gourock Ropework Company in Port Glasgow and he invested in shipbuilding companies on both the Clyde and the Tyne, including the yards of his son-in-law, William Todd Lithgow. Birkmyre also invested in steam fishing fleets, and the Gourock Ropework Company continued to operate New Lanark until 1968.[94]

There were also new developments in Glasgow. In 1871, James Patterson and his brother Robert built a new spinning mill complete with modern machinery for their firm, James Paterson and Co., in Cotton Street, Dalmarnock, Glasgow. They produced fine yarns for the cotton thread industry. Significantly, the mill was equipped with machinery from Manchester.

Eight years later, in 1883, Thomas Reid founded the Glasgow Cotton Spinning Company in Bridgeton, which specialised in producing high-count yarns for the Turkey red dyeing industry. The firm was described as 'the only concern (in Scotland) which meets the Lancashire establishments on their own ground, and . . . its experience proves that commercial success is possible with capital, experience and the right methods'.[95] The factory was modelled on the 'Oldham Limiteds' and embodied a new type of fireproof construction, with hollow tiles in place of brick arches. Reid's family firm was a dyeing firm, Alexander Reid, and his partner was John Colville, who became chairman of A. and A. Galbraith Ltd., one of the few early nineteenth-century Glasgow cotton spinning firms to survive into the twentieth century.[96]

The success of the North of England firms in this period spawned imitators in Scotland, using Lancashire and Yorkshire architects to design textile mills. Reid's Cotton Spinning Works in Bridgeton was designed by Joseph Stott of Oldham in 1883, and Coats' No 1 Spinning Mill at Ferguslie, Paisley, by Woodhouse and Morley of Bradford in 1887. Similarly, Clark's Anchor Thread Mills in Paisley boasted the giant Mile End Mill, built in 1899–1900 to the designs of Morley of Bradford.[97]

In 1868, the Galbraith mills at Oakbank and St Rollox in Glasgow were 'among the most extensive cotton factories in Scotland'. The cotton used was mainly American, Indian and Egyptian. The spinning department contained 95,000 mule and throstle spindles, and the weaving department 1,532 power looms, the whole powered by steam engines of up to 1,600 horse power. The workforce was heavily feminised, with 1,600 females (94%) out of a total of 1,700. The mills produced 17 million yards of plain cloth a year, which was sent for printing and dyeing. The type of cloth produced was varied, ranging 'from fine muslin for summer dresses to stout calicoes'.[98]

The growth of limited liability companies and the decline of the family firm

By the late nineteenth century, the family firm, the staple of manufacturing industry in Britain, was beginning to be replaced by the limited liability company, which offered greater access to capital. In 1881, the Glasgow cotton spinners James Paterson and Co. became the Clyde Spinning Company Ltd.; and Thornliebank Print Works, Renfrewshire was floated as a limited company in 1886, with a nominal capital of £250,000.[99] The Paisley thread firm of J. and P. Coats became a limited company in 1890.[100] By 1903, the Gourock Ropework Company had been floated as a limited company, with a nominal capital of £720,000 which included the New Lanark cotton mills.[101] The cotton mills at Stanley, Perthshire, became a limited liability company in 1915, linked with Manhattan Jute Works, Dundee under the title Frank Stewart Sandeman and Sons Ltd.[102] Although many of these limited companies were dominated by family members, limited liability did leave the door open to the slow rise of the professional manager with few or no connections to the founding family, to takeover by larger firms and to amalgamation in larger units.[103]

The combination and amalgamation of several firms into a larger unit was another favoured survival strategy. By the third quarter of the nineteenth century, the bleaching, dyeing and finishing trades contained some of the largest and most dynamic firms in the textile sector. Under the management of Alexander Crum, Thornliebank Printworks, Renfrewshire became the largest in the UK. After Crum's death in 1893 the firm joined the Manchester-based Calico Printers' Association in 1899, which marked a loss of momentum and of Scottish control. The subsequent history of Thornliebank was a melancholy one of 'decline and gradual closure in favour of its less distinguished English counterparts'.[104]

Similar strategies took place in dyeing, when the Vale of Leven dyeing firms combined in 1898 to form the United Turkey Red Company, although in this case there was no loss of Scottish control. The United Turkey Red Company was headed by a trained chemist, John Christie, who had begun working for the dyeing firm of John Orr Ewing and Co. in 1859. Christie, the son of a Barrhead joiner, attended the Andersonian College, Glasgow part time and began his working life with his cousin, John Hyde, who ran a silk manufacturing and dyeing firm in Port Dundas, Glasgow. Christie carried out research into the Steiner method of dyeing, which he introduced to Alexandria in 1863, and on artificial madder, the dye used in the Turkey red process. He worked in 1868 with Sir Robert Pullar, head of the Perth dyeing company and pioneer of dry cleaning in Scotland, on aniline dyes. However, in a telling example of successful foreign competition, the Germans gained a monopoly of producing artificial dyes in 1882 and the Scottish industry was forced to rely on German imports.[105]

A similar loss of momentum occurred at the giant chemical works of Tennant and Co. in St Rollox, Glasgow, which had made its reputation producing dry bleaching powder and sulphuric acid for the textile finishing trades. In 1890, it led a combination of 45 chemical firms into the United Alkali Company. However, the firm remained stubbornly committed to the older Leblanc process of alkali production, whereas its English rival, Brunner-Mond, made an early switch to the more efficient ammonia-soda process, invented by the Belgian Ernest Solvay.[106]

A success story – the Paisley thread trade

Knox has divided the Scottish cotton industry at this time into 'losers, hangers on and winners'.[107] The major success story was the Paisley cotton thread industry, dominated by a handful of family firms, particularly Coats and Clarks. These two firms grew to virtually monopolise the world market in cotton thread, governed by the introduction of the domestic sewing machine in the 1850s and the increasing demand for industrial thread.

From the late 1850s, a 'new paternalism' began to emerge amongst cotton thread firms in Paisley, aimed at their increasingly female workforce and stressing the dynastic and paternalistic relations between employers and employed. This was part of a British and indeed a European phenomenon. In 1851, James Hudson praised 'the unexampled efforts now being made in every part of the kingdom for the intellectual and physical improvement of the lower classes of the community' and went on to explain how 'the manufacturer finds it profitable to form schools and factory libraries, to rear amateur bands of musicians amongst his workmen, to encourage frugality by savings banks, benefit societies, sick clubs, clothes clubs, burial associations and by occasional tea meetings, at which he and his family partake, to destroy that barrier between men, which pride and wealth sometimes ungraciously erect'.[108] This is a telling description of the largely successful attempts by the Victorian middle classes to create a cultural hegemony.

The period from 1850 to 1875 was the 'golden age' of dynastic capitalism across Europe, with the family firm as the dominant form of industrial organisation. This type of paternalistic capitalism began to decline with the arrival of the limited liability company, often combined with a tendency towards monopoly and the amalgamation of firms, from the 1890s onwards. In Britain, it was also affected by the growth of alternative state welfare systems – the Workmen's Compensation Acts of 1895 and 1907, and Liberal reforms from 1906 onwards, which included pensions (1908), Trade Boards (1909), Labour Exchanges (1909) and National Insurance (1911).[109] However, paternalism continued to have a vigorous existence in Paisley, where it was associated with the collapse of hand loom weaving, the rise of the thread trade and power loom weaving and the increasing feminisation of the workforce. Paternalism was much more a feature of a burgh like Paisley than of a city like Glasgow, which resembled Manchester in having a larger, less settled, more anonymous and diverse population.

By 1857, J. and P. Coats employed 1,000 people and the total value of thread manufactured in Scotland was estimated at £400,000. There were ten factories with a total workforce of 3,000, 77% female. These factories produced about 11 million bobbins of thread, each holding 100 to 300 yards. This required huge amounts of wood for the bobbins – about 13,000 tons annually, worth £13,000. Paisley cotton thread was 30% cheaper than French thread and won prizes at the Paris Exhibition of 1855, where the Paisley firms involved were Coats, Clarks, Carliles, Clappertons, and Kerr and Clark.[110]

From this group of competitors emerged two major firms – Coats and

Clarks. Both firms were well served by innovative textile engineers. Thomas Coats was the main innovator in his family firm, whilst the main technical mind behind Clarks was Peter Kerr. The dominant figure in the later development of the industry was the German-born Otho E. Phillipi, who ran the sales side of Coats. Phillipi typified the new breed of professional managers who were beginning to come to the fore in limited liability companies. He masterminded the merger with Clarks and also reorganised the Calico Printers' Association in 1899.[111] Initially, Clark and Coats formed a joint sales combination called the Sewing Cotton Agency in 1889, which functioned as a sales regulator and account collector. In 1896, the firm of Coats, which had become a limited liability company in 1890, amalgated with Clarks of Paisley, Jonas Brook of Meltham and James Chadwick of Bolton to form J. and P. Coats Ltd, with a capital of nearly £11 million and 17,000 shareholders.[112] The firm claimed an 80% share of world markets in cotton thread and had manufacturing bases all over Europe and in the USA. By 1913, J. and P. Coats had a market value of £22 million, with 25,000 shareholders, although half of both preference and ordinary shares remained in family hands.[113] This helps to explain why an analysis of wealth holders in Britain revealed that of 23 cotton millionaires, no fewer than 56% were Paisley based.[114]

The thread industry was heavily export orientated. In 1840, 75% of Coats' output went to the USA, and Andrew Coats was based there for 20 years to supervise sales. George Clark, from the rival Paisley thread firm, followed Andrew Coats to the USA and set up a thread manufacture in Newark, New Jersey in 1864. In 1870, the Coats followed suit and built a cotton thread mill at Pawtucket, Rhode Island.[115] Both firms were concerned about their rivals undercutting them in the highly competitive American market, and circled around each other in wary fashion with a view to coming to an (illegal) agreement on prices. Archibald Coats wrote from Paisley to James Coats in the USA in 1870:

> It is no use, however, talking of our going to Clark regarding prices, that we never will do. If a settlement is come to they must come to us, or it must be proposed by [a] neutral partner, in which case we will be glad to meet them after a few months of present 6 cord prices. If you see George Clark a few months hence, say about May, and *he* speaks to you about a settlement you can easily say our position was such that we could be willing to meet them in a fair way, but for heaven's sake, don't you go and put us in a humiliating position by being the first to propose such a settlement. You know how the Clarks 'blow' and after the position by them individually and as a firm taken up, we must be in a position to deny that we made any overtures to them.[116]

Both these families had strong religious convictions and their philanthropy owed a good deal both to this and the desire to create loyalty amongst the workforce by creating a 'company culture'. However, behind the cosy façade of paternalism, there lurked an iron fist and a ruthlessly competitive attitude. In November 1870, Archibald Coats recorded: 'Had a strike of night workers a week ago on Friday night, shut them out on Saturday, they were glad to get back on Monday. Kept out thirty of the ringleaders and got plenty to fill their places and pulled up seven. Two fined £3 5s each on 14 days and evenings out for their case who did not appear, two got off'.[117]

It seems likely that the Coats and Clark thread dynasties were influenced in their paternalistic management styles not only by the Lancashire cotton industry but by early exposure to the American cotton industry, where paternalistic firms were the norm.[118] In 1857, the Coats' workers turned out in their 'hundreds . . . late at night' to welcome James Coats and his American bride back from their honeymoon.[119] There was also a strong element of competitive philanthropy, with the Clarks and the Coats vying with each other in endowing buildings, facilities and organisations in Paisley. Paisley Museum and Library was donated to the burgh in 1871 by Peter Coats, who received a knighthood for his endowment. This was countered when George Clark, who died in Newark, New Jersey in February 1873, left a bequest of £20,000 for the erection of a Town Hall in Paisley.[120] The Town Hall was finally opened in 1882, the occasion marked by a parade of all the town's trades, including blacksmiths, joiners, bricklayers, engineers and organisations such as friendly societies, public authorities and officials. They carried banners bearing inscriptions such as 'Wher'er the Town Hall chimes do ring, the Donors to our minds they bring' (threadworkers), 'Long live the Brothers [Clark] one and all, the Donors of the new town hall' (joiners), and 'Combine to support but not to injure' (bakers).[121]

The Paisley 'threadocracy' used part of their immense wealth to provide a comprehensive welfare system for their workforce, including pensions, schooling and housing, as well as donating a wide range of civic amenities to the town, part of a conscious attempt to stabilise industrial relations. A contemporary described how 'the leading men in the thread trade have at all times taken a lively interest in the affairs of the town' and how 'their names are to be found on the governing boards of every institution and society, educational, philanthropic and religious in the town'. Thomas Coats presented the Fountain Gardens in 1868 to the burgh, together with an endowment of £5,000. This combined a seven-acre park with a Geological Museum. He also gifted £6,000 for the Coats Observatory, a public observatory, which was transferred to the Philosophical Institution in October 1882, shortly before his death.[122] Thomas Coats died in Paisley on 15 October 1883. His funeral was a highly ritualised event, attended by 'from 7,000 to 8,000 children belonging to the Board Schools of the town, the Grammar School, the John Neilson Institution and the Ragged School'. There were nearly 1,000 men in the funeral procession and thousands of spectators. The Coats Memorial

4 Anchor Mills, Paisley, c. 1890. Workers 'skailing' (leaving) the works at 2.00 p.m. after the early shift

Baptist Church was erected to his memory by his family, at a cost of between £100,000 and £150,000.[123]

McIvor has argued that paternalism was blatantly selective, 'the supervisors, clerical staff and skilled workers were the major beneficiaries of company largesse around 1880, though significantly, there was usually something for all workers'.[124] This certainly applied to Paisley, where the thread firms favoured their skilled male workers with bowling greens near the Anchor and Ferguslie Mills, whilst Coats also provided men with facilities for tennis, cricket and football near the Ferguslie Works. Similarly, George Clark specified that Paisley Town Hall should be provided with 'a large reading room for working men, where they can sit in comfort and enjoy smoking; and the room shall be open from five o' clock in the morning till twelve o'clock at night', whilst Coats supported a reading room for working men, known as the Artisans' Institution.[125]

By contrast, women, the majority of the workforce, were provided with a (closely supervised) hostel for young single women at Coats' Ferguslie Works and works outings on 'Sma' Shot Saturday', the first Saturday in July, which they organised and paid for themselves. These involved 'six or seven different excursions, which frequently require two to three trains to each place . . . as many as ten thousand trippers connected with the thread trade will sometimes enjoy a holiday in this manner'. Each of the flats in the thread mills had a 'Holiday Bank', where the women saved their money on a weekly basis for the holidays.[126]

The decline of the Scottish cotton industry

Whilst J. and P. Coats and Co. thrived, the rest of the cotton industry in Scotland was in terminal decline. By 1896, there were only two cotton spinning mills left in Glasgow and two weaving factories with spinning departments. Even in weaving, 'the bulk of the plain calico weaving trade has practically gone and it is only in the finer goods, known as "fancies" . . . that Glasgow has been able to hold her own'.[127] Cotton yarn production in Scotland fell from 0.95 million pounds in 1867 to 0.19 million in 1907 and the number of spinners fell from 17,000 to 3,000. In England, yarn output grew from a weekly total of 17.5 million pounds to 29 million pounds between 1867 and 1907, whilst the workforce increased from 200,000 to 219,000. In the same period, the number of cotton weavers in England doubled from 153,000 to 304,000, whilst in Scotland the weaving workforce halved from 22,000 to 11,000. Output of cotton piece goods almost doubled in England, from 68.25 million yards in 1867 to 134 million in 1907, whilst in Scotland they more than halved, from 5.19 million to 2 million yards.[128] The decline is mirrored in employment figures. Employment in Scottish cotton factories fell from 10% of UK employees in 1867 to 6% in 1889, and the total number of employees in the Scottish cotton industry fell from 24% of the UK total in 1841 to 3% in 1891.[129]

The reasons for this decline have been debated at length by historians. The industry exhibited a fatal combination of 'a recalcitrant labour force and an unmotivated management'.[130] Some contemporaries blamed the workforce. Wages in the Scottish cotton industry were lower than in England. In 1886, the highest-paid cotton workers in Britain were in Burnley, with 35.4% of its workforce consisting of men and an average wage of £42 per year. In Scotland, only 10.6% of the workforce were men and average wages were £28.[131] However, as will be demonstrated in Chapter 5, productivity was much higher in England.

Others blamed the decline of the Scottish cotton industry on the failings of the employers, rather than on the inefficiency and restrictive practices of the workers. Until recently, many historians shared this view of entrepreneurial failure as an explanation for the loss of Britain's economic dominance in the last quarter of the nineteenth century. However, historiography in the 1980s provided a more favourable view of Victorian entrepreneurs and argued that most of them made the best of changing circumstances.[132] Well-informed contemporaries were not so indulgent towards the Scottish cotton manufacturers. The *Textile Trade Review*, in 1883, contrasted the hard-working, practical, first-generation Glasgow cotton masters with their spoilt successors with gentlemanly aspirations: 'Born with silver spoons in their mouths . . . with little love for the practical work of their fathers.' Margaret Irwin, writing in 1893, believed the Scottish cotton manufacturers had made their fortunes and the next generation were 'lacking in commercial enterprise'.[133]

By contrast, Campbell believed that the Scottish industry's decline was due to its 'relative backwardness in the introduction of the mechanical devices' and its dependence on textile machinery developed and manufactured in Lancashire. Henry Houldsworth, a prominent Glasgow cotton manufacturer, had acknowledged this as early as the 1830s, having 'no doubt that Manchester is the leading place for machinery' and that 'good improvements' there in the previous two or three years were adopted only slowly in Glasgow.[134]

Bolin-Hort has argued that the decline of the industry in Scotland was due to better incentives for workers and greater worker efficiency in Lancashire, based on regional piece rates after 1850. These agreements, which were upheld by unions and management in Lancashire, meant that greater worker efficiency, such as minding more looms, led to increased earnings. After the Glasgow Cotton Spinners' strike of 1837, piece rate lists were abolished and every employer fixed his own rates. After 1837, there appeared to be organised trench warfare between workers and management in the west of Scotland and all attempts at increasing efficiency were resisted by workers because there was no guarantee that it would increase earnings.[135] Another factor may have been the presence of large numbers of Irish workers in the west of Scotland cotton industry, leading to sectarian and racist attitudes by employers and corresponding responses from workers, which were less prevalent (although certainly not unknown) in Lancashire.[136]

Another explanation is that of comparative advantage – the advantages given to Lancashire by geographical concentration and economies of scale. Geographical concentration took place within the Scottish cotton industry itself, as early cotton manufacturing centres further from the Clyde ports, such as Dundee and Fife, gradually declined and reverted to linen production, whilst the cotton industry became increasingly concentrated in Lanarkshire and Renfrewshire. The English woollen industry provides another example of increasing industrial concentration, as the West Riding of Yorkshire rose to a dominant position in woollen manufacturing, at the expense of regions such as East Anglia and the West Country.[137]

The Lancashire cotton industry was always on a larger scale than its counterpart in Scotland, leading to many comparative advantages, from a thriving textile engineering industry to a larger market for commercial activities such as sales or credit. This was picked up early on by Scots merchants and manufacturers, some of whom moved south to work in various parts of the cotton industry in Manchester, Liverpool and London. Archibald Prentice, for example, who began in a cotton warehouse in Glasgow, was appointed in 1811 as a commercial traveller to sell Scottish muslins in England. He spent three years in sales, travelling the length and breadth of England, then concentrated on the wholesale houses of London and Manchester. In Manchester he quickly found 'that I met in the street in one day more country drapers than I could with the utmost industry meet in their shops in two and it struck me that if we kept our manufactured stock in Manchester we could considerably increase our business and at a great saving in travelling expenses'.[138]

By September 1815, Prentice was predicting that Manchester 'would become so much the market for all kinds of goods, in cotton, woollens, linen and silk, as to attract every respectable country draper in England several times a year'. The young man had spotted the importance of geographical concentration and the advantages of a much larger and wealthier market for fashion items and he:

> spoke of the coal fields of Lancashire and of the industry, the enterprise of the hard headed shrewdness of the inhabitants. He said, 'We have coal and industry and intelligence and shrewdness here.' 'Yes', I replied, 'you have, but you have not centrality; you are in a corner, you have nothing but Glasgow and Paisley; Manchester has about a dozen of Paisleys – Wigan, Preston, Blackburn, Bolton, Bury, Rochdale, Ashton, Stockport and numerous fast growing villages, all increasing in importance and likely come time or other, if fair play is given to their industry, to form one enormous community.'[139]

His arguments convinced his employer, who gave the go-ahead for a Manchester warehouse, to which the Glasgow stock was transferred in only three weeks. This was an early example of a trend which was to intensify throughout the nineteenth century.

By the 1890s, Margaret Irwin believed that Lancashire was able to concentrate on producing larger quantities of cheaper fabrics, involving long 'runs', whereas in Scotland the emphasis was on producing smaller quantities of more expensive 'fancy' goods, with shorter production runs. She argued that whilst the cotton industry was the major outlet for manufacturing energy in Lancashire, in Scotland, it was only one of many outlets.[140]

There were only nine cotton spinning firms left in Scotland in 1914, excluding the highly successful Paisley thread industry. A similar decline had taken place in the finishing trades. After 1851, when the number of Scottish textile printworks had peaked at 81, the industry went into steady decline and by 1919 there were only 10 printworks in Scotland, 8 belonging to the Calico Printers' Association, which the Scottish firms had joined in 1900. Thornliebank Printworks in Renfrewshire had declined from being 'the largest and best equipped print works in the world' to a subsidiary of a Lancashire conglomerate.[141] The Scottish cotton industry had changed from being the innovative launch pad for the country's industrialisation to a relic of a bygone era. The reasons for this still remain elusive, in spite of numerous attempts to explain them. Partly this is because there are still major gaps in our knowledge of the industry, such as the lack of detailed comparison with the Lancashire industry, and an absence of reliable material on the marketing of Scottish cotton goods. These issues will be discussed in the next three chapters.

Notes

1. P. L. Payne, *British Entrepreneurship in the Nineteenth Century* (London, 1988); and S. Gunn, 'The "Failure" of the Victorian Middle Class: A Critique', in J. Wolff and J. Seed (eds), *The Culture of Capital: Art, Power and the Nineteenth Century Middle Class* (Manchester, 1988).
2. For Paisley see J. Blair, *The Paisley Thread Industry* (Paisley, 1907). For more recent discussion see R. H Campbell, *The Rise and Fall of Scottish Industry, 1707–1939* (Edinburgh, 1980); A. Slaven, 'Entrepreneurs and Business Success and Business Failure in Scotland', in D. Aldcroft and A. Slaven (eds), *Enterprise and Management: Essays in Honour of Peter L. Payne* (Aldershot, 1995); W. W. Knox, *Hanging by a Thread: The Scottish Cotton Industry, c. 1850–1914* (Preston, 1995); P. L. Payne, *Growth and Contraction: Scottish Industry, c. 1860–1990* (Dundee, 1992); and P. L. Payne, 'Industrialisation and Industrial Decline', in A. J. Cooke et al. (eds), *Modern Scottish History, 1707 to the Present. Volume II, The Modernisation of Scotland, 1850 to the Present* (East Linton, 1998).
3. Report of Select Committee on Manufactures, Commerce and Shipping, *Parliamentary Papers* (*PP*), 1833, VI, Q652.
4. Mitchell Library, Glasgow (ML), Glasgow Chamber of Commerce Correspondence (GCC), 9 July 1784.
5. A. Brown, *A History of Glasgow and of Paisley, Greenock and Port Glasgow* (Glasgow 1795), III, 239–44.
6. Factory Inquiry Commission, Employment of Children in Factories, *PP*, 1834, XX, A1, 227–8.
7. *PP*, 1834, XX, A1, 144–5.
8. Factory Inquiry Reports. Evidence taken by Mr. Stuart, *PP*, 1833, XX, A1, 105.
9. Factory Inquiry Reports. Evidence taken by Mr. Mackintosh, *PP*, 1833, XX, A2, 49.
10. *PP*, 1833, XX, A1, 98.
11. Report of Select Committee on Bill to regulate the Labour of Children in Factories, *PP*, 1831–2, XV, 241–8 and 264.
12. *PP*, 1833, XX, A1, 103–4.
13. *PP*, 1833, XX, A1, 36–7.
14. *PP*, 1833, XX, A1, 104.

15. A. Slaven, *The Development of the West of Scotland, 1750–1950* (London, 1976), 96–100; and N. Murray, *The Scottish Handloom Weavers, 1790–1850. A Social History* (Edinburgh, 1978).
16. *New Statistical Account of Scotland* (*NSA*) (Edinburgh, 1845), VI, 153–4.
17. Glasgow University Archives (GUA), Lancaster, Duncan and Co., UGD, 189/4/9, Discharge 28 February 1834.
18. *PP*, 1834, XX, 195.
19. A. K. Cairncross and J. B. K Hunter, 'The Early Growth of Messrs J. and P. Coats, 1830–83', *Business History*, 1987, XXIX, 175.
20. P. Joyce, *Work, Society and Politics: The Culture of the Factory in later Victorian England* (London, 1980).
21. *Ibid.*
22. A. C. Howe, *The Cotton Masters, 1830–1860* (Oxford, 1984), 109–114.
23. *PP*, 1834, XX, A1, 14.
24. *PP*, 1834, XX, A1, 5.
25. *PP*, 1834, XX, A1, 27.
26. *PP*, 1834, XX, A1, 188–9.
27. *PP*, 1834, XX, A1, 155–6 and 135.
28. *PP*, 1834, XX, A1, 196.
29. S. Pollard, *The Genesis of Modern Management, A Study of the Industrial Revolution in Great Britain* (London, 1965), 201.
30. *PP*, 1834, XX, A1, 199.
31. *PP*, 1834, XX, A1, 79.
32. *PP*, 1834, XX, A1, 102.
33. *PP*, 1834, XX, A2, 89.
34. *PP*, 1834, XX, D1, 227.
35. *PP*, 1834, XX, A1, 230.
36. *PP*, 1834, XX, A1, 94.
37. *PP*, 1834, XX, A1, 82.
38. *PP*, 1834, XX, A1, 93–7.
39. *PP*, 1834, XX, A1, 76–8.
40. G. Turnbull, *A History of the Calico Printing Industry in Great Britain* (Altrincham, 1951), 94.
41. National Archives of Scotland, Edinburgh (NAS), SC 65/34/7, fols 183–200, Will of James Ewing, 21 February 1854.
42. *PP*, 1834, XX, A1, 227.
43. Report on the State of the Irish Poor in Great Britain, 1835, *PP*, 1836, XXXIV, Appendix G, Scotland, Evidence of Henry Houldsworth.
44. J. L. Carvel, *The Coltness Iron Company: A Study in Private Enterpris* (Edinburgh 1948), 9–13; and C. Brogan, *James Finlay and Company Ltd., 1750–1850* (Glasgow 1951), 154.
45. *NSA*, VI, 154 and NAS, SC 65/34/6/117, Will of William Dunn, 4 October 1849.
46. Brogan, *James Finlay*, 140, 71 and 18.
47. Cairncross and Hunter, 'Coats', 169.

48. S. G. Checkland, *Scottish Banking: A History, 1695–1973* (Glasgow, 1975), 419.
49. W. H. Fraser, 'The Glasgow Cotton Spinners, 1837', in J. Butt and J. T. Ward (eds), *Scottish Themes* (Edinburgh, 1976); and M. Winstanley, 'The Factory Workforce' in M. B. Rose (ed.), *The Lancashire Cotton Industry: A History since 1700* (Preston, 1996), 136.
50. J. Butt, 'The Industries of Glasgow', in W. H. Fraser and I. Maver (eds), *Glasgow, Volume II, 1830–1912* (Manchester, 1996), 183–4.
51. S. D. Chapman, *The Cotton Industry in the Industrial Revolution*, 2nd edition (London, 1987), 43.
52. Murray, *Handloom Weavers*, 23.
53. Butt, 'Industries of Glasgow', 100.
54. M. Lochrie, 'The Paisley Shawl Industry', in J. Butt and K. Ponting (eds), *Scottish Textile History* (Aberdeen, 1987), 104.
55. Blair, *Paisley Thread*, 30.
56. GUA, UGD 199/7/2/1, J. and P. Coats Ltd, Letterbook of James Clark, 1821–42, James Kerr to A. and I. Reid, 31 July 1841.
57. I. Levitt and T. C. Smout, *The State of the Scottish Working Class in 1843* (Edinburgh, 1979), 156.
58. Report of the Select Committee on Distress (Paisley), 1843, *PP*, 1843, VII; and T. C. Smout, *A Century of the Scottish People, 1830–1950* (London, 1986).
59. A. J. Robertson, 'The Decline of the Scottish Cotton Industry, 1860–1914', *Business History*, 1970, XII (2), 117–18; and R. H Campbell, *Scotland since 1707: The Rise of an Industrial Society* (reprinted Oxford, 1971), 108–9.
60. E. Gordon, *Women and the Labour Movement in Scotland, 1850–1914* (Oxford, 1991), 45–6.
61. Slaven, *West of Scotland*, 105.
62. GUA, UGD 91/1/5/1/1/3, James Finlay and Co., Statements and Calculations relating to Ballindalloch, Catrine and Deanston, 1835–56.
63. J. Maclehose, *Memoirs and Portraits of 100 Glasgow Men* (Glasgow, 1886), Vol. I, 94.
64. Butt, 'Industries of Glasgow', 101.
65. Robertson, 'Decline', 118.
66. Butt, 'Industries of Glasgow', 106.
67. Anon, *Famous Fabrics 1822–1952. David and John Anderson, Atlantic Mills, Bridgeton, Glasgow* (Glasgow 1952).
68. A. Slaven, 'A Glasgow Firm in the Indian Market: John Lean and Sons, Muslin Weavers', *Business History*, 1969, XLIII (4). A dhoti is a Hindu loincloth (as worn by Mahatma Ghandi). A lappet is a little lap or flap made of cloth. Mull is soft muslin and jaconet is a cotton fabric similar to muslin, originally from Jagannath in India.
69. *Ibid.*
70. Turnbull, *Calico Printing*, 82.
71. D. Bremner, *The Industries of Scotland: Their Rise, Progress and Present*

Condition (Edinburgh, 1869), 297–304; and A. Clow and N. Clow, *The Chemical Revolution: A Contribution to Social Technology* (London, 1952).

72. Bremner, *Industries of Scotland*; and N. Tarrant, 'The Turkey Red Dyeing Industry in the Vale of Leven', in J. Butt and K. Ponting (eds), *Scottish Textile History* (Aberdeen, 1987), 37–47.
73. Bremner, *Industries of Scotland* .
74. Tarrant, 'Turkey Red', 44.
75. National Library of Scotland, Edinburgh (NLS), Account Books of Milton Printworks, Dunbartonshire.
76. Clow, *Chemical Revolution*, 191–3.
77. G. Stewart, *Curiosities of Glasgow Citizenship* (Glasgow, 1881), 44.
78. J. G. Kohl, *Scotland* (London, 1844), 7.
79. Bremner, *Industries of Scotland*, 308.
80. R. E. Tyson, 'The City of Glasgow Bank and the Crisis of 1857', in Aldcroft and Slaven (eds), *Enterprise and Management: Essays in Honour of Peter L. Payne* (Aldershot, 1995), 151–70.
81. Bremner, *Industries of Scotland* .
82. B. Collins, 'Sewing and Social Structure: The Flowerers of Scotland and Ireland', in R. Mitchison and P. Roebuck (eds), *Economy and Society in Scotland and Ireland, 1500–1939* (Edinburgh, 1988), 247.
83. W. O. Henderson, *The Lancashire Cotton Famine, 1861–1865*, 2nd edition (Manchester, 1969), 35, 13, 53 and 23–6.
84. *Ibid.*, 120–3.
85. *Ibid*, 131; and H. Hamilton, *The Industrial Revolution in Scotland*, 2nd edition (London,1932).
86. Knox, *Hanging by a Thread*, 23 and 37.
87. GUA, UGD 91/1/5/3/1/3, James Finlay and Co., Statements relating to Ballindalloch, Catrine and Deanston.
88. Brogan, *James Finlay*, 45.
89. A. J. Cooke, *Stanley. From Arkwright Village to Commuter Suburb, 1780–2003* (Perth, 2003), 108.
90. I. Donnachie and G. Hewitt, *Historic New Lanark. The Dale and Owen Industrial Community since 1785* (Edinburgh, 1993), 144.
91. A. Slaven and S. G. Checkland (eds), *Dictionary of Scottish Business Biography, Volume I, The Staple Industries* (*DSBB*) (Aberdeen, 1986), 297.
92. Cooke, *Stanley*, 112.
93. Donnachie and Hewitt, *New Lanark*, 169.
94. *DSBB*, Vol. I, 298.
95. Robertson, 'Decline' 126; and *DSBB*, Vol. I, 383–4 and 396.
96. *DSBB*, Vol. I, 297; and J. Hume, *Industrial Archaeology of Glasgow* (Glasgow, 1974), 29.
97. J. Hume, *The Industrial Archaeology of Scotland, Vol. I, The Lowlands and Borders* (London, 1976), 218–20.
98. Bremner, *Industries of Scotland*, 290–3.
99. *DSBB*, Vol. I.

100. Cairncross and Hunter, 'Coats'.
101. G. Blake, *The Gourock. A History of the Gourock Ropework Company* (Glasgow, 1963).
102. Cooke, *Stanley*, 115.
103. P. L. Payne, *The Early Scottish Limited Companies, 1856–1895* (Edinburgh, 1980); Payne, *British Entrepreneurship*; Payne, *Growth and Contraction*; Payne, 'Industrialisation'. See also Slaven, 'Entrepreneurs and Business Success'.
104. *DSBB*, Vol. I, 384.
105. *DSBB*, Vol. I, 300 and 321–2; and W. Harding, *Pullars of Perth* (Perth, 1991).
106. N. Crathorne, *Tennants Stalk. The Story of Tennants of the Glen* (London, 1973) 143–4; and *DSBB*, Vol. I, 288–9.
107. Knox, *Hanging by a Thread*, 173.
108. J. W. Hudson, *The History of Adult Education* (1851) (reprinted London, 1969), vi.
109. Joyce, *Work, Society and Politics*, 134–57; Payne, *British Entrepreneurship*; and A. J. McIvor, *A History of Work in Britain, 1880–1950* (London, 2001), 87.
110. J. Parkhill, *The History of Paisley* (Paisley, 1857), 108.
111. *DSBB*, Vol. I, 299.
112. Blair, *Paisley Thread*, 62–3.
113. *DSBB*, Vol. I, 330–1.
114. W. D. Rubinstein, *Men of Property: The Very Wealthy in Britain since the Industrial Revolution* (London, 1981), 82.
115. Anon, *Coats the Threadmakers, 1830–1980, 150th Anniversary Exhibition* (Paisley, 1980).
116. GUA, UGD 199/1/2/2, J. and P. Coats Ltd, Correspondence 1868–1872, Archibald Coats to James Coats, 21 January 1870.
117. GUA, UGD 199/1/2/2, J. and P. Coats Ltd, Letter from Archibald Coats, 26 November 1870.
118. T. Dublin, *Women at Work: The Transformation of Work and Community in Lowell, Massachusetts, 1826–1860* (New York, 1979); and W. Gordon, *Mill Girls and Strangers: Single Women's Independent Migration in England, Scotland and the United States, 1850–1881* (New York, 2002).
119. W. W. Knox, *Industrial Nation. Work, Culture and Society in Scotland, 1800–Present* (Edinburgh, 1999), 110.
120. Anon, *Coats*.
121. Knox, *Industrial Nation*, 109.
122. Blair, *Paisley Thread*, 85–100.
123. R. Brown, *The History of Paisley* (Paisley, 1886), 393.
124. McIvor, *History of Work*, 85.
125. Brown, *History of Paisley*, 391 and Blair, *Paisley Thread*, 85–90.
126. Blair, *Paisley Thread*, 81–3.
127. M. H. Irwin, 'Women's Industries in Scotland', *Proceedings of the Philosophical Society of Glasgow*, XXVII, 1895–6, 73 and 77.
128. Knox, *Hanging by a Thread*, 89–92.
129. Butt, 'Industries of Glasgow', 99–100.

130. Payne, *Growth and Contraction*, 9.
131. Knox, *Hanging by a Thread*, 89–91.
132. Payne, *British Entrepreneurship.*
133. Irwin, 'Women's Industries', 78.
134. R. H. Campbell, 'The Making of the Industrial City', in T. M. Devine and G. Jackson (eds), *Glasgow. Volume I, Beginnings to 1830* (Manchester, 1995), 197.
135. P. Bolin-Hort, 'Managerial Strategies and Worker Responses: A New Perspective on the Decline of the Scottish Cotton Industry', *Journal of the Scottish Labour History Society*, 1994, XXIX.
136. A. J. McIvor, 'Work, Wages and Industrial Relations in Cotton Finishing, 1880–1914', in J. A. Jowitt and A. J. McIvor (eds), *Employers and Labour in the English Textile Industries, 1850–1939* (London, 1988), 127–152.
137. P. Hudson, *The Industrial Revolution* (London, 1992) 116–17; and M. Berg, *The Age of Manufactures, 1700–1820: Industry, Innovation and Work in Britain*, 2nd edition (London, 1994), 98–115.
138. R. Prentice, *Historical Sketches and Personal Recollections of Manchester* (London, 1851), 66.
139. *Ibid.*, 67.
140. Irwin, 'Women's Industries', 73–4.
141. Turnbull, *Calico Printing*, 93.

4

Technology

When capital enlists science in her service, the refractory hand of labour will always be taught docility. (Andrew Ure, *The Philosophy of Manufactures*, 1835)

Introduction

From the late 1730s a series of remarkable inventions in textile machinery took place in the Midlands and the North of England. They revolutionised the emerging process of cotton manufacturing and ushered in the modern factory system. Wrigley has characterised industrialisation as a move from an 'organic' to a 'mineral' economy and Whatley has stressed the importance of the shift from human, animal, wind and water power to the use of coal-powered steam engines in the Scottish economy.[1] However, Scotland, with its rich resources of water power, was slower to change in this direction than the North of England and water power remained important in the Scottish cotton industry long after steam power had become dominant in Lancashire.

Originally, all the technology of cotton manufacture had to be brought in from England. Gradually the Scots began to play a more proactive role in textile technology. Mokyr has identified the phenomenon of 'clustering' of inventions, comparable to clustering in the cultural realm, and has argued that 'the driving force in the industrial revolution was a similar clustering of a relatively small number of macro-inventions in a relatively small corner of north-west Europe. These macro-inventions, by raising the rate of return on further improvement and development, unleashed waves of micro-inventions and "learning by doing" phenomena, which jointly provide the technological basis of the industrial revolution.'[2] By 'macro' inventions Mokyr meant major breakthroughs in an industrial process, such as the inventions of Hargreaves, Arkwright, Cartwright and Crompton in cotton spinning and weaving. 'Micro' inventions were defined as ongoing developments and improvements in technology following major breakthroughs. In cotton spinning and weaving, the Scots were particularly prominent in developing various 'micro' inventions. For example, William Kelly at New Lanark and James Smith at

5 Old Mill, Johnstone, Renfrewshire (1782)

Deanston both made improvements to the spinning mule. Kelly invented a semi-automatic mule and in 1790 successfully applied water power to the mule.[3]

The diffusion of technology

However, the diffusion of technology took place at very different rates in the different branches of the cotton industry. Industrialisation was a complex process, involving more than simply the rapid replacement of hand methods and small-scale working units by factories and machine processes. It has been described as a 'complex web of improvement and decline, large and small scale production, machine and hand processes'.[4] The carding and spinning of cotton were rapidly mechanised, using first horse power to drive the new machinery, then water power and increasingly, from the late 1790s,

6 Finishing mill, Anchor Mills, Paisley (1886)

steam power. Not all parts of the preparatory stages were as quick to mechanise, however. Cotton picking remained a part-time, largely female occupation, often carried on by hand in workers' homes rather than in factories. At Catrine in Ayrshire in the early 1790s, there were 226 women picking cotton at home, whilst at New Lanark there were 109 women who 'work at picking cotton in their own houses and for the most part have families, some of whom are employed at the mills'.[5] David McVicar, the Stanley manager, wrote in 1789 that a tailor who wished to settle in the village would be welcome, his children would find work in the mill and 'if he has a wife who will be at the trouble of learning to pick cotton I could give her constant employment and our women earn and have employment from 3 to 6s a week'.[6] Nor was the system confined to rural areas. Henry Houldsworth, the owner of steam-powered spinning mills at Anderston in Glasgow, described in 1816 how he employed over 100 women picking cotton in their own homes.[7]

Pirn winding was another low-paid manual job carried out often by married women at home. Walter Freer's mother worked as a pirn winder in Glasgow. The mill supplied a board with wire pins on it, together with yarn, and the women spun this yarn onto pirns with a pirn wheel in their own homes. This was rewarded by 'shockingly low wages, about a shilling a week'.[8]

Weaving remained overwhelmingly hand powered until the 1830s, in spite of the introduction of power looms from the 1810s. Hand loom weaving was initially the preserve of the skilled male artisan, for which an apprenticeship was served. The process was heavily gendered, with women and children, often from the weaver's family, making up the support team for each weaver. The centre of the fancy weaving trade in Scotland was Paisley, where in 1805 the muslin trade employed 6,750 weavers, each creating work for at least two additional people, engaged in winding, warping, clipping, tambouring, sewing, bleaching and calendering.[9] Hand loom weaving took place in the home and in small workshops, but also in hand loom weaving factories controlled by capitalist employers who often ran spinning mills. This was the case in Aberdeen, where in 1814 William Thom entered the hand loom weaving factory in School Wynd owned by Gordon, Barron and Co., the owners of water-powered spinning mills at Woodside, on the edge of Aberdeen.[10] Similar conditions prevailed in the west of Scotland, where many of the steam-powered spinning mills in Glasgow and Paisley employed large numbers of hand loom weavers as outworkers, who could be easily laid off in times of trade depression. By the 1830s, Glasgow and Paisley capital in the form of merchant and manufacturing houses controlled the work of virtually all the hand loom weavers in Scotland, from Ayr and Kilmarnock in the West to Perth and Stirling in the East.[11]

The third major component of the cotton industry, the finishing trades, including bleaching, dyeing and textile printing, adopted new technology much more quickly than did the weaving process. The Scots were in the forefront of developments such as new machinery, new power systems and the replacement of organic bleaching and dyeing agents by new and faster-working chemical agents. By 1812, there were 56 bleachfields in Renfrewshire alone, using bleaching liquor and bleaching powder, and a contemporary writer boasted that 'Their art has derived much benefit from chemical discoveries, and they have wisely availed themselves of the aids which science affords.'[12] Whyte has explained this propensity to innovate as due to a more extensive and practical system of education in Scotland, as compared to England: 'Scots did not simply copy English ideas and technology; they made their own distinctive contribution to the Industrial Revolution, due in part to the more practical slant of the Scottish education system.'[13]

Cotton manufacture – preparing and spinning

Cotton had been manufactured in Lancashire since the early seventeenth century, often mixed with Scottish or Irish linen yarn to strengthen the cloth. Raw cotton is the downy fibre surrounding the seed pod of a tropical plant.

It came into the country in bales and had to be disentangled, cleaned and blended before carding. A new machine for cleaning cotton, called a scutching or blowing machine, was invented by Neil Snodgrass of Glasgow in 1797 and was first used by Johnston and Co. of Houston in Renfrewshire.[14] It was introduced into Manchester about 1808 and was improved by the firm of Arkwright and Strutt, with the introduction of an air fanner and sieve. In 1817, Archibald Buchanan of Catrine, Ayrshire made further improvements to the opening and blowing machines and was claimed, with some degree of hyperbole, to have created a blowing room 'as free of dust as a drawing room'.[15]

Carding was the process of combing the cotton to straighten the fibres into a long rope called a sliver. The process was originally done manually, using hand cards, which were brushes made of wire mounted in leather and then stuck onto a flat piece of wood with a handle. In the late 1730s, the stock cards used in woollen manufacture were adapted to cotton carding, which meant that one of the two cards was made a fixture and later the moveable card was attached to a pulley. This greatly increased productivity. A major breakthrough came with the invention of the carding cylinder, patented by Lewis Paul of Birmingham in 1748. This was introduced into Lancashire in the 1760s and improved by James Hargreaves, a Blackburn weaver. In 1775, Richard Arkwight took out a patent for an improved carding machine, which included a feeder belt for feeding the cotton onto the cylinder.[16] However, this patent did not apply in Scotland.

At Catrine Mills in Ayrshire, a letter to Claude Alexander in 1788 described the proposed construction of a carding house: 'Mr Dale has sent us no plans of the carding house it is uneccessary to wait for his plan let it be built of the dimensions he mentions within walls and place the windows in it in the same way they are in the Large Mill and then we cannot go wrong as we can shut up windows if they are not wanted.'[17] Incidentally, this seems to contradict claims made by Robert Owen that his father-in-law, David Dale, 'knew little about cotton spinning'.[18]

Some of the early carding machines were driven by horses. The Paisley radical Arthur Sneddon went to work in 1797 at the age of 10 as a piecer in the Underwood cotton mills in Renfrewshire. After a year, he moved on to the carding room, 'driven by a horse and gin at this time; hand jennies being entirely used in the mills'. Other parts of the carding operation were powered by 'a water wheel in rather a primitive way'. A steam engine pumped water into a cistern, which then drove the water wheel. Sneddon had to attend 'two finishers and a breaker'.[19] Carding machines powered by horse gins are recorded in the 1790s in Dundonald, Ayrshire and Douglas, Lanarkshire, and water-powered carding machines at Dalry in Ayrshire and Cambuslang, Lanarkshire.[20]

At Stanley, Perthshire, the owner James Craig began to set up mechanical carding in February 1808 with advice from Robert Owen at New Lanark. Owen advised Craig to buy his carding machines from Whitley and Co. at Halifax and thought that 70 carding machines would be enough for Craig's operation. At New Lanark, half the carding machines were made of wood, half of cast iron, which made little difference to quality. Owen advised that Demerara or other coarse types of cotton should be put two or three times through the carding machines, thin and well spread.[21] Further improvements to the carding machine were made by James Smith of Deanston, Perthshire in 1815 and again in 1829, which were confirmed by patent in 1833.[22] By the 1830s, John Bartholomew's spinning and weaving factory in the Barony parish, Glasgow was using ventilation funnels to carry off the dust from the carding and scutching rooms.[23]

The slivers from the carding machines were fed into tall cans. Drawing was the next stage, which took four slivers to be stretched into longer and straighter fibres. Roving was carried out on a flyer frame. The fibre was drawn out yet again and slightly twisted, then wound onto a bobbin. Roving underwent several improvements, culminating in the development of the bobbin and fly frame by Henry Houldsworth Junior in Glasgow in 1825.[24] Spinning took the yarn from the bobbins and stretched and twisted it onto cops (the conical ball of thread on a spindle) to make a finer thread. In the 1790s, there were three types of spinning machinery to be found in Scotland. The first was the jenny, usually called 'jeannie' in Scotland, invented by the Lancashire weaver James Hargreaves in 1767. It was a machine driven initially by hand, later by horse gins, consisting of a large wooden frame with a single large wheel with eight vertical spindles. It mimicked the actions of a hand spinner but enabled several spindles of yarn to be produced simultaneously. The eight threads could be spun using female and child labour. However, the jenny was only suitable for spinning weft (the short thread carried on the shuttle) for weaving, not the stronger warp (the thread stretched lengthwise on the loom.)[25]

At New Lanark, William Kelly improved the jenny so the machine could be driven by water power. By 1793 there were four mills at New Lanark, the first containing 4,500 spindles, the second 6,000 spindles. The third mill housed 'patent jennies' modified by Kelly. The rationale was to cut down the dependence on expensive and potentially disruptive male labour: 'the great improvement arising from Mr. Kelly's invention of Jennies going by water, reduces very considerably the number of men that formerly were necessary in working the common Jennies. Such being the case, widows with large families are much wanted here, as children can manage the patent Jennies with great ease, while their mothers are employed in other branches.' [26] At Luncarty, Perthshire, in 1795, the company 'spins cotton by jeanies, constructed after

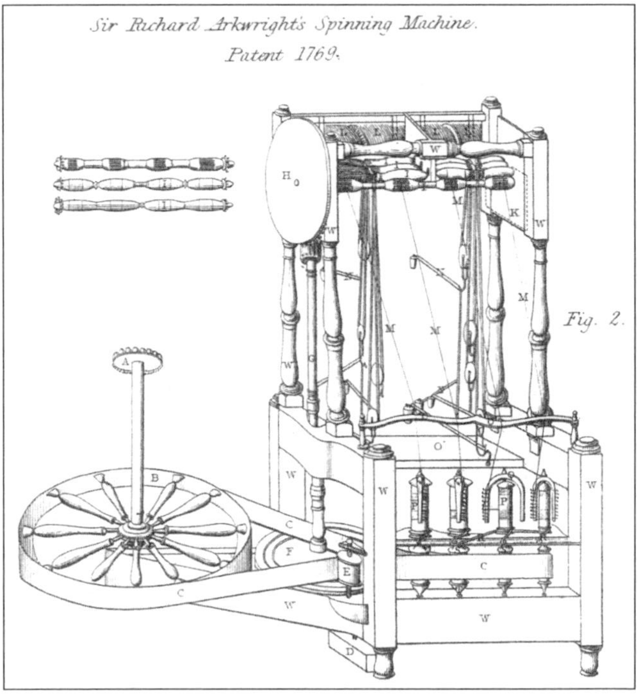

7 Richard Arkwright's Spinning Frame, patented 1769

the most approved plan; the carding and spinning are performed by water. They employ about a thousand spindles'.[27]

The second cotton spinning machine was the water frame, patented by Richard Arkwright in 1769. The water frame had two sets of leather rollers, the second revolving faster than the first and drawing out the fibre to the required thickness or 'count' before it was twisted. Spinning by rollers had been developed in Birmingham by Charles Wyatt and Lewis Paul as early as 1738. The water frame required more power than the jenny but produced a strong cotton yarn suitable for warp and therefore complemented the jenny. Originally, Arkwright specified that the machine would be driven by horses but, as its name suggests, the water frame was better suited to be driven by water power and required greater capital investment than the jenny.[28] At New Lanark in 1807, the top rollers used for water spinning were leather covered with sheepskin, which had been oiled and dried, from Cummings of Kilmarnock.[29]

A modification on the water frame, popular in rural Scottish water-powered mills, was the spinning throstle, a lighter and simpler machine, which could be more easily altered to spin different counts of yarn.[30] In December 1802, Robert Owen recommended to James Craig at Stanley, Perthshire that he should replace some of his water frames by throstles, 'because you can put more spindles in the same space' and they would work with less power and cost less to make. Owen promised to send drawings of the throstles and Craig could have castings of most parts of the machine.[31] However, the major improvement to the spinning throstle came, significantly, not from Britain but from the USA, in 1831. This was the Danforth Throstle, named after its American inventor and introduced into Scotland by Alexander Carrick, a native of Glasgow. Its great advantage over the conventional spinning throstle was its speed – it ran at 8,000 to 9,000 revolutions a minute, compared to 4,000 to 5,000 revolutions a minute for the traditional throstle.[32] In 1831, the ratio of mule spindles to throstles in Lanarkshire was 12 to 1, with 591,288 mule spindles and 48,900 throstles. Andrew Ure believed that the proportion of throstles in England at this time was higher because of the demand 'for throstle yarn for the fustian and velveteen fabrics'.[33]

The third type of cotton spinning machine was the mule, a cross between the jenny and the water frame, invented by Samuel Crompton of Bolton, Lancashire in 1779, which produced finer and stronger yarn. This combined the leather rollers of the water frame with a moving carriage and spindles mounted on wheels, so that the thread was stretched and twisted when the carriage moved away from the rollers and wound onto the spindles when it moved back again. Mule spinning required greater strength than water spinning and was generally carried out by men.[34] The mule was originally worked by hand, but in 1792 William Kelly of New Lanark took out a patent for a type of self-acting mule worked by machinery. The main idea behind this was to replace more expensive male labour by women and children. However, after a trial it was found 'that a greater amount of produce might be obtained and at a cheaper rate by taking the men back as spinners and employing them to return the carriage as formerly while the machine performed the other operations. In this way one man might spin two mules.'[35]

In 1795, Archibald Buchanan was engaged by Finlay and Company to fit out its cotton works at Ballindalloch, Stirlingshire. He built 'very light mule jennies' and, as a result, 'dispensed altogether with the employment of men as spinners, and trained young women to the work. These he found more easily directed than the men, more steady in attendance to their work and more cleanly and tidy in the keeping of their machines, and content with much smaller wages.' When Buchanan moved to Catrine in Ayrshire in 1802 he took the same system with him there and introduced female spinners.[36] At Rothesay Mills, Bute, the spinning machinery in the 1830s had been adapted for use by children between 9 and 12 years old, ' there being many poor widows with small families in the place in consequence of the father being lost at sea and otherwise'.[37] This reflected the ingenuity of William Kelly, the

Lanark clockmaker and Dale's former manager at New Lanark, who was a partner at Rothesay until his retirement in 1826.

Scottish cotton mills contained a wide range of spinning machinery, depending on the fineness of the yarn required. A valuation of 39 Scottish water-powered mills in 1791 estimated that they housed a total of 124,800 spindles on water frames, working day and night, an average of 3,200 spindles per mill. In addition there were 1,200 'common jennies' with an average of 84 spindles each, working by day, valued at £6 each, and 600 'mule jennies' with an average of 144 spindles each, valued at £30 each. This resulted in a total count of 312,000 spindles. Water frames accounted for 40% of spindleage in the Scottish industry at this time, jennies for 32% and mules for 28%. Most of this was used to produce finer yarns. A fourth of the spindleage was 'spinning warps and wefts' with an average count of No. 25, producing 3,479,563lbs of coarser yarn valued at an average 4s 1d a pound. The other three-fourths of the spindles produced finer yarns with an average count of 75 and worth an average 9s 6d a pound for the estimated 1,149,475lbs produced. However, because the industry produced about three times as much coarse yarn as fine, the coarse yarn sector was worth more than the fine.[38]

The type of machinery installed in cotton mills could change over time, as products changed and new improvements came in. In 1793, No. 3 Mill at New Lanark contained water-powered 'patent jennies' developed by William Kelly.[39] By 1819, No. 3 Mill, which burned down that year, was devoted to mule spinning.[40] In June 1813, when Stanley Mills, Perthshire were offered for sale, the two mills contained 'about 16,000 Mule and Water spindles in excellent condition and now going' as well as 60 power looms ready to be put up.[41] The efficiency of the mule improved greatly, so that by the 1830s one spinner could operate up to 1,200 spindles, compared to the average of 144 spindles in 1791. Eventually, a virtually automatic (self-acting) mule was developed by the Manchester engineer Richard Roberts, who took out patents in 1825 and 1830.[42]

The self-acting mule was used as an example by Marx to demonstrate the use of technology by capital to dominate and subdue labour. A number of inventions, he argued, had 'the sole purpose of supplying capital with weapons against the revolts of the working class. At the head of these in importance stands the self acting mule, because it opened up a new epoch in the automatic system.'[43] Andrew Ure made a similar point in 1835: 'the effect of substituting the self acting for the common mule, is to discharge the greater part of the men spinners, and to retain adolescents and children', which he hoped would 'put an end to . . . the folly of trades unions'.[44] However, whatever the intentions of employers, male mulespinners maintained their position in both Britain and the USA for most of the nineteenth century. Some historians have claimed that the self-acting mule deskilled mule spinning.[45]

However, Freifeld has argued that looking after a 'self actor' remained skilled work, with spinners being responsible for larger numbers of spindles. The 'doubling up' of mules began in Lancashire in the 1820s, but only after 1837 in Scotland. Scottish mule spinners remained highly paid – in Glasgow in 1838 they were paid 22s a week for 300 spindles and 24s for 600. However, by the 1880s and 1890s, mule spinning flats in Scotland were dominated by women, although men continued to supervise the work.[46]

Between 1885 and 1914, the USA was much quicker than Britain to adopt ring spinning, an invention by the American John Thorp (1828) that saved labour, speeded up cotton spinning and eventually replaced spinning mules. By 1905 there were 17.9 million ring spindles in American cotton mills, as compared to only 5.2 million mule spindles. By contrast, in Britain, as late as 1913–1914, there were only 10.4 million ring spindles, as compared to 45.5 million mule spindles. This was despite the fact that by the early 1880s all the leading Lancashire machine makers were producing ring frames, mainly for export.[47] Scotland was actually quicker than England to adopt the new technology. In 1901, ring spindles made up some 30% of total spindleage in Scottish mills, compared to only 14% in England. This was largely due to the widespread use of ring spindles in the manufacture of cotton thread in Paisley and Renfrewshire. The ratio of mule to ring spindles in 1901 was four to one in Lanarkshire, whilst in Renfrewshire it was nearer two to one. At the Glasgow Cotton Spinning Company, the most advanced works in Glasgow, ring spindles amounted to some 28% of total spindleage, well above the average for Lanarkshire.[48]

Central heating in Scottish cotton mills

The best temperature conditions for cotton manufacture were between 65 and 80 degrees Fahrenheit, depending on the nature of the process and the quality of the spinning being carried out. William Shanks, a cotton spinner from Johnstone, Renfrewshire, testified that 'cotton will not spin well below seventy degrees'.[49] The finer spinning and processes such as warp dressing required higher temperatures. Some cotton mills had complicated arrangements for different temperatures in different parts of the building, depending on the processes being undertaken. In the 1830s, James Oswald's Barrowfield Cotton Works in Glasgow consisted of three steam-powered mills spinning mule twist. The wright shop, mechanic shop, reeling, winding and warping rooms were heated to between 60 and 70 degrees Fahrenheit. The picking rooms were kept at between 70 and 76 degrees, the four card rooms at 78 degrees and the eight spinning rooms at 81 degrees. The temperature for fine spinning was kept around 85 degrees and was reduced to around 83 degrees for coarser yarn.[50] Dugald McPhail and Company's power loom weaving factory in Glasgow, which produced cotton cloth for printing, reported that high temperatures were not required for weaving, except for dressing the yarn.[51] The Factory Inspectors who visited the three Glasgow factories for spinning and weaving owned by the McPhails in 1833 commented: 'It seems singular that although a high temperature is necessary in some part of each of these establishments, a thermometer has never been seen, by the overseers or workmen, in any one of them.'[52] Another Glasgow power loom factory, that of John King, heated the dressing flat to between 80 and 90 degrees, but elsewhere the heat was for the comfort of the workers and was regulated by them.[53]

At Gordon, Barron and Co's Woodside Mills in Aberdeen, in the 1830s, the temperature varied between 65 and 70 degrees Fahrenheit. The highest temperature required was in the warp dressing room, where the warp for the power looms was dressed with starch. This process required the stifling temperature of between 86 and 90 degrees Fahrenheit.[54] The highest temperatures in the whole industry were in dyeing. At Blantyre works in Lanarkshire, which combined cotton spinning, weaving and Turkey red dyeing, the lowest temperatures were in the weaving factory, between 60 and 70 degrees. In spinning it was between 70 and 80 degrees, whilst in the dyeworks it was occasionally an astonishing 150 degrees, but was claimed to be never over 90 degrees when people were involved. Because of the high temperatures required, Turkey Red dyeing stopped in 'severe winter weather'.[55]

These processes required the installation of stoves for central heating in cotton mills. A memorandum from the late 1780s quoted different insurance rates for cotton mills heated in different ways. The lowest rate was for 'Stoves fixed in Arches of Brick or Stone on the Lower Floors, with upright metal pipes, carried to the whole Height of the Buildings, through Brick Flues or Chimnies, or having common Grates, or close or open Metal stoves or Coakles, standing at a distance of not more than one foot from the wall, or Brick or Stone Hearths, surrounded with fixed Fenders, and not having more than two Feet of Pipe leading therefrom into the Chimney.' This type of heating was expensive to install but cost only 10s per cent to insure. A more expensive rate was for 'stoves with metal pipes and Drying Stoves contained in an arch of brick or stone'. The most expensive rate was for cheaply installed 'Pot or Kettle Stoves', which presented a greater fire risk and cost double the rate of the first type – 20s per cent to insure.[56]

George Dempster, MP, a partner in Spinningdale mills, Sutherland, wrote to Sir Adam Fergusson in 1794 that he was introducing central heating at his Dunnichen house along the lines of the Sutherland mill. Dempster described 'a curious experiment I am trying at Dunnichen to heat the saloon, dining room, drawing room and principal bed chambers by means of an oven that bakes the air and diffuses it in tubes thro' all the house. Our cotton mill here (Skibo) is warmed in this way. One oven bakes more air than is sufficient in half an hour to make a story of the mill too hot for human habitation.'[57] At New Lanark, William Kelly claimed in 1796 to have solved the problem of overly high insurance premiums by inventing a stove with a series of hot air ducts, which 'was sufficient to warm a mill of 150 feet by 30 or upwards'.[58] In Renfrewshire in 1812, heating 'by metal tubes from a furnace' had been replaced in many cotton mills by steam pipes.[59] In 1816, Houldsworth's mills in Anderston, Glasgow were heated by steam pipes, those at Woodside 'by rarefied air and stoves partly and partly by steam'.[60]

Artificial lighting in Scottish cotton mills

Because of long working hours in cotton mills, some form of artificial lighting was necessary, particularly in winter. In the early days, candles or oil lamps were used – a dangerous business in a mill, where cotton waste could easily ignite. At Stanley, Perthshire, Robert Owen told James Craig in 1802 it was advisable to find candles for the spinners, as 'there is not any thing lost by a fair encouragement of work people'.[61] In September 1810, Owen received a letter from Craig about his project for lighting and heating the mills by gas. Owen hoped to visit Stanley that week and see Mr Maiken, whose ideas 'if all prove true' might be used at New Lanark. Three weeks later, Owen told Craig that he would speak to Houldsworth in Glasgow about Maiken's gas lighting. However, Owen feared that Maiken was ignorant of what Murdoch of Boulton and Watt had accomplished.[62] In fact, gas lighting at Stanley had to wait until the coming of the new regime of Denniston, Buchanan and Company in the early 1820s.

In 1812, cotton mills in Renfrewshire were generally lit by candles, with some using oil lamps and one using gas.[63] As late as the 1830s, some of the smaller spinning mills in Renfrewshire were still using oil lamps for lighting. Thomas Mitchell's water-powered spinning mills in Neilston, rebuilt in 1813 after a fire, were lit by 'oil lamps and glass tops'. Another cotton company in Neilston, the water-powered Crosshouse Mills of James Orr and Co., was lit by 'oil and candles in the morning and evening'. Oil was also used to light the spinning mills of Brown, Malloch and Co. in Paisley.[64] The *Parliamentary Papers* record the size and distribution of the different power systems installed in Scottish cotton mills in the early 1830s, together with the installation of gas lighting. Table 15 shows that only 6 out of 18 spinning mills (30%) in Renfrewshire had gas lighting at that date, compared to 9 out of 12 spinning mills (75%) in Paisley and 7 out of 13 of cotton factories (54%) in Glasgow. If the transfer from candles and oil lamps to gas lighting can be seen as evidence of modernity and of a propensity to innovate, then the failure of

Table 15 Scottish cotton mills by location, function, type and hp of power used, and use of gas lighting, 1833–1834

	Spinning mills				Weaving factories				Combined spinning mills and weaving factories			
Location	Mills	Steam	Water	Gas	Mills	Steam	Water	Gas	Mills	Steam	Water	Gas
Glasgow	8	236		2	3	91		3	2	75		2
Paisley	12	279		9								
Renfrewshire	18	88	509	6					1	30		
Other	5	51	136	1					4	36	610	3
Total	43	654	645	18	3	91		3	7	141	610	5

Source: Parliamentary Papers, 1833, XX and 1834, XX, Factory Inquiry Commission Reports.

most cotton mills in Renfrewshire, outside Paisley, to install gas lighting by the 1830s suggests that firms in this area were beginning to fall behind in the innovation stakes.

One of the earliest Scottish mills to install gas lighting was Catrine in Ayrshire, where it was introduced as early as 1814.[65] A number of cotton mills fitted gas lighting as part of expansion programmes in the early 1820s. At Deanston in Perthshire, the Managing Partner, James Smith, built Deanston House as his residence in 1820 and laid out a new lade (water course), dam, new roads, a gas works, a new mill and weaving shed and new water wheels. The total expenditure on all this was around £100,000.[66] A change of ownership at Stanley, Perthshire in 1823 ushered in a similar ambitious expansion programme. The new owners, Denniston, Buchanan and Company, began a large investment programme, which involved a new lade, three new mills and a new street (Store Street) in the village. The cotton mills formed a square, 'in the centre of which an extensive Gas works has been constructed for the purpose of lighting them, the vent of which is upwards of one hundred feet in height'. The whole building programme was said to have cost £160,000.[67] The gas works chimney at Stanley still survives, the earliest surviving example in Scotland. At New Lanark, the gas lighting came later, 'at some point before 1851', to provide lighting for the mills and village.[68] Rothesay Mills on Bute were 'lit by gas in winter evenings and mornings' by the early 1830s.[69]

Cotton mills in urban centres such as Glasgow, Greenock and Paisley had less need to manufacture their own gas, as commercial gas works grew up to supply the towns and cities. In Glasgow, the shops of a baker, a bookseller, a spinning mill and the lecture theatre in the Andersonian Institution were lit by gas as early as 1805. Two years later a weaving factory in Pollockshaws was lit by gas generated in an old steam cylinder. The Glasgow Gas Light Company, one of the first public gas companies in Britain, obtained an Act of Parliament in 1817 and by the end of that year had 25 cast-iron retorts in operation at Townhead.[70] Greenock followed the example of Glasgow in 1827, when a joint stock company was formed to produce coal gas. In 1836 the gas works was transferred to the corporation and by 1840 it employed 20 men and produced 16 million cubic feet of gas a year.[71]

By the 1830s, gas lighting was being used at many cotton mills in Glasgow, including May and Dennistoun's spinning mills in Calton, Stronach's Burnside Mills in St John's, Robert Marshall's spinning and weaving factory in the Gorbals, and the power loom weaving factories of Dugald McPhail and Co., John Sommerville and Sons in Govan and the Barrowfield Weaving Company. At John Miller's Wellington Factory, Hutchesontoun, a mixed spinning and weaving factory, the works were lit 'with gas from the Glasgow

Company'.[72] At Finlay and Company's Ballindalloch mills, Stirlingshire gas lighting was used 'from the middle of the month of September until the end of the month of March'.[73]

Many cotton mills in Renfrewshire also used gas lighting, including John White's spinning mills at Eaglesham, John Freeland and Co's mills at Houston, Fulton, Buchanan and Co.'s mills at Lochwinnoch, and John Graham's mills at Neilston. It was also installed in the spinning mills of Robert Montgomery in Johnstone and James Crum at Thornliebank.[74] In Paisley, gas lighting was used in the spinning mills of John Orr Junior and Co., N. and P. Pollock, Joseph Twigg's Sneddon Mills, the Floors Throstle Mill, Mathew Brown and Company and Arthur Ross, a thread twining factory, as well as cotton and silk thread manufacturers such as Joseph Clark, John Kerr and Sons, Peter Kerr, and Mathew and George Carswell.[75] However, a smaller proportion of mills in Renfrewshire (excluding Paisley) used gas lighting, as compared to Glasgow or Paisley.

Cotton manufacture – winding, warping and weaving

If the yarn was going to be woven into cloth, it had to go through a number of other processes. Winding was the process of winding the yarn from cops onto bobbins and passing it through water en route. This produced the weft to be attached to the weaver's shuttle. Warping took the same yarn and strengthened it by passing it through a solution of hot starch, a process known as dressing. This produced a smoother and stronger yarn, which could be used as warp on power looms. Cotton weaving was initially carried out on hand looms, and hand loom weaving continued on a large scale until the 1830s. Long before the introduction of power loom weaving, numerous improvements had been carried out on the hand loom. In 1738, John Kay replaced the old method of throwing the shuttle by hand with a fly shuttle, which threw the shuttle by the simple device of a peg and two strings. This greatly speeded up production and meant that the weaver could now produce nearly twice as much cloth as before. It also meant that one man on his own could produce the widest cloth, which had previously required two men to produce.[76]

At Cambuslang, Lanarkshire, muslin weaving was introduced about 1783, and the use of the fly shuttle about the same time.[77] Similarly in Kilsyth, Stirlingshire, a muslin manufacturing centre, the fly shuttle was used by hand loom weavers in the 1790s and hailed as a great improvement.[78] In Paisley, 'the plan of the fly shuttle and lay' was introduced from England about 1797 by Herbert Buchanan of Arden, a Paisley silk manufacturer. Buchanan sent one of his workers, John Robertson, to Manchester to see the model, and since then Paisley weavers had made many 'micro' improvements to it, including the 'ten box lay' in 1812, 'by which a weaver can work with the greatest facility with ten shuttles without shifting them. The original "fly lay" could be wrought with only one shuttle.'[79]

In 1785, the Rev. Dr Cartwright invented a power loom, introduced into Glasgow in 1793 by James Lewis Robertson of Dunblane. A year later, 40 power looms were installed at a bleaching and calico printing works at Milton, near Dumbarton, to weave calicoes for printing. In 1801, John Monteith of Glasgow got a pair of looms from Milton and two years later had 200 looms at work in his mills in Pollockshaws, Glasgow. Three years later, Monteith persuaded Archibald Buchanan of Catrine, Ayrshire to take a pair of looms from him to improve them and the machines for dressing the warps. Buchanan did this with such success that by 1807 Catrine was the first place in Britain where warping, dressing and power weaving were carried on under the same roof. Buchanan also increased the speed of the power looms from 70 to 80 shots or picks a minute to 140 shots a minute. Other Scottish firms to adopt power looms early on included Foster and Corbett of Glasgow and Crum of Thornliebank. In 1808, power looms were introduced at Deanston, Perthshire, and a year later the weaving of tweels (twills) and then checks on power looms was successfully introduced.[80] By March 1810, the dressing and weaving operations at Deanston and Catrine were almost complete, and by May, Deanston works produced on average six pieces per loom weekly, or about 1,800 pieces weekly.[81]

By 1831, power looms were well established in the west of Scotland and were used to weave a great variety of cotton fabrics. Four large companies in Glasgow and the west of Scotland – the Lancefield Spinning Company, Johnston and Galbraith, James Finlay and Company, and William Dunn of Duntocher had over 3,000 power looms between them.[82] However, for a long time power looms coexisted with hand looms, which could produce more complex patterns and required less capital outlay.

In the last quarter of the nineteenth century, there was a great contrast between the British and American cotton industries in their willingness to adopt the newest technology in spinning and weaving. The reluctance of the British industry to adopt ring spinning has been discussed earlier and a similar attitude applied to the latest developments in weaving. The Northrop or automatic loom was developed in the USA to simplify the weaving process, so that less-skilled labour was required. It also made it possible to increase the worker/loom ratio. By 1914, 40% of cotton looms in the USA were Northrop automatics, whilst in Britain they amounted to only 1–2 % of the total.[83] In Scotland, the reluctance of employers to adopt the automatic loom was partly explained by the fact that it was not well adapted to the production of 'fancy goods', the staple of the Scottish industry.[84]

Cotton manufacture – sources of power

Water power

The early Scottish cotton industry used a wide variety of power sources. The first jenny factories were hand powered, and carding mills were driven by horses in Dundonald, Ayrshire and Douglas, Lanarkshire, whilst in Dalry, Ayrshire the carding was water powered.[85] In Cambuslang, Lanarkshire a cotton mill was built in Flemington in 1787, consisting of a water-powered carding machine and 17 jennies, and employing about 50 people 'old and young'.[86] However, once water frames were introduced they needed a constant supply of water to power them, involving considerable investment in dams, lades and water wheels.

Much of the technical and engineering expertise in these examples came from England, but the Scots also possessed a good deal of expertise in mill construction and the installation of water power systems. Scottish bleachfield owners had considerable experience in modifying the landscape and diverting rivers and water courses for industrial use. Between 1752 and 1754, the Perthshire linen dealer and bleacher William Sandeman of Luncarty spent £1,300 on 'levelling and laying out twelve acres of bleaching ground' on the site of a bog by the River Tay known as the 'Myretoun of Luncarty'. This involved major alterations in the landscape, and Sandeman was praised for replacing a 'quagmire' by 'lawns, orchards, grass parks, cornfields and bleaching greens' and building 'commodious villages' for his workers. Luncarty lay on the junction of the Shochie and the Ordie Burns with the River Tay. To stop flooding, a new channel was dug for the course of the burns and the old channel was converted into a 'neat canal' for the bleachfield.[87]

As well as changes to the landscape carried out by Scottish bleachers, a small-scale industrial revolution had already taken place in Scotland with the introduction of water-powered lint mills for preparing flax for spinning. Here the slow and tedious business of teasing out the fibres from the flax plant by hand had been replaced by water-powered machinery. By 1772, there were 252 water-powered lint mills distributed throughout Scotland, scutching flax mechanically, with 29% in Perthshire.[88] Some of these mills were later used to house cotton spinning machinery, as at Rothesay on Bute, or Deanston, Perthshire, where John Buchanan acquired land alongside the River Teith. Here, 'a lint dressing mill had been long established on this spot, and there was a good weir or dam dyke attached to it. The building of the lint mill was immediately filled with machinery for carding and roving cotton wool, which rovings were spun into yarn upon hand jennies, which were placed in a new building erected at some distance from the lint mill.'[89]

However, the larger Arkwright mills demanded heavy capital investment and substantial changes to the landscape in the name of 'improvement' and profit. At New Lanark, a difficult, boggy site in the Clyde Gorge, 'a mere morass, situated in a hollow glen of difficult access', the landscape was transformed by building a planned village and mills and engineering 'a subterranean passage of near 100 yards in length through a rocky hill' to provide the mill lade.[90] By 1793, William Kelly, the New Lanark manager, had modified the water wheel design to use a fourth less water than previously needed.[91] In 1802, a Swedish visitor described how, 'at each of the above mentioned four spinning mills was a low overshot water wheel a few feet wide, which drove the whole of the machinery, which was made entirely of cast iron, from the largest to the smallest hand wheels. The head for the water wheel was obtained from the River Clyde by means of a water way which went for almost an English mile, partially undergound.'[92]

At Stanley, Perthshire, a similarly ambitious programme of capital investment and landscape alteration and 'improvement' was required for the construction of cotton mills on the Atholl estates. As early as 1729, a tunnel had been driven through the hillside on the great bend of the Tay to drive a corn mill.[93] In 1785 the Duke of Atholl's factor, James Stobie, designed a new lade in the form of a tunnel through the hillside, 776 feet long, with a modest fall of 1 foot 4 inches overall, running at a maximum depth of 127 feet below the hill.[94] The guiding light behind this scheme was Richard Arkwright, who trained Andrew Keay, Managing Partner at Stanley, at his Cromford Mills in Derbyshire. Keay wrote from Cromford in 1785 to William Sandeman that:

> We must on no account be Short of Water for the Cotton mill but do not you think that it would be proper to begin the work according to Mr. A.s directions when on the spot by repairing the old one – he says you will have plenty of water for the whole mill which I hope we shall but if not a new Cutt can be made and surely it ought to be as wide as you mention in that case . . . The water which according to the plan I sent is intended to use about 70 tons of water . . . so that some judgement may be formed of whether more water will be necessary than there is in the old Canal – 40 tons however will drive all the machinery we shall have for sometime.[95]

For a water-powered site, location was all important. At Rothesay on Bute, the manager, Robert McFarlane, complained in 1785: 'I despair of seeing, even in rainy seasons, a constant regular supply of water, sufficient to drive the mills both day and night'. The original Rothesay mill was situated so close to the sea that the water supply could be disrupted by a high tide. Eventually, the Company had to construct a reservoir and build a new mill higher up, at a cost of £30,000.[96]

In 1811, Robert Owen wrote to James Craig that since Owen's under manager, Robert Humphreys, had returned to New Lanark, he had been trying to arrange to cast and fit up a new water wheel for Stanley. Owen insisted that 'the first moving power is of so much importance in a Cotton

Mill that no expense should be spared to have it in all respects perfect and compleat. It would be the greatest folly imaginable to erect a wheel twelve feet diameter where there is a fall of 18 feet – you may preserve the light by placing the water wheel at somewhat greater distance from the Mill.' Owen promised to send the wheel to Leith, then ship it to Perth, and a man from New Lanark would fit it together.[97]

A large number of water-powered sites for cotton spinning were situated in Renfrewshire. Dovecothall Mill, in Neilston parish, built in 1780, was three stories high and 'the outer great wheel is sixteen feet in diameter, and three feet thick'. Two years later, a larger, five-story mill was built in Johnstone, powered by a water wheel six feet broad and eighteen feet in diameter.[98] At Catrine, Ayrshire, Arkwright recommended his millwright, Thomas Lowe of Nottingham, to Claude Alexander and David Dale. Alexander and Dale built a weir on the River Ayr and sluices at Glenbank Loch, the source of the river.[99] Lowe installed four water wheels 'at different parts of the building, with a divided fall of 48 feet'.[100] A millwright called Abercrombie tendered in 1787 'to direct and oversee the cutting of the Canal and lead including the Dam compleat to the Mill. The building the House the water wheel and principal machinire [*sic*] brought up as far as sufficient to place the spinning frames and the apparatus thereto belonging upon such principles as Mr. Dale shall point out.'[101]

The Lowe water wheels powered Catrine Mills until the 1820s, when William Fairbairn, the Scots-born founder of the Manchester engineering firm of Fairbairn and Co., replaced them. Fairbairn described Lowe's work as 'heavy and clumsy' and thought the water wheels were 'ill constructed, deficient in power and constantly breaking down or getting out of repair'. However, they had 'in a certain way answered their purpose, and as cotton mills were then in their infancy he was the only person qualified from experience to undertake the construction of the gearings'. Fairbairn designed two water wheels for Catrine, installed in June 1827. He boasted that 'they have never lost a day since that time, and they remain . . . probably the most perfect hydraulic machines of their type in Europe'. Each wheel was 52 feet in diameter, generating a total of 240hp.[102]

This was part of a 'second generation' of water wheels installed in Scottish cotton mills some 40 years after the 'first generation' of the 1780s, to take advantage of improvements in engineering since that time and to fight strong competition from firms running steam-powered cotton mills in urban centres and overseas. By 1840, the cotton mill at Eaglesham, Renfrewshire was driven by 'a magnificent water wheel of iron forty five feet in diameter and of fifty horse power' installed by the Glasgow engineering firm of Murdoch and Aikin. Some 740 cubic feet of water fell on the wheel every minute 'and yet it is so artfully introduced and carried away, that no water is seen within the walls'.[103]

The 'new generation' of civil engineers who made huge improvements in the efficiency of water power systems included people like Robert Thom (1775–1847), 'civil engineer and proprietor of the Rothesay Cotton Works, a man of great facility of invention and extraordinary mechanical genius'.[104] Thom was born at Tarbolton, Ayrshire in 1775 and studied at the Andersonian Institution, Glasgow. He became manager and partner of the Blackburn cotton mill, West Lothian and in 1813 bought the Rothesay mills on Bute in partnership with William Kelly, the former manager of New Lanark. On Kelly's retirement in 1826, Robert Thom became sole partner at Rothesay. In 1821, he devised an elaborate system of aqueducts at Rothesay leading into Loch Fad, which doubled the storage capacity. This increased the water power available to the mills to 70hp. Thom planned a similar scheme at the Blackburn cotton mills, West Lothian, in 1824, with a reservoir supplying 600,000 cubic feet of water a day, but the prospective Edinburgh investors got cold feet and pulled out of the scheme.[105]

Thom's most ambitious scheme was Shaw's Water Works at Greenock, Renfrewshire, a large-scale water storage and supply project, 'altogether singular in the history of manufactures in this or any other country; executed at comparatively small expense' under the patronage of Sir Michael Shaw Stewart. It was designed to overcome Greenock's chronic shortage of water for domestic and industrial use, and involved an Act of Parliament on 10 June 1825, which set up a joint stock company with a capital of £31,000. An artificial lake (the Great Reservoir, later Loch Thom) was created high above Greenock, which together with six auxiliary reservoirs held 337 million cubic feet of water. From this holding system, designed to withstand an eight-week drought, aqueducts ran down to the town of Greenock. The system opened in 1827 at a cost of £90,000, and by 1845 was generating 569hp and driving 13 water-powered mills of different kinds.[106] Robert Thom died at Ascog on Bute on 14 December 1847, leaving a modest estate of £2,669.[107]

The largest operation on the Greenock aqueduct system was the Shaws Water Cotton Spinning Company, completed in 1840. It was a large, fireproof mill, with 14,000 throstle spindles and space for 10 pairs of mule jennies, each containing 1,000 spindles. The mill was steam heated, with a gas works and workers' housing. James Smith of Deanston built the water wheel, made of 'malleable and cast iron', 70 feet in diameter and 12 feet broad. It weighed 180 tons and generated 120hp, providing power at a yearly rental of £1 1s per horse power. The advantages of the Greenock site were that Glasgow, the principal source of raw cotton and the major market for the yarn produced by the mill, was only an hour away by rail and the Liverpool markets were 16 or 17 hours' sail from Greenock. There was also 'an abundant population for carrying on the work and an excellent port for importing cotton, or exporting yarns to the continent or to India'.[108]

At Deanston, Perthshire, James Smith installed a new lade, dam and water wheels in the 1820s and 1830s. The waterwheels were built by William Fairbairn of Manchester and modelled on those of Catrine, although they were not so large. When the first two wheels opened in 1830, the event was marked by a procession of the Deanston Friendly Society accompanied by the Deanston Band of Music. The third and largest new wheel at Deanston, named 'Hercules', began to turn on Christmas Eve 1833. In 1844, Deanston had four water wheels 36 feet in diameter, generating 300hp. They drove 14,184 throstle spindles (9,916 Danforth's patent) 12,384 self-acting mules (Smith and Orr's patent) and 302 power looms.[109]

At Stanley, Perthshire, the new owners, Denniston, Buchanan and Company, invested and reorganised the power system along similar lines when they bought the mills in 1823. The company built a new lade to give a fall of 16 feet and generate 200hp from seven water wheels. This was a substantial piece of engineering and capital investment. The lade was carried under a 150-foot high hill by means of a 'mine' 800 feet long, 8 feet high and 10 feet wide, arched and paved throughout. The water supply from the Tay never failed, 'though sometimes it is in such superabundance as to stop the wheels'.[110] These major investment programmes were designed to help firms in the long-established water-powered factory villages to compete with the expansion of the steam-powered cotton industry in the cities and abroad.

Steam power

As long as water power remained the main source of power, the cotton industry would always be limited in scale and in location. The key to the large-scale expansion of the industry was the adoption of steam power, although von Tunzelman believed that there was little perceptible fall in the cost of power used by cotton manufacturers from the 1790s to the mid 1830s, and possibly for a decade after that. Tunzelman further argued that the high cost of power delayed the introduction of more fully automated machinery in cotton manufacturing and the finishing trades.[111]

The Scottish cotton industry was slower than its English counterpart to change over to steam power. This was largely because of superior water power resources in Scotland, which possessed large rivers like the Clyde, the Don, the Tay and the Teith. However, Glasgow's water power resources were limited and one of the few early cotton mills in the city, built in 1784 on the River Kelvin at South Woodside, suffered from a shortage of water.[112] Not until the introduction of steam power could Glasgow become a major cotton manufacturing centre. The first steam engine manufactured by Boulton and Watt for a cotton mill in Britain was in 1785 for Robinson's mills in Papplewick, Nottinghamshire[113]. In Glasgow the first steam-powered mill was built in 1792 on David Todd's land at Springfield, by the harbour.

Table 16 M'Taggart's list of steam engines and horse gins at present in use for cotton machinery – Glasgow, Paisley, Johnston and Strathaven, August 1798

Location	Company	Power
Glasgow	Scott Stevenson and Co. Coal quay	8hp
	Alex Henery, Greenhead	4hp
	John Brand and Co., Calton	4hp
	John Pattison and Co., Brigton	8hp
Paisley	W Leach Twigg and Co	8hp
	Mr. Twigg and Co.	24hp
	The Underwood Co.	
Johnston	Campbell Spier and Co., 38" cylinder	10hp
Stravethen	and Smith and Currie.	
	NB The last two are used about 3 months in the year having water the remainder	
	Horse gins used by	
Glasgow	Chadwick and Whyte, Grahams Square	24 mules
	M'Tierlie and M'Taggart, do	14 mules
	John M'Taggart, Ruthglen	14 mules
	James Monach Canon Street	Jennies and mules
	Peter Buchanan George Street	Jennies and mules
Paisley	Mathew Corse and Co. Newtown	20 mules
	David Finlay and Co	14 mules
	Wm Clarke Sneddon	20 mules
	John Davidson	14 mules
	John Dalyel and Co	14 mules
	A. Pollock and Co	24 mules

Source: J. Tann (ed.), *The Selected Papers of Boulton and Watt*, Volume I, *The Engine Partnership, 1772–1825*, 1981, 309–310.

The managing partner was William Scott, otherwise known as 'Swearing Wully'.[114] The steam engine here was built not by Boulton and Watt but by a local man, Robert Muir.[115]. In the same year a steam-powered mill was built in Govan, which employed 100 people[116].

By August 1798, there were steam engines installed in at least nine Scottish cotton mills – four in Glasgow, three in Paisley, one in Johnstone and one in Strathaven, although the last two were used only three months of the year to supplement water power. None of these engines was built by Boulton and Watt – they were locally built and of modest horse power, varying from 4 to 24hp . This suggests that engineering skills were well developed in Glasgow, although Boulton and Watt engines were more reliable. The largest steam engine was one of 24hp in a mill in Paisley owned by Twigg and Company. Another significant source of power was horses, used to drive horse gins in 11 cotton mills – 5 in Glasgow and 6 in Paisley. They were generally used to drive spinning mules, although two Glasgow mills used them to power jennies as well as mules. The number of mules driven by horse gin varied between 14 and 24.[117]

Another early steam-powered mill in Glasgow was built in 1800 by John Pattison in Mile End. It measured 130 feet by 48 feet, was five stories high and had a 32hp steam engine by Boulton and Watt.[118] Two years later William Murdoch or Murdock, one of Boulton and Watt's most trusted engineers, was routinely installing steam engines in Glasgow cotton mills and nearby print-works. He wrote to Boulton and Watt on 18 August 1802:

> Mr Houldsworth and Co of Anderston Cotton Mill gives your orders for a 45 or 50 horse Engine to be executed within 11 months from the date of this with Iron beam Cross plate and pillars a drawing of the premises will be sent and they will determine which they will have the price and Execution they Leave to yourselves. Mr. Hamilton thinks this Company may be depended on.[119]

Houldsworth's Anderston Cotton Work in Cheapside Street was the first large brick building in Glasgow. The steam engine was 45hp and in May 1804, 'Great care is intended to be taken in making every thing firm in the [engine] house which with the mill and the machinery is all to be incombustible . . . they intend to begin building shortly.'[120] A year later a Belfast banker touring Scotland described the new mill:

> I saw a new Cotton Mill at Anderston near Glasgow, one half of which was built, this half was seven stories high 30 feet wide & 14 windows in length – the floors were supported by metal pipes – which at the same time served the purpose of conveying Steam for Heating the House – the joists are also of metal likewise the window frames & sashes, & not a piece of Timber in the House except the roof – as the floors were to be laid with tiles. I was told the expence of metal exceeded Timber 25 p ct which was saved in three years by the difference of Insurance – the pipes & c only cost 16/- per cwt.[121]

Murdoch also built an engine in 1802 for 'Messrs Stirlings printers [calico] on the River Leven' for 16 or 20hp, which they wanted completed in nine months. The firm wanted to know the cost of:

> a ram that will raise about 120 Gallons of water per minute the fall in 60 feet is 18 inches and the height to be raised is 10 feet – I think much may be done with Rams in this river for all the bleach fealds; I have been at the Shaws with Mr. Monteith the Engine house will be finished in 4 weeks he wished to have Joseph Varley [?] to erect his Engine. Mr Paterson complains of his Engine not doing the work although it is short of its load some thousand spindles he begs I will put it in good repair before I leave this place which I shall do.[122]

A good deal of Murdoch's repeat business depended on installing steam engines which worked reliably and impressed the many visitors who came to see them. He had arrived in Glasgow on 6 August 1802:

> and found Mr. Fulton's Engine not finished and will require ten days from the date of this to finish the Blowing part I hope to see It work before I leave this as there is many People waiting to see the performance of this before they give orders.[123]

On 8 September Murdoch reported:

> Mr Fultons Engine Set to work on the 2 and gives Satisfaction to all it has a great many visitors I intend to set out the 4 and shall attend to your orders at Bolton.[124]

By 1800, there were 23 steam engines installed in Scotland. Only eight of them, with a total of 128hp, were in cotton mills. Most of these powered spinning mules, whilst the water frame and its improved version (the throstle) remained water powered.[125] In November 1808, James Watt Junior wrote to Mathew Boulton from Edinburgh reporting on the condition of steam engines installed by the Boulton and Watt Company in Scotland. Most of them worked well, although many were not kept in good condition. Henry Houldsworth's engine, of 45hp, erected at the Anderston Mills in 1805, was experiencing problems, 'The irregular Motion of the pump had occasioned the fracture of one of the Connecting Wheels a few days before I called and although it was got mended and to work again, the house was rather in confusion'.[126]

The 14hp engine at Finlay's cotton works at Balfron was 'Not at work, having plenty of water. It is pretty well put up and gives satisfaction but there are symptoms of incipient dirt, which Mr. Finlay has promised to correct. The throttle valve is not very good'. The engines the company had installed at William Stirling's printfields on the River Leven received a mixed report. The 14hp engine was 'a very firm job and working well, but dirty', whilst the larger one of 20hp was 'still worse and out of order'. Other steam engines had been installed at the cotton works of John Pattison, Dunlop and Co. and Houldsworth and Hussey, but were 'in very indifferent order'.[127]

A firm like Boulton and Watt had to keep a sharp eye on the changing credit status of firms. In the depression year of 1811, James Watt Junior wrote that 'The present circumstances of many of the Commercial houses at Glasgow affords an additional motive for the detention of Messrs Gushen and Sons 2nd Boiler at the Foundry.' He was also concerned about the debts of the cotton manufacturer Monteith, Bogle and Co., who bought a 30hp engine from Boulton and Watt in 1802 and another of 53hp in 1809.[128]

On occasion, steam power was used to supplement water power in Scottish cotton mills. As early as 1805, Boulton and Watt erected a 14hp steam engine at James Finlay's cotton mills at Ballindalloch, Stirlingshire to supplement the water power in summer.[129] When the mills were advertised for sale in 1844, a water wheel of 28 feet diameter generated 35hp, assisted by a 16hp steam engine in summer. This drove 10,752 mule spindles, of which only 1,248 were self-acting.[130] At Catrine, Ayrshire, Archibald Buchanan installed two 40hp steam engines to eke out the power shortfall caused by the frequent breakdowns of the water wheels.[131] Even when more reliable water wheels were installed in 1828, two steam engines of 45hp each were kept in reserve 'for dry seasons'.[132] Similarly, at Woodside Cotton Mills, Aberdeen, where water power from the Don drove three large water wheels and two smaller ones, a marine steam engine named 'Victoria' was installed in 1837 to supplemement the water power.[133] Even in the rainy west of Scotland, the Rothesay Mills on Bute suffered from water shortages and used a steam engine to supplement their water wheel in dry weather.[134]

The cotton industry in Renfrewshire also used steam engines to supplement water power. At Houston Mill, an expansion programme saw the installation of a steam engine for dry spells and a similar solution was required at the New Mills, Lochwinnoch. At Linwood, a 20hp steam engine supplemented the 48hp available from water wheels. As late as 1838, the Renfrewshire cotton industry was still heavily dependent on water power. In that year 28 water wheels produced 798hp (41.5% of the total power in cotton mills in the county). Fifty steam engines produced 1,124hp , of which 333hp was in the town of Paisley.[135] However, there was a steady growth in the amount of steam power used in Scottish cotton mills. In 1800, there were only eight Boulton and Watt steam engines in Scottish spinning mills. By 1831, Glasgow alone possessed 107 steam-powered mills.[136]

The second half of the nineteenth century saw the erection of large steam-powered mills in Britain, particularly the 'Oldham Limiteds' in Lancashire. The Oakbank and St Rollox mills in Glasgow, owned by A. and A. Galbraith, were housed by 1868 in 'two immense ranges of somewhat irregular buildings'. They employed 1,700 people, with 95,000 mule and throstle spindles and 1,532 power looms, producing 17 million yards of plain cloth a year for printing and dyeing. The operation was powered by 'several large steam engines' producing 1,600hp altogether.[137] Apart from a few Glasgow mills and the large thread mills in Paisley, there were few in Scotland to compare with the giant cotton mills built in Oldham during the 'Indian Summer' of the Lancashire industry, from 1870 down to the First World War.[138]

In the last quarter of the nineteenth century, a new generation of owners began to install water turbines in Scottish cotton mills to replace less efficient water wheels. At Stanley Mills, Perthshire, a new owner, Frank Stewart Sandeman, took over the firm in 1876.[139] He installed a 200hp Jonval turbine in 1878, followed by another of 400hp a year later. They replaced seven water wheels installed 50 years earlier that had frequently been brought to a halt by flooding on the Tay.[140] At New Lanark, Henry Birkmyre of the Gourock Ropeworks, Port Glasgow, bought the mills in 1881. He installed Jonval water turbines in 1884, followed by a second set in 1898, generating 827hp . These turbines initially powered machinery by rope and belt drive and later generated electricity for power and lighting for the mills and village.[141]

Cotton manufacture – the finishing trades

The greatest technological contribution made by locally based Scots in the cotton industry was in the bleaching and finishing trades. One of the advantages the Scots enjoyed over the English in this period was a more practical, scientific and generally more accessible system of education. The Scottish Enlightenment had an intensely practical side to it and an industrialist like Charles Macintosh, FRS, a key player in the textile finishing trades, received an excellent part-time education in chemistry from Dr Joseph Black, who held a Lectureship in Glasgow, and from 1766 a Chair at Edinburgh University. Black's lectures were open to outsiders who were not matriculated students, and in addition to his influence on Charles Macintosh, Black was noted for his friendship and support for James Watt.[142]

The finishing trades have not generally received the attention they deserve from historians. They went through a genuine scientific revolution in this period to keep pace with the rapidly growing output of cloth and yarn, and their transformation was a key factor in the success of the cotton industry. It also laid the foundations for the modern chemical industry. A number of historians have characterised industrialisation as a shift from organic to inorganic raw materials and power sources.[143] This was particularly true in dyeing, bleaching and calico printing. Landes claimed that 'the transformation of the textile manufacture, whose requirements of detergents, bleaches and mordants were growing at the same pace as output, would have been impossible without a corresponding transformation of chemical technology'.[144] The Clows believed that 'the capitalisation of bleaching is every bit as important as the capitalisation of the cognate spinning and weaving industries'.[145]

Bleaching, the process of whitening cloth to make it more attractive for sale, was originally carried out using natural materials and was a slow process using large amounts of land to expose the cloth. It involved boiling linen in water or weak alkali, a process known as 'bucking'. The linen was then spread out on the 'green', a process known as 'crofting'. Finally, the yarn or cloth was treated by a weak acid in the form of sour milk, known as 'souring'. The whole process could take between 6 and 18 months to complete. In 1756, Dr Francis Hume of Edinburgh, encouraged by the Board of Trustees, publicised the use of sulphuric acid (vitriol) as a substitute for sour milk in the final 'souring' process. This speeded up the bleaching process to about four months.[146]

The next stage was the discovery of a cheaper and more efficient chemical alkaline substitute for the initial 'bucking' process. Following the discovery and development of chlorine as a bleaching agent by Swedish and French scientists, it was introduced into Scotland by James Watt, who had met Claude Louis Berthollet in France and seen the use of chlorine for bleaching in 1786. On his return to Scotland, Watt communicated his discovery to his father-in-law, a Glasgow bleacher. A year later, the Aberdeen firm of Gordon, Barron and Company introduced the same process. In 1798, Charles Tennant developed a portable version of chlorine by combining slaked lime with chlorine to produce chlorine liquor, and in 1799 he went into partnership with Charles Macintosh to produce a dry bleaching powder. At the same time, the partners bought two acres of ground at St Rollox on the north side of Glasgow and built a chemical works there. Land on that side of Glasgow was cheap and the site was also close to supplies of lime and bordered by the Junction Canal, which connected the Forth and Clyde Canal with the Monkland.[147]

Production at St Rollox grew rapidly and by the 1840s it was the largest chemical works in Europe, covering 100 acres and employing over 1,000 people. Tennant's chimney (known as 'The Big Stalk'), built in 1841 and 455 feet high, was one of the landmarks of the Glasgow skyline.[148] This dominance did not last. By the late nineteenth century Tennant and Company was facing difficulties. The firm remained stubbornly committed to the older Leblanc process of alkali production, whereas its great English rival, Brunner-Mond, made an early switch to the more modern and efficient ammonia-soda process, invented by the Belgian Ernest Solvay. Alkali production at St Rollox fell from 14,000 tons a year in 1877 to 9,000 tons in 1890 and the workforce halved to 600 in the same period. In 1874, world production of alkali was 525,000 tons, of which 94% was produced by the Leblanc method. By 1902, world production was 1.8 million tons, of which only 8% was produced by the Leblanc method. In 1891, the United Alkali Company was formed by a merger of 45 firms, of which St Rollox was the largest, with a capital of £8.2 million and Sir Charles Tennant as chairman. However, this did not slow the relative decline of the company, and by 1893 the profits of Brunner-Mond had overtaken those of United Alkali.[149]

In the dyeing process, Turkey red dyeing had been commercialised by George Macintosh in 1785 in partnership with David Dale at Dalmarnock on the Clyde. Macintosh, the son of a Ross-shire farmer, built up a large shoe making business in Glasgow employing some 500 people and then branched out into the manufacture of cudbear. Cudbear was a purple dye manufactured originally from lichen and used particularly to dye wool and silk. It was manufactured from a mixture of lichen and ammonia, the latter supplied by the collection of large quantities of human urine. George Macintosh built a high wall around his factory in Dennieston and employed Gaelic-speaking Highland workmen in order to try to keep trade secrets. The firm was very export orientated and in 1786 George's son, Charles, travelled to the Continent to introduce the use of cudbear and to sell sulphuric acid for the Prestonpans Vitriol Company.[150]

Turkey red dyeing was introduced into England by Borelle, a Frenchman, who set up a dyeworks in Manchester and received a reward from the government for his efforts.[151] In Scotland, George Macintosh hired another Frenchman, Monsieur Papillon, a Turkey red dyer from Rouen in Normandy, to develop his Barrowfield dyeworks in Dalmarnock, 'where cotton is dyed a real Turkey red, equal in beauty and solidity to East India colours'. This proved more successful than the Manchester dyeworks. However, Macintosh and Papillon soon fell out and Macintosh wrote to his son Charles in 1787: 'Papillon has now left us entirely. We could not manage his unhappy temper. I have made a great improvement in his process. I dye in twenty days what he took twenty five to do. We paid him his salary up to October, so as to be quite clear of him'.[152] Papillon continued to live and work as a dyer in Glasgow and eventually retired in 1799, leaving a fortune of £20,000.[153]

In 1805, Dale and Macintosh sold the Barrowfield Dyeworks to Henry Monteith.[154] Until 1810, the Turkey red process could only be used on thread and yarn. In that year, Koechlin, of Mulhausen in Alsace, developed a method of Turkey red dyeing on cloth and a year later improved calico printing to incorporate colour designs.[155] By the 1830s, the Barrowfield Dyeworks employed 20 'stove girls', earning 7s 6d a week and working in temperatures of up to 140 degrees Farenheit, to hang up cloth in stoves to dry and fix the Turkey red colour.[156]

The Scottish dyeing industry continued to innovate, although it faced increasing competition from Germany. John Hyde Christie (1836–1926), a trained chemist, was an influential figure in John Orr Ewing and Co., a major Turkey red dyeing firm in Alexandria, Vale of Leven, Dunbartonshire. Christie carried out research into the Steiner method of dycing, introduced in 1863 at Alexandria. He also carried out experiments on aniline dyes with Robert Pullar in Perth in 1868 and on artificial madder.[157] John Orr Ewing and Co. developed an improved yarn dyeing machine, and in 1868 reported that 'some of our opponents in the Turkey Red trade are anxious to adopt these machines and we of course are unwilling to allow this unless they pay us a very smart Royalty'. In the following year, the company wrote to Messrs Stuart and McKenzie that they would have no objection to their manufacturing 'one of our bowl liquoring machines' for H. Monteith and Co. at Blantyre, but would charge a royalty of 100 guineas.[158]

Tarrant has claimed that by the end of the nineteenth century the Vale of Leven Turkey red trade was 'a highly specialised and sophisticated industry, geared to its markets and able to withstand most competition'.[159] However, it was vulnerable to superior German technology and to changes in export markets. In 1882, German firms gained a monopoly of producing artificial dyes and the Scottish industry had to rely on imports. A major export market was India, where the government wished to introduce tariffs in the 1890s. To combat these threats the Vale of Leven dyeing firms and Alexander Reid of Milngavie formed the United Turkey Red Company in 1897, a virtual British monopoly.[160]

There were close links between Turkey red dyeing and textile printing in Scotland. The earliest printworks in Scotland were for linen and were operating in the late 1720s at Gorgie and Bonnington on the Water of Leith, close to the affluent Edinburgh market.[161] The industry was driven by fashion and feminine taste. It was claimed that 'taste, chemistry and mechanics were the three legs of calico printing'.[162] Early printfields in the west of Scotland were at Pollockshaws, on the River Cart on the edge of Glasgow and at Dalsholm on the Kelvin. By 1784–1787, the west of Scotland, with 27 calico printing firms, was a major centre of the industry in Britain, which had a total of 111 firms at that time, Manchester being the largest centre, with 45 firms.[163] Printing was at first done by block presses, but copperplate presses were introduced, driven by hand. As this required a great deal of effort and required three men for every press, water power was substituted, and by the early 1790s many processes were driven by water.[164]

Berg has described calico printworks as 'proto factories', a transitional stage between the domestic workshop and the factory. Textile printing combined labour-intensive technologies with an advanced and heavily gendered division of labour. The printing was done by wooden blocks, which were patterned by pins or studs tapped into the blocks. This was specialised work carried out by women, who earned 12s to 14s a week. Another labour-intensive process done by women was pencilling or handpainting patterns directly onto the cloth.[165] Women were employed in 'a range of specific sex stereotyped tasks', such as hand and machine needlework, sewing silk borders, embroidery, washing, folding and parcelling.[166]

In 1769, printing by wooden blocks was replaced at Pollockshaws by engraved copper plates, and two years later the nearby Carntyne printfield invented a paste for printing different colours side by side.[167] The industry showed an advanced division of labour and one firm incorporated no fewer than 24 skills in its different processes.[168] This was true across the whole of the finishing trades. In the 1890s, the Amalgamated Society of Dyers, Bleachers, Finishers and Kindred Trades monitored the earnings of 66 distinct occupational groups.[169]

In his *Philosophy of Manufactures* (1835), Andrew Ure described calico

8 Calico printing, 1835

printing as a prime example of technical change driven by high wages and a highly skilled, strike-prone workforce. The first major technical breakthrough was the introduction of cylinder printing, the invention of a Scot named Bell, in 1785 at the printworks of Livesey, Hargreaves and Hall, at Mosney, near Preston, Lancashire. This resulted in enormous gains in productivity. It was estimated that one cylinder machine, attended by a man and a boy, could produce as much as 100 block printers and tear boys.[170] Cylinder printing was introduced into Lennoxmill printfield in Stirlingshire in 1810, and by 1841 the printfield contained seven printing cylinders and the employment of women for pencilling the cloth had been 'entirely abandoned'.[171]

One of the largest and most successful printfields in the UK was J. and W. Crum at Thornliebank in Renfrewshire, on the edge of Glasgow. The firm prospered under the ownership of Alexander Crum and became a limited liability company in 1886. After his death in 1893, profits fell from £43,044 to £4,607 four years later and the firm became part of the Lancashire-based Calico Printers Association.[172]

The relationship between technology, innovation and industrial expansion was rarely a simple or linear one. Much of the expansion in the Scottish cotton industry took place because of the increasing division of labour and the breakdown of manufacturing into many specialised processes, which could be carried out at low cost by female and child labour, often as outworkers outside the factories. This will be further examined in the next chapter.

Notes

1. E. A. Wrigley, *Continuity, Chance and Change: The Character of the Industrial Revolution in England* (Cambridge, 1988), 5; and C. A. Whatley, *The Industrial Revolution in Scotland* (Cambridge, 1997), 51.
2. J. Mokyr, 'Technological Change, 1700–1830', in R. Floud and D. McCloskey (eds), *The Economic History of Britain since 1700. Volume I, 1700–1860*, 2nd edition (Cambridge, 1994), 41.
3. I. Donnachie and G. Hewitt, *Historic New Lanark. The Dale and Owen Industrial Community since 1785* (Edinburgh, 1993), 53–4; and G. Timmins, 'Technology', in M. A. Rose (ed.), *The Lancashire Cotton Industry: A History since 1700* (Preston, 1996), 43.
4. M. Berg, *The Age of Manufactures, 1700–1820: Industry, Innovation and Work in Britain*, 2nd edition (London, 1994), 280.
5. Sir J. Sinclair (ed.) *[Old] Statistical Account of Scotland* (*OSA*) (Wakefield, 1973-83), 1982, VI, 562; and 1973, VII, 462.
6. National Archives of Scotland, Edinburgh (NAS), Graham of Fintry Papers, GD 151/11/24, David McVicar to Robert Graham, 17 October 1789.
7. Report of Select Committee on the State of Children Employed in Manufactures, *Parliamentary Papers* (*PP*), 1816, III, 249.
8. W. Freer, *My Life and Memories* (Glasgow, 1929), 16. Pirn winding was the task of winding the yarn onto a bobbin for use by the weaver.
9. W. Carlile, 'Sketches of Paisley', *Scots Magazine*, July 1806, 43.
10. W. Thom, *Rhymes and Recollections of a Handloom Weaver* (Paisley, 1880), v and 1.
11. N. Murray, *The Scottish Handloom Weavers, 1790–1850. A Social History* (Edinburgh, 1978).
12. J. Wilson, *A General View of the Agriculture of Renfrewshire* (Paisley, 1812), 267.
13. I. D. Whyte, *Scotland's Society and Economy in Transition, c. 1500– c. 1760* (London, 1997), 160.
14. J. Cleland, *Enumeration of the Inhabitants of the City of Glasgow and County of Lanark* (Glasgow, 1831), 109.
15. *New Statistical Account* (*NSA*) (Edinburgh, 1845), Vol. VI, 146–7.
16. E. Baines, *History of the Cotton Manufacture in Great Britain* (1835, reprinted London, 1966), 170–80.
17. Mitchell Library, Glasgow (ML), Dale/Alexander Correspondence, Letter to Claude Alexander, 7 April 1788.
18. I. Donnachie, *Robert Owen. Owen of New Lanark and Harmony* (East Linton, 2000), 78.
19. J. Parkhill (ed.), *The Life and Opinions of Arthur Sneddon, An Autobiography* (Paisley, 1860), 27.
20. *OSA*, 1982, VI, 158 and 177; and VII, 99 and 265.
21. Blair Castle, Perthshire, Atholl Mss., Box 25, II, fols 100–2, Robert Owen to James Craig, 16 February 1808.

22. *NSA*, VI, 147.
23. Factory Inquiry Commission Reports, *PP*, 1834, XX, A1, 128.
24. *NSA*, VI, 147; and J. Shaw, *Water Power in Scotland, 1550–1830* (Edinburgh, 1984), 318.
25. Baines, *Cotton Manufacture*, 155–64.
26. *OSA*, 1973, VII, 461–4.
27. *OSA*, 1976, XI, 528.
28. Baines, *Cotton Manufacture*, 147–55; and R. S. Fitton, *The Arkwrights, Spinners of Fortune* (Manchester, 1989), 22–46.
29. Atholl Mss, Box 25, III, fols 83–4, Owen to Craig, 17 February 1807.
30. *NSA*, VI, 141–2.
31. Atholl Mss, Box 25, III, fols 19–21, Owen to Craig, 23 December 1802.
32. *NSA*, VI, 145–6.
33. A. Ure, *The Cotton Manufactures of Great Britain* (London, 1836), Vol. II, 400–1.
34. Baines, *Cotton Manufacture*, 197–205; and W. Lazonick, 'Industrial Relations and Technical Change: The Case of the Self Acting Mule', *Cambridge Journal of Economics*, 1979, III.
35. Cleland, *Glasgow*, 108–9; and Baines, *Cotton Manufacture*, 205–7.
36. *NSA*, VI, 143.
37. *PP*, 1834, XX, A1, 27.
38. A. Brown, *A History of Glasgow and of Paisley, Greenock and Port Glasgow* (Glasgow 1795), III, 240.
39. *OSA*, 1973, VII, 461.
40. Donnachie and Hewitt, *New Lanark*, 5 and 91.
41. *Perthshire Courier*, 10 June 1813.
42. Timmins, 'Technology', 43.
43. K. Marx, *Capital* (New York, 1967), Vol. I, 435–6.
44. Andrew Ure, *The Philosophy of Manufactures* (1835, 3rd edition London, 1861), 23 and 368.
45. J. Foster, *Class Struggle and the Industrial Revolution* (London, 1974); and Lazonick, 'Industrial Relations'.
46. M. Freifeld, 'Technological Change and the "Self Acting" Mule: A Study of Skill and the Sexual Division of Labour', *Social History*, 1986, XI, 335; and W. W. Knox, *Hanging by a Thread: The Scottish Cotton Industry, c. 1850–1914* (Preston, 1995).
47. D. J. Jeremy, 'Lancashire and the International Diffusion of Technology', and A. Marrison, 'Indian Summer, 1870–1914', both in Rose (ed.), *Lancashire Cotton Industry*, 236 and 254.
48. Knox, *Hanging by a Thread*, 57–8.
49. *PP*, 1834, XX, A1, 210.
50. *PP*, 1834, XX, A1, 138–9.
51. *PP*, 1834, XX, A1, 141.
52. *PP*, 1834, XX, A1, 71.
53. *PP*, 1834, XX, A1, 150.

54. *PP*, 1834, XX, A1, 13.
55. *PP*, 1834, XX A1, 142–3.
56. ML, Houston of Johnstone Papers, TD 263/218, Insurance Rates for Cotton Mills, undated.
57. J. Fergusson (ed.), *Letters of George Dempster to Sir Adam Fergusson, 1756–1813* (London, 1936), 248–9.
58. Donnachie and Hewitt, *New Lanark*, 54.
59. Wilson, *Renfrewshire*, 253.
60. *PP*, 1816, III, 249.
61. Atholl Mss, Box 25, III, fol. 14, Owen to Craig, 31 August 1802.
62. *Ibid.*, fol. 157, Owen to Craig, 27 September 1810 and fols 150–5, Owen to Craig, 17 October 1810.
63. Wilson, *Renfrewshire*.
64. *PP*, 1834, XX, A1, 193–9.
65. C. Brogan, *James Finlay and Company Ltd., 1750–1950* (Glasgow, 1952), 63.
66. *Ibid.*, 70.
67. *Scots Magazine*, 14 September 1825, 496.
68. J. Hume, 'The Industrial Archaeology of New Lanark', in J. Butt (ed.), *Robert Owen, Prince of Cotton Spinners* (Newton Abbot, 1971), 215–53; and Donnachie and Hewitt, *New Lanark*, 157.
69. *PP*, 1834, XX, A1, 260.
70. J. Hume, *Industrial Archaeology of Glasgow* (Glasgow, 1974), 137.
71. *NSA*, VII, 442.
72. *PP*, 1834, XX, A1, 131–59.
73. *PP*, 1834, XX, A1, 222.
74. *PP*, 1834, XX, A1, 177–92 and 206–16.
75. *PP*, 1834, XX, A1, 196–213.
76. Baines, *Cotton Manufacture*, 116.
77. *OSA*, 1973, VII, 98.
78. *OSA*, 1978, IX, 502–3.
79. *NSA*, VII, 270–1.
80. *NSA*, VI, 152–3.
81. Atholl Mss, Box 25, III, fols 144–52, Letters from Owen to Craig, 13 March to 14 May 1810.
82. *NSA*, VI, 153–4.
83. Marrison, 'Indian Summer', 254.
84. Knox, *Hanging by a Thread*, 75.
85. *OSA*, 1982, VI, 177 and 158, and *OSA*, 1973, VII, 265.
86. *OSA*, 1973, VII, 99.
87. National Library of Scotland, Edinburgh (NLS), Saltoun Mss, 17564, fols 255–6, Account of Luncarty Bleachfield from 1752.
88. A. J. Warden, *The Linen Trade, Ancient and Modern* (London, 1864), 455; and N. E. McLain, 'Scottish Lint Mills, 1729–1770', *Textile History*, 1970, I.
89. Fitton, *Arkwrights*, 79.
90. Donnachie and Hewitt, *New Lanark*, 23–5.

91. *OSA*, 1973, VII, 461.
92. Donnachie and Hewitt, *New Lanark*, 75.
93. *NSA*, X, 434.
94. Atholl Mss, D1/2, Plan of Stanley.
95. NAS, Graham of Fintry Papers, GD 151/12/21, Andrew Keay to William Sandeman, 17 June 1785.
96. Signet Library, Edinburgh (SL), 411/62, Robert McFarlane to Brown and Cairnie, 5 February 1785.
97. Atholl Mss. Box 25, III, fols 160–2, Owen to Craig, 8 January 1811.
98. *OSA*, 1973, VII, 811–2.
99. Brogan, *James Finlay*, 55.
100. Fitton, *Arkwrights*, 80.
101. Mitchell Library, Glasgow (GL), Mss 63/3, Dale/Alexander Correspondence, Abercrombie's Proposal, 10 February 1787.
102. W. Pole, *The Life of William Fairbairn* (London, 1877), 122–3.
103. *NSA*, VII, 401.
104. *NSA*, VII, 432.
105. J. Shaw, *Water Power*, 482.
106. *NSA*, VII, 432–3.
107. NAS, SC 8/35/5/107, Will of Robert Thom.
108. *NSA*, VII, 443.
109. Brogan, *James Finlay*, 70–2.
110. *NSA*, X, 440.
111. G. N. Von Tunzelman, *Steam Power and British Industrialisation to 1860* (Oxford, 1978), 212–24.
112. Hume, *Glasgow*, 26.
113. Baines, *Cotton Manufacture*, 226.
114. R. Reid, *Glasgow Past and Present* (Glasgow, 1884), Vol. III, 371.
115. Hume, *Glasgow*, 26–7.
116. *OSA*, 1973, VII, 359.
117. J. Tann (ed.), *The Selected Papers of Boulton and Watt, Volume I, The Engine Partnership, 1775–1825* (London, 1981), 309–10.
118. Hume, *Glasgow*, 27.
119. ML, TD 605/2, William Murdoch to Boulton and Watt, 18 August 1802.
120. Hume, *Glasgow*, 27.
121. Hume, *Glasgow*.
122. ML, TD 605/2.
123. *Ibid.*
124. *Ibid.*
125. H. Hamilton, *The Industrial Revolution in Scotland*, 2nd edition (London, 1966), 131–2.
126. Tann (ed.), *Boulton and Watt*, 395–6.
127. *Ibid.*
128. *Ibid.*, 404–6.
129. *Ibid.*

130. *PP*, 1834, XX, A1, 221; and Brogan, *James Finlay*, 61–2.
131. Pole, *Fairbairn*, 12.
132. Brogan, *James Finlay*.
133. P. Morgan, *Annals of Woodside and Newhills* (Aberdeen, 1886), 30.
134. *PP*, 1834, XX, A1, 26.
135. Shaw, *Water Power*, 335.
136. A. Clow and N. Clow, *The Chemical Revolution: A Contribution to Social Technology* (London, 1952), 169.
137. D. Bremner, *The Industries of Scotland: Their Rise, Progress and Present Condition* (Edinburgh 1869), 291.
138. Marrison, 'Indian Summer', 238–64.
139. *Dundee Advertiser*, 8 November 1898.
140. *Perthshire Courier*, 18 March 1879.
141. Donnachie and Hewitt, *New Lanark*, 169.
142. G. Macintosh, *Biographical Memoir of the late Charles Macintosh FRS by his son* (Glasgow, 1847); and T. C. Smout, *A History of the Scottish People, 1560–1830* (London, 1969), 482–3.
143. D. Landes, *The Unbound Prometheus* (Cambridge, 1969), 41 and 109; and Wrigley, *Continuity*.
144. Landes, *Unbound Prometheus*, 108.
145. Clow and Clow, *Chemical Revolution*, 172.
146. *Ibid.*, 169; A. E. Musson and E. Robinson, *Science and Technology in the Industrial Revolution* (Manchester, 1969), 256; and N. Crathorne, *Tennants Stalk. The Story of Tennants of the Glen* (London, 1973), 58–9.
147. Clow and Clow, *Chemical Revolution*; Musson and Robinson, *Science and Technology*; Crathorne, *Tennants Stalk*; and A. Durie, *The Scottish Linen Industry in the Eighteenth Century* (Edinburgh, 1979), 103.
148. J. G. Kohl, *Scotland* (London, 1844), 4; G. Stewart, *Curiosities of Glasgow Citizenship* (Glasgow, 1881), 37; and Crathorne, *Tennants Stalk*.
149. Crathorne, *Tennants Stalk*, 143–4; and A. Slaven and S. G. Checkland (eds), *Dictionary of Scottish Business Biography, Volume I, The Staple Industries*, (*DSBB*) (Aberdeen, 1986), 288–9.
150. Macintosh, *Charles Macintosh*, 116–21; and Clow and Clow, *Chemical Revolution*.
151. Bremner, *Industries of Scotland*, 299.
152. Stewart, *Glasgow Citizenship*, 73.
153. P. McKenzie, *Reminiscences of Glasgow and the West of Scotland* (Glasgow 1868), Vol. III, 418–9.
154. Macintosh, *Charles Macintosh*, 121.
155. Bremner, *Industries of Scotland*, 299.
156. Ure, *Philosophy of Manufactures*, 392.
157. *DSBB*, I, 320–1.
158. GUA, UGD, 13/4/4, United Turkey Red Company, Letter Book, 1868–1890, fol. 3, John Orr Ewing and Co. to Macgregor, Stevenson and Fleming, 6 November 1868 and fol. 12, Orr Ewing and Co. to Stuart and McKenzie, 30 March 1869.

159. N. Tarrant, 'The Turkey Red Dyeing Industry in the Vale of Leven', in J. Butt and K. Ponting (eds), *Scottish Textile History* (Aberdeen, 1987), 45.
160. *DSBB*, I, 321.
161. Shaw, *Water Power*, 343.
162. Clow and Clow, *Chemical Revolution*, 224.
163. S. D. Chapman and S. G. Chassagne, *European Textile Printers in the Eighteenth Century: A Study of Peel and Oberkampf* (London, 1981), 8.
164. *OSA*, 1978, IX, 13.
165. M. Berg, *The Age of Manufactures*, 152 and 213.
166. A. McIvor, 'Work, Wages and Industrial Relations in Cotton Finishing, 1880–1914', in J. A. Jowitt and A. J. McIvor (eds), *Employers and Labour in the English Textile Industries* (London, 1988), 143.
167. A. Brown, *A History of Glasgow* (Glasgow, 1795), Vol. II, 216.
168. Chapman and Chassagne, *European Textile Printers*, 15.
169. McIvor, 'Work, Wages and Industrial Relations', 130.
170. Baines, *Cotton Manufacture*, 259–66.
171. *NSA*, VIII, 254–5.
172. *DSBB*, I, 347–9.

5

Workers

> The textile manufactures consist of two distinct departments; one carried on by multitudes of small independent machines belonging to the workmen, another carried on by concatenated systems of machinery, the property of the masters. (A. Ure, *The Philosophy of Manufactures*, 1835)

Introduction

Edward Thompson argued that between 1780 and 1832 'most English working people came to feel an identity of interests as between themselves, and as against their rulers and employers'. It was a period which saw the 'making' of the English working class, who developed an increasing 'disposition to behave as a class'.[1] Since the 1960s, other narratives have entered the story – those of divisions created by gender, race and religion. Modern historiography has also challenged the older view of industrialisation as a decisive break with the past, and emphasised continuity and uneven rates of change between different regions and different sectors of the economy. In Scotland, which Thompson specifically excluded from his analysis, the experience of industrialisation was probably more dislocating than in England, because of the greater speed of industrial change and urbanisation in Scotland, the reliance on migrant labour from peasant societies such as Ireland and the Scottish Highlands and the resulting linguistic, religious and sectarian divisions. However, even within the Scottish cotton industry, the experiences of working people in this period varied greatly, according to the occupations they followed, their age and gender, and where they lived.

Recruitment

The workforce in the Scottish cotton industry was recruited from diverse origins, depending on whether it was factory based or (the great majority for many years) outworkers. The factory-based workforce was heavily dependent on migrant labour, and both factory workers and outworkers were recruited to a large extent from the pool of cheap labour provided by women, children and young adults. The west of Scotland drew heavily not only on workers from the neighbouring Lowlands but from the Highlands and from Ireland, particularly Ulster.[2] In these ways, the Scottish cotton industry was intimately linked with far-reaching changes taking place in agriculture and land use, such as clearances of population in both the Scottish Highlands and the Lowlands, and similar changes in Ireland.

In Ayrshire, Renfrewshire and Lanarkshire, the linen industry offered an abundant supply of labour with skills in textile production, used to a semi-capitalistic system of production, with raw materials and sometimes looms provided by the linen merchant, who marketed the finished product. This workforce had the skills to transfer to the cotton industry, but frequently not the inclination to move into factory-based production, with its rigid systems of time management and work discipline.[3] Many Scots preferred to remain in home-based industries, such as hand loom weaving or tambouring, which gave them some independence, even if they paid less than factories. Factory work became heavily dependent on 'vulnerable' groups of workers, such as migrant workers from the Highlands or Ireland, widows with large families to support, or children from the urban poorhouses. It recruited and retained workers by targeting these 'vulnerable' groups and by paying higher and more regular wages than domestic textile production or agricultural labouring. This led to complaints from contemporaries that factory work was luring people away from agriculture to better-paid jobs in towns and was raising wages all round to levels that farmers could not afford.

In 1792, Carluke in Lanarkshire had lost population to Glasgow and Paisley, 'As there is a constant drain from the parish, both of young men and women to the neighbouring cotton mills, iron works etc., the farmer is often at a loss for labourers.'[4] Similarly at Carnwath, the introduction of iron and cotton manufactures nearby had increased the price of labour, whilst Auchinleck parish in Ayrshire had lost population to 'the Muirkirk Iron and local Tar Works, but especially to the Cotton Mill at Catrine, which have attracted inhabitants from this parish'.[5] In Beith, Ayrshire, people had moved to 'the extensive cotton works erected in the neighbourhood, particularly in the parish of Lochwinnoch and at the town of Johnstone, in the parish of Paisley', whilst at Old Cumnock there had been migration to Glasgow, Paisley and Kilmarnock, Catrine and Muirkirk.[6]

At Drymen, Stirlingshire, Balfron cotton mills and the printfields and bleachfields on the Leven near Dumbarton, 'perhaps the most extensive in Scotland', had pushed wages so high that farmers found it hard to compete. In the 1770s the wages of a man servant were about £4 a year, which by the 1790s had risen to £10 a year 'and frequently a good deal higher'. Female wages had increased in proportion and day-labourer rates had gone up from 8d to 10d a day, to 1s 6d.[7] However, industrial change was not always straightforward or linear. Because of the cyclical nature of the cotton industry and the way in which it was affected by wars and economic depression, these occupational and population shifts could reverse themselves. In Gargunnock, Stirlingshire, in 1793, 'The cotton mills at Balfron and Doun and the great demand at Glasgow a few years ago for weavers, masons and day labourers' had lured people away by 'the hope of regular employment and better wages'. The outbreak of the French Wars had changed all this, and 'By the late stagnation of trade, however, many have been obliged to return to their former occupations.'[8]

The effects of industrialisation were felt far beyond the Central Belt. Large numbers of people were displaced by clearances for sheep in the Highlands and by enclosures in the Lowlands. From Reay in Caithness, 'some poor people and one or two reduced families went from this parish to the cotton mills in Lanark and Stanley in 1788'.[9] At Weem, in Highland Perthshire, the local minister claimed in 1791 that 'Few or none have emigrated from this parish, but whole troops of boys and girls go annually to the low country for service, and of late to the cotton works, many of whom settle there.'[10]

The process of agricultural change and the resulting displacement of population was particularly traumatic in the west Highlands and Islands. From Campbelltown, Argyll, in 1792:

> upwards of five hundred persons young and old have left Kintyre and gone to Glasgow, Paisley, Bridge of Johnstone etc. in order to be employed in the cotton works at these and neighbouring places. The whole inhabitants of Canna have left the island and embarked on board of a vessel for the Clyde, being from four to five hundred persons, old and young, to seek employment in the Low Country, the island being let it is said to two persons for grazing their sheep by which they were all turned out of their small possessions.[11]

At New Lanark, 'a great proportion of the inhabitants are Highlanders, mostly from Caithness, Inverness and Argyleshire. Few of those from the west understand English. In 1791 a vessel carrying emigrants from the isle of Sky to North America, was driven by stress of weather into Greenock; about 200 were put ashore in a very destitute situation. Mr. Dale, whose humanity is ever awake offered them immediate employment, which the greater bulk of them accepted.' Dale recruited workers for New Lanark from Argyll and the Isles and housed 200 families during 1792, a year when sheep walks were being established in the Highlands.[12]

At Deanston in Perthshire, James Smith looked back on the initial process of recruitment in the late eighteenth century:

> from the great wages which the people earned, the better part of the surrounding population were ultimately attracted to the works. The first supply was

chiefly from the Highlands, where, from the introduction of sheep, the farmers and small cotters were forced away to seek employment in such establishments ... It has been uniformly found that the people of the immediately surrounding neighbourhood have proved the best population, and these works have been an asylum for many a reduced farmer, with his family, and for the widows and orphans of the agricultural and village population.[13]

Enclosures in the Lowlands led to the clearance of smaller and poorer tenants, who could not measure up to the 'new farming' and were often steered towards the textile industries. The fourth Duke of Atholl wrote to tenants on the Nairne estate, Perthshire, in November 1786, that they must move with their families to the newly developing factory village of Stanley or face eviction:

Encouragement held out to any of the tennents in the above farms who follow trades are industrious and have families of three children and upwards the Duke will give them as much ground near Stanley as will be sufficient to erect a house upon with a little garden behind for potatoes the Duke will . . . give them that and the ground gratis for their prospective lives the neighbouring works [Stanley cotton mill] will give constant employment to their children who instead of being a burthen to their parents will help materially to support them. Any old tenant having no family who can bring proof of his being on the ground 30 years upwards the Duke will . . . give a small piece of ground to at an easy rate provided he bear a good character. Those of the above tenants who are wise enough to see their own interests in accepting the above conditions will give notice to Commissary Bisset [the factor] . . . Those that do not accept of them will do well to look out for possessions elsewhere as the Duke is determined not to let his lands again in such small farms.[14]

These close links between agricultural change, population movement and industrialisation are illustrated by accounts from parishes, such as Little Dunkeld, Perthshire. Here, the fall in population between 1776 and 1792:

can in no way be accounted for but by the uniting of farms, and by the migration of some of the inhabitants to Perth and its neighbourhood, for employment at the bleachfields and extensive manufactories lately erected there, and to the village of Stanley in the parish of Auchtergaven, where there is a considerable cotton work carrying on.[15]

Cotton mills provided 'a convenient asylum' for the human casualties of agricultural change. In Stirlingshire, a contemporary highlighted the benefits to landowners of having spinning mills on their estates:

It cannot be questioned that these establishments are of advantage to the agricultural interests of the district in which they are set down. They afford a convenient asylum and the means of subsistence to the small occupants who

> have been ejected from their farms, to make way for tenants of proper skill and capital, who are now so generally introduced. They increase the consumption of the produce of the ground and furnish a ready market for every article that is produced on them.[16]

Some cotton mills conducted advertising campaigns to attract skilled labour. Gordon, Barron and Co. of Woodside Mills on the edge of Aberdeen, advertised in the *Aberdeen Journal* on 11 October 1790. They were seeking skilled workers, women and children, and young men to serve apprenticeships in weaving and spinning: the company clearly placed a high premium on skills, which challenges presumptions by some historians that the Scottish cotton industry was largely staffed by unskilled labour.

> Gordon, Barron and Co. continue to give encouragement to journeyman weavers in manufacturing cotton goods of different kinds, light, easy and profitable work to the weaver. Country weavers wishing to remove to the town will be assisted with money or looms by applying to James Ferguson at their Manufactory, Belmont Street, Aberdeen. They who have families will get employment for their wives and children. Young men from 16 to 25 years of age wanted as apprentices to the weaving and spinning.[17]

This advert suggests a shortage of skilled labour for cotton mills, which is reinforced by a later advert by New Lanark Mills, who were looking for workers (excluding the Irish), where there was an existing textile industry. An advert in the *Dundee, Perth and Cupar Advertiser* on 6 December 1806 set out to attract familes with large numbers of children:

> cleanly, industrious and well behaved families, in which there are three or more children, upwards of ten years of age, natives of the Highlands or Lowlands of Scotland only, and who can procure properly authenticated testimonials of their good character, may have constant employment, with every comfort that workpeople can desire, by applying at the New Lanark Cotton Mills, or at the Lanark Twist Company's Warehouse, Glasgow.[18]

Skilled labour, particularly men who could build and repair expensive machinery, was in short supply in this period. Landes has claimed that 'the first decades of industrialisation saw a ceaseless war against breakdown'.[19] This is confirmed in the letters of Robert Owen to James Craig at Stanley. In January 1808, when Craig was struggling to keep Stanley going, Owen enquired: 'Have you any steady valuable mecanics leaving you at the time you mention, either millwrights clockmakers or others?' as Owen would be glad to offer them employment.[20]

Glasgow and Paisley acted as magnets for migrant labour. In the Paisley textile industry, 'there are a few from England, more from Ireland, a great many from Ayrshire, and probably still more from the Highlands'.[21] Family, community and kinship networks acted as recruitment and training agencies. In the 1830s, the Glasgow cotton spinner Hugh Cogan described how 'the Irish send over for their relations, or acquaintances, or townspeople, and take them in as lodgers, and train them to weaving, which is now so easily acquired, that a person of ordinary acuteness can do common work in a very short time'.[22]

Migrant workers – the Irish and Highlanders

There were few people of Irish birth in the west of Scotland in the early 1790s and they mostly worked as agricultural labourers in the south-west.[23] In the Barony parish of Glasgow, out of a population of 18,451 in 1794, there were only 20 Roman Catholics, although there were doubtless Ulster Protestants amongst the overwhelmingly Protestant majority.[24] This began to change with Irish immigration into the west of Scotland, often beginning as seasonal harvesters, then as permanent settlers, aided by cheap steamboat travel. In Glasgow, the Catholic population rose from about 30 in 1778 to 2,300 in 1808, to 27,000 in 1831, to be followed by an even larger wave after the Irish Famine.[25]

From the late 1790s to the early 1850s, the overwhelming majority of Irish immigrants into Scotland came from the nine counties of Ulster. After the United Irish Rebellion of 1798, many political refugees fled Ulster, seeking work as weavers or in cotton spinning mills.[26] In the early nineteenth century, the decline of the Irish linen and cotton industries created many economic migrants seeking work in the rapidly expanding cotton industry in the west of Scotland. As early as 1821, out of 5,680 households in Paisley, 603 (10.5%) had an Irish-born head of household, and a further 558 (9.7%) a Highland-born household head. However, although there were 603 households with Irish-born heads, there were only 246 Catholic households, which suggests that a majority (59%) of the Irish incomers to Paisley were Protestants.[27] By 1841, Irish-born residents made up over 13% of the populations of Lanarkshire and Renfrewshire.[28]

Ulster Protestants made up a significant proportion of Irish migration. In Glasgow in 1831, out of a total population of 202,426, some 35,554 were Irish. Of these 19,333 were Catholics, a ratio of 55% Irish Catholic, 45% Irish Protestant.[29] Blantyre in Lanarkshire was an Irish Protestant stronghold. In the early 1830s, the workforce totalled 1,000 and 'about half the persons employed in the mills are Irish or of Irish extraction; there are more females than males, about two to one'. The manager at Blantyre added that 'Most of the Irish in this mill have been born in Scotland. The Irish at Blantyre are almost all Protestants.'[30]

There were numerous family ties and considerable population movement between Ulster and the west of Scotland. William Hammond was born in County Tyrone in Ulster to Presbyterian parents from south-west Scotland. He moved to Scotland in the 1840s, travelling from Belfast to Ardrossan by paddle steamer, then in an open cattle truck to Glasgow, 'completely filled with Irish immigrants like myself'. Hammond found work as a hand loom weaver in Calton, Glasgow, but encountered anti-Irish prejudices even though he was a Protestant, so that 'it was not all smooth sailing my settlement in the Calton. Some lads, weavers like myself, helped me to better my skill at the craft, so did the old men with whom I worked, but some of the baser sort made me understand that it was not an advantage to have been born in Ireland.'[31]

Irish migrant labour kept wages down and costs low in the Scottish cotton industry. John Orr, a Paisley spinner, described how, when his mill opened in 1810, all the workers were Irish, as 'the native people had an objection to work in cotton mills and other work was so plenty they did not require it'. Irish labour was essential to the cotton industry's success, and 'It would in the early stages of the business, have decidedly interfered with the prosperity of the manufacture, if the Irish had not come here, we could not have got on without them.' By 1834, Orr employed 199 Irish workers, 71% of the workforce in his spinning mill.[32] Henry Houldsworth in Glasgow agreed that 'if it had not been for the Irish, the manufactures of Glasgow could not have grown as rapidly as they have . . . Wages in the spinning department of the cotton trade have been kept down by the Irish.'[33] Lowland Scots were said to shun factory work. Alexander Carlile, a Paisley thread manufacturer, claimed:

> Most natives of Paisley would I believe, sooner earn 12 shillings a week at weaving with their own looms . . . than work in a cotton factory for 20 or 25 shillings a week. Our weavers, however destitute, seldom think of applying for employment in cotton factories. A cotton spinner does not hold the same rank in society as a fancy weaver; the cotton spinners in Paisley and its neighbourhood are in general, a dissipated set of men.[34]

The manager of Blantyre Mills agreed:

> Few Scotch families could be prevailed on to go into a cotton mill, they looked on it as a sort of degradation, hence the large numbers of Irish in spinning and weaving mills. This is in great measure owing to the aversion that the Scotch have of allowing their children to go into a cotton mill when the trade was started in the West of Scotland.[35]

The Irish were also prominent in the cotton outworking trades, particularly hand loom weaving. In Stranraer, there were 50 hand loom weavers in 1834 weaving cotton pullicates and gingham for Robert Walker in Glasgow. Most of them were immigrants from Down, Armagh, Antrim and Derry and their quarter of the town was known as Little Ireland.[36] In Glasgow, John George Hamilton of Henry Monteith and Co. noted that 'a great proportion of the hand loom weavers in Glasgow are Irish', whilst the muslin manufacturer James Hutchison, who employed 1,500 to 2,000 hand loom weavers in and around Glasgow, observed that 'a good many of them are Irish'. Hutchinson, who also employed 100 hand loom weavers in Belfast, noted that the Glasgow population was 'chiefly formed of natives of Lanarkshire, of Highlanders and of Irish'.[37] Another Glasgow cotton manufacturer, Hugh Cogan of John Bartholomew and Co. in the Calton, thought that about half of all Glasgow hand loom weavers were Irish, although outside Glasgow fewer than 10% were. Cogan agreed that without Irish immigration, the cotton industry would have struggled to find sufficient labour and keep wages down: 'in the cotton trade, particularly in the weaving department, we could not have done without the Irish'. Joseph Browne, a Glasgow dyer, echoed this: 'I do not see how we could have done without them [the Irish]. The Highlands and country villages could not have given us a sufficiency of hands.'[38]

Contemporaries were divided about the impact of the Irish on industrial relations in the cotton industry. Some characterised them as more prone to daring and violent behaviour than the Scots, others as more likely to act as strike breakers and blackleg labour. Until recently, historians have characterised Irish workers as less likely to join trade unions, to be involved in radical politics and more likely to act as strike breakers. Recently, Mitchell has challenged this view and shown that Irish-born workers played a prominent role in trade unions and in radical politics in the west of Scotland. One of the most prominent figures in the Glasgow Cotton Spinners' Association in the 1830s was Patrick Magowan, an Irish Catholic, who was active in the Grand General Union of Cotton Spinners of the United Kingdom and in factory reform.[39]

An analysis of the geographical origins of heads of households employed in the cotton industry in Bridgeton, Glasgow and Paisley showed that in Bridgeton in 1851, 28% of heads of household employed in cotton were Irish born. The comparable figure for Paisley was only 2.8%, and 77% of heads of household working in the cotton industry there in 1851 had been born in Paisley[40]. However, this is misleading, as most of the workforce in cotton mills consisted of women, children and young adults, not adult male heads of households. Another analysis, for Anderston, Glasgow in 1851 revealed that 52.5% of females and 13.4% of males worked in textiles. Almost half of these women were employed in the expanding power loom factories, where women had largely supplanted male hand loom weavers by mid century. The Anderston figures also showed the extent to which the Glasgow cotton industry was an Irish stronghold. In 1851, 13% of Irish-born men in Anderston were employed in textiles, whilst only 3.5% of Highland-born men were similarly employed.[41]

In Renfrewshire, labour for the textile industry was supplied by migrants from Ireland and the Highlands. Between 1851 and 1881, approximately 40% of Paisley's adult population had been born outside Renfrewshire and between 13% and 16% were Irish migrants. Out of a sample of four bleachfields in the Paisley/Renfrewshire area in 1851, almost 43% of single women who worked there were Irish and some 20% were Renfrewshire born. The other 37% were Scottish born, split between Highland and Lowland origins. Because the Renfrewshire bleachfields were sited on isolated sites close to water supplies, the single women stayed in dormitories, known as 'womanhouses'. They were recruited through family, friendship and community networks. At Foxbar bleachfield, near Paisley, most of the residents of the womanhouse in 1851 and 1861 came from Lochgilphead, Argyllshire.[42] This was similar to the company boarding houses of the Hamilton Company in the cotton town of Lowell, Massachusetts, USA, where, in 1836, 95% of the boarders were single women from the rural areas of New England. The New England boarding houses were strongly patriarchal, with a strict religious regime and a 10 p.m. curfew.[43] By 1851, 34% of the Highland-born population in the Paisley area worked in textiles, contrasting with Anderston in Glasgow, where there were few Highlanders employed in the local printworks or power loom weaving factories.[44]

The Lancashire cotton industry also drew on the Irish as a source of labour, but much less than in Scotland. In Preston, 32% of men over 20 and 28% of women over 20 worked in cotton manufacturing in 1851. The number of Irish-born in the Preston population more than doubled, from 3.3% in 1841 to 7.4% 10 years later. However, the great majority of workers were local. In 1851, 70% of the adult population of Preston had been born outside the town but 70% of them had travelled less than 30 miles from their birthplace, indeed 40% had travelled under 10 miles.[45] This contrasted with Paisley, where between 20% and 25% of the population between 1851 and 1881 were migrants – the figure for Preston over this period was around 10%.[46]

In Lowell, Massachusetts, the proportion of migrants in the population was higher, peaking at 46% in 1851, then falling to 25% in 1881.[47] The New England cotton mills initially recruited farm girls, and in 1836 only 3.6% of the workforce at the Hamilton Company, Lowell were foreign born. This began to change radically with mass migration from Ireland after the Potato Famine. From the late 1840s, there was increasing dependence on Irish labour. By 1850, 25% of the Hamilton workforce was Irish born and by 1860 this had risen to 46.9%.[48]

The composition of the workforce

The male mule spinner, a skilled and highly paid male artisan whose entry to the trade was restricted by apprenticeship, may have been iconic but he

Table 17 Workforce composition of three Scottish cotton spinning mills, 1791–1793

	Boys under 15	Girls under 15	Total under 15	Percentage under 15	Males over 15	Females over 15	Total over 15	Total workforce	Percentage of female workers
Busby, Renfrews	100	110	210	58	60	90	150	360	55
Neilston, Renfrews	94	78	172	57	29	100	129	301	59
New Lanark	376[a]	419[a]	795[a]	69[a]	145[b]	217[b]	362[b]	1157	55
Total	570	607	1177	65	234	407	641	1818	56

Notes: [a] New Lanark under 16; [b] New Lanark over 16.

Source: OSA, 1973 edition, Vol. VII, 462, 795 and 812.

was not typical. The workforce in cotton was dominated by female and child labour. In 1791, 181,753 men, women and children were employed in the Scottish cotton industry, excluding those working in bleaching and finishing. Of these, only 25,000 (14%) worked in factories. The remaining 156,753 were outworkers, including 38,815 hand loom weavers (probably 75% adult men), 12,938 women winding warp and weft, and no fewer than 105,000 women and children engaged in tambouring and needle decoration of muslins.[49]

A more detailed breakdown of workforce composition is given by figures from New Lanark and Busby and Neilston in Renfrewshire, where the workforce in the 1790s was largely made up of women and children, as shown in Table 17. Children under 15 averaged 65% of the workforce in the three mills, and women workers averaged 56%. The percentage of women and children in the three mills was 87%, similar to Stanley, Perthshire where they made up 86% of the workforce.[50] Feminist historians have argued that workplace arrangements in the cotton industry, with male foremen exercising authority over women and children, closely replicated patriarchal arrangements in the home.[51]

By 1816, the cotton factory workforce had fallen from 25,000 in 1791 to 10,000, reflecting the depressions and disruptions to trade from the French Wars, and also undercounting, as New Lanark was excluded from the 1816 figures. Of 10,000 workers employed by 41 factories in 1816, 6,854 (68%) were female and 4404 (44%) were under 18. Of these, 415 (4%) were under 10 years old. The use of child labour in cotton factories had declined between 1791 and 1816, although it had not disappeared. There were also 694 under 10 years of age employed in power loom factories and 1,366 in printworks.[52]

By the early 1830s, William Smith, a member of the Glasgow Cotton Spinners' Association, claimed that 75% of workers in Glasgow spinning

Table 18 Workforce composition of cotton spinning mills and power loom factories, William Dunn and Co., Dunbartonshire (4 mills) and Neilston, Renfrewshire (6 mills) and printfields and bleachfields, Neilston, 1835–1837

	Under 12		Under 18		Above 20		
	Males	**Females**	**Males**	**Females**	**Males**	**Females**	**Total**
Spinning mills and weaving factories, Dunn and Co., Dunbartonshire	180[a]		120[a]	235[a]	256	626	1,417
Spinning mills and weaving factories, Neilston, Renfrewshire	37	39	220	445	296	622	1,659
Printfields, Neilston	290	139	195	122	511	86	1,343
Bleachfields, Neilston	17	29	49	232	126	259	712
Total	524	207	584	1,034	1,189	1,593	5,131

Note: [a] Dunbartonshire figures refer to 'boys 11–14', '14 and upwards', and 'girls'.

Source: New Statistical Accounts, 1845, Vol. VII, 337 and Vol. VIII, 26.

mills were children and young people and the ratio of women of men was two to one. Each mule spinner employed three piecers under 18, and each spinner needed seven support staff – carders, clerks, mechanics and others.[53] According to James McNeish, another Glasgow mule spinner, the work was physically debilitating: 'I believe there are none, generally speaking, employed in the factories beyond the age of 40; their constitutions are so broken down by that age, that they cannot produce the quantity that the younger hands do.' A survey by the Association of 1,600 men in cotton factories in Lanark and Renfrewshire discovered only about 10 workers over the age of 45.[54]

Table 18 shows the impact of factory legislation on the cotton industry. After the Factory Acts of the 1830s, the strongholds of child labour in the industry were no longer the regulated spinning mills and power loom factories but the unregulated printfields, where in Neilston parish, Renfrewshire, children under 12 made up 32% of the workforce in 1837, compared to a mere 4.5% in the mills and factories. Table 18 also reveals the striking gender differences in the workforce between different branches of the industry. Spinning mills and power loom factories in Dunn and Co's four works in Dunbartonshire and in six mills in Neilston, Renfrewshire were dominated by female labour (61% in Dunbartonshire and 66% in Neilston). Calico printing works in Neilston were dominated by male labour (74% of the total), with adult males making up 38% of the total workforce. In the Neilston bleachfields, women made up 73% of the workforce in 1837.

In Scotland, the cotton industry became increasingly feminised in the second half of the nineteenth century. By 1868, the steam-powered spinning and weaving mills of A. and A. Galbraith in Oakbank and St Rollox in Glasgow had a workforce of 1,700, of whom 94% were female.[55] During the 'Great Depression' of 1873–1896, male workers moved out of cotton, into the expanding heavy industries. Between 1871 and 1881, the number of men working in cotton manufacturing in Glasgow declined by 50%, whilst the number of women increased over three times. As the century progressed, the proportion of women working in cotton manufacture as a proportion of the total female working population fell dramatically, particularly in Lanarkshire, where it was 23% in 1851, compared to only 4.7% in 1901. In Renfrewshire, the decline in the proportion of women employed in cotton manufacture from 25% in 1851 to 1.7% in 1901 is balanced out by the increasing proportion of women in thread manufacture, which rose from 3.5% in 1851 to 16.5% in 1891. By 1891, 30% of the female workforce in Renfrewshire were in cotton-related employment, including thread manufacture, weaving and factory hand (textiles).[56]

Labour turnover

From the few statistics available, it appears that the early cotton spinning mills experienced a high turnover amongst their youthful employees. A fragment of a wages book from the cotton mills of William McCormick in Kirkintilloch, Dunbartonshire, reveals that of 15 workers employed there on 1 July 1789, only three were still on the payroll on 27 July 1790.[57] Butt has shown that at Douglas, Dale and McCall's cotton mill in Newton Stewart, Wigtonshire, out of a total workforce of 177, only 85 (48%) completed a full year's employment in 1800–1801. The majority of the workforce (92 or 52%) left within a year or joined during the year.[58]

The difficulty of retaining workers was highlighted by Robert Barr, manager of Crosslee cotton mills, Renfrewshire. It proved difficult to attract and retain workers at Crosslee, a relatively isolated water-powered mill on the River Gryfe; without providing housing for workers:

> It is wonderful that a mill of this size daily making machinery into which so little has been advanced in this period should be hampered for money . . . no human being can do well 'till we have more housing. Ever since the winter

Table 19 List of people employed at Catrine Works, 1 January 1813 with a description of the present employment of residents and numbers who have died, September 1833

In the works, resident, Catrine	196	23%
Married and have families, Catrine	132	15%
Married and have no families, Catrine	9	1%
Left the works, Catrine	85	10%
Left the works and parish	241	28%
Left the works and parish, married and families	49	6%
Left the works and parish, married, no family	3	
Lost sight of	1	
Died at Catrine	151	17%
Total	867	100%

Source: GUA, UGD 91/1/5/2/6/3/1.

> weather set in we have not been able to keep our card room and water spinning room going for two days for want of hands, particularly children for the spinning room and piecers for the water jennies, which are often standing for want; besides when some come, they will stay for a few weeks as learners and for want of quarters go. Some children, who have been with us thro' summer come perhaps a mile or more every morning and return every evening, left us so soon as the bad weather set in.[59]

Labour turnover was lower in the early nineteenth century at Catrine, Ayrshire, due to a paternalistic management which provided housing, gardens, schooling etc. for workers and their families. Here, paternalism can be seen as a management strategy designed to cut down on high labour turnover. Table 19 shows that out of a total Catrine workforce of 867 in 1813, 422 or 49% were still living in the village in 1833 and a further 151 people (17%) had died there in the interim. The extent of paternalism can be gauged by the fact that of the 294 (34%) who had left Catrine, only one had been 'lost sight of'. Glasgow was the main destination for those leaving the area. Of the 294 who had left Catrine, 52%, had gone to Glasgow, with 8% going to Kilmarnock and 4% emigrating to America.[60]

Better records have survived for the New England cotton industry, which show a high labour turnover. At the Hamilton Company in Lowell, Massachusetts more than a quarter of the workforce either entered or left the mills in the five weeks from 23 July 1836. In the Hamilton Company's Mill A, male workers had been employed on average for 2.17 years and women workers for only 1.75 years in 1836. Because of a chronic labour shortage, Hamilton workers could work for short periods and leave without giving proper notice, only to be rehired again a few months later, in spite of company regulations.[61]

Women and children

Female and child labour was a defining feature of the early cotton factories and of the outworkers servicing the industry – in fact, of all manufacturing industry in Scotland, where, in 1826, women, youths and children formed 63% of the workforce.[62] It seems likely that a higher proportion of women and children were employed in manufacturing industry in Scotland than in England and that they played a key role in a Scottish economy based on low wages. The importance of female and child labour in Scotland was partly based on the fact that male wages were often so low that they could not support a family and had to be supplemented by the earnings of other family members.[63]

Why were women's wages so low? There was a deep-seated attitude amongst employers and male workers that female labour was worth less than male labour. This was buttressed by beliefs that men's wages should support a family, that women were 'inferior' in physical strength and general health, and that for many women work was a temporary phase before they married and had children. Amongst many male artisans, the test of 'respectability' was to be able to afford to keep a wife at home. The cult of female domesticity, the 'angel at the hearth', was a potent symbol in Victorian Britain.

The Paisley hand loom weaver William Taylor, like many other skilled male artisans, disliked the employment of women in cotton mills, or anywhere else – 'the female sex are formed to superintend domestic affairs and this alone is their proper province'. He also feared the moral consequences of men and women working so closely together in the mills for long hours.[64] The status hierarchy of work amongst women in the Paisley textile industries closely replicated the nineteenth century ideal of female domesticity.[65] Top of the tree in the Paisley hierarchy was 'sewing or fringing shawls in warehouses' or at home for a shilling a day, then working in a cotton thread works, which was preferred by natives of Paisley. Next down the ladder was working in a cotton spinning mill, which was mainly the preserve of Irish women. Women working in domestic service were nearly all Scottish, mainly local, but including some Highlanders.[66]

Child labour was a vital element of early industrialisation. Isolated rural mills like Blantyre, Catrine, New Lanark or Stanley had to find some way of attracting and retaining families and did so by paying higher wages, providing housing and often schooling. However, this still left a shortfall of child labour and an alliance was formed between rural cotton mills and the urban poorhouses. New Lanark provides the best known example of the recruitment of pauper apprentices, but places such as Blantyre in Lanarkshire, Stanley in Perthshire and Woodside Mills on the edge of Aberdeen all used pauper labour. At Blantyre and Woodside they were known as 'barracks children' and this quasi-military reference underlines the strict discipline imposed on women and children by the factory system. Indeed, William Cobbett complained about 'this sort of soldiership discipline' imposed on the New Lanark workers when he visited in the 1830s.[67]

In 1791, Blantyre employed 368 people, of whom 60 (16%) were 'Barracks children, employed at the mill'. They were orphans aged 8 to 12, bound to the works for a few years by their relatives and housed by the company, who employed a doctor, and a school master to teach them 'in their spare hours'.[68] At Woodside, a large building called the Barracks housed children who worked at the calico printing works. The boys were called the 'bun boys' (bound boys) because they were apprenticed to calico printing.[69] Barracks were also found in urban cotton mills, such as Houldsworth's mills at Anderston in Glasgow, which housed 500 workers in a barracks built by the company.[70]

At New Lanark, David Dale was praised for his humane treatment of child workers and the attention given to their education, housing and health. There were 507 children at school in New Lanark and most lived with their parents, either in the village or in Lanark. They were paid weekly and engaged for four years. Children from the poorhouses of Edinburgh and Glasgow received bed and board in lieu of wages and were bound for between four and seven years, depending on their age, as the apprenticeships finished at 15. They worked an 11½ hour day, slept three to a bed and were dressed in cotton in summer, wool in winter. The supply of child labour from Edinburgh and Glasgow was assured 'by the number of destitute children these places constantly afford'.[71] At Deanston, Perthshire, the English Quaker owner, Benjamin Flounders, was praised in 1798 for transforming a cotton mill distinguished by 'looseness and corruption of manners' and turning it around so, 'the workmen were now sober and respectable and the children are watched with vigilance and care'.[72]

However, not all contemporaries were so sanguine in their view of child labour. The Rev. Robert Boog, minister of Paisley Abbey, feared the effects of the rapid expansion of cotton manufacturing on the health, education and morals of children:

> It is painful to think, that a manufacture which gives employment to so many hands and which may be a source of great wealth to individuals, may be productive of very unhappy effects upon both the health and morals of the childen employed in it . . . Tempted by the wages, parents send their children to this employment at a very early age, when they have got little or no education; and the close confinement deprives them of the opportunity of acquiring more.[73]

Others were concerned about the expansion of outwork and its effects on the health and welfare of children. At Strathvathen, Lanarkshire, 'The great wages made by weaving, induces many parents to put their boys too early to that business, which stunts their growth, occasions swellings about their legs and hurts their morals, by rendering them too soon independent of their parents.' [74] In Paisley, in 1791, children could find employment in cotton weaving and bleaching from 8 to 9 years old and 'hence, in general, they marry young'.[75]

Girls were also affected by being sent into 'the flowering of muslin, which by confining them too soon to a sedentary life, makes them pale and sickly, and is likely to subject them to nervous complaint all their lives'.[76] Large numbers of women and girls were employed in tambouring, which involved needle decoration by hand carried out on a frame called a tambour, a technique originally used in the silk industry.[77] In 1791, it employed 105,000 women and children, 58% of the total Scottish workforce in cotton (excluding bleaching and finishing).[78]

Tambouring provided a useful replacement for the domestic hand spinning industry. In Dalziel, Lanarkshire, there was a shift in female employment from spinning fine yarn to tambouring, where young girls 'have learned to flower muslin, in large frames made for the purpose, which they find more profitable'.[79] In Galt's *Annals of the Parish*, when a cotton spinning mill was built on the Brawl Burn in 1788, the schoolmistress, Miss Sabrina Hooky, 'was touched with the enlivening rod and set herself to learn and teach tambouring, in such a manner as to supersede by precept and example that old time honoured functionary, as she herself called it, the spinning wheel'.[80] In Paisley, tambouring was done by girls in the home and in 'schools that are kept by a mistress . . . from 7 o'clock in the morning till 8 o'clock at night', where girls earned on average 6s a week in 1809.[81]

Muslin sewing or tambouring was widely distributed across Scotland, although generally controlled by Glasgow or Paisley companies, who distributed outwork as far away as Ulster.[82] In the early 1790s, it was to be found in Kilsyth and Kippen in Stirlingshire, and in Stirling itself.[83] In Ayrshire, it was found in Ayr and Beith, whilst in West Monkland parish, Lanarkshire, 'the boys and girls get wages for tambouring, sewing, muslins etc. at so early a period, that there is great danger of their education being neglected'.[84] By the mid nineteenth century, the trade was controlled by the Glasgow warehouses, who employed girls on site and as outworkers over a widely dispersed area.[85]

In Glasgow and Paisley, there was a plentiful supply of child labour, and cotton mills had little need to use the apprenticeship system, which was expensive and only resorted to in rural areas because of labour shortages.[86] By the early 1830s, the Glasgow and Paisley cotton mills employed tiny numbers of pauper apprentices, and the great bulk of their child workers lived at home with their families. Exploitation was not simply found between employer and worker. It could also apply to the relationship between male mule spinners and their child piecers, whether family members or not. Children could easily become the victims of physical and sexual abuse if they had no one to speak up for them. The Glasgow mule spinner James McNish, who worked at a spinning mill in the Calton, produced a strap or tawse 'about three feet long and with a heavy end, which might certainly be used to inflict a severe blow', whilst a piecer from the same mill, 11-year-old John Gibb, testified that 'the spinners often lick him, when he is in fault, with taws of leather'. Two girl piecers, Bell Sinclair and Mary Ann Collins, aged 13 and 10, had been beaten with the tawse and by spinners using the back of their hands. James McNish further testified that a male spinner in the Calton mill had recently been tried and found guilty of the rape of a 10-year-old girl piecer.[87]

However, even child workers were not always powerless victims. In the early 1830s, child piecers at the cotton spinning and weaving works of Couper, Maitland and Co. in Lanark went on strike for higher wages: 'our piecers, the youngest in our employment (but whose wages are paid by the spinners) turned out lately and would not work another day until their wages were advanced, from which we think that they are more capable of regulating their treatment and hours of labour than any law can'.[88]

Worker narratives

On the evidence of surviving autobiographies, working in a cotton mill was often a temporary phase in a working life, particularly for boys. The Paisley radical, Arthur Sneddon, started work at 10, in 1797, as a piecer in the Underwood cotton mills, Renfrewshire. After a year, he was transferred to the carding room, and by the age of 13 he had moved on to hand loom weaving. Another radical activist, Charles Campbell, was born in 1793 in Tarbert, Argyll. His Gaelic-speaking family moved to Johnstone, Renfrewshire, where his father worked in the warehouse of a cotton mill. When his father fell sick, Campbell had to work in the mill, where he earned 8s to 10s a week. His way out was to become an active self-improver, joining a subscription library and a debating society. He led an eventful later life, working for a time as an overseer on a slave plantation in the West Indies and standing trial for the murder of his wife in Glasgow.[89]

The missionary and explorer David Livingstone is the best known example of a child cotton worker who changed his life through the route of self-improvement. Livingstone's family, originally from the West Highlands, settled in Blantyre in Lanarkshire, where his father worked as a salesman. David started his working life in 1823 at the age of 10 as a piecer in the Blantyre cotton mills. He continued his education by attending the factory evening school and eventually the Andersonian Institution, Glasgow, where he studied chemistry, then medicine at Glasgow University.

He supported himself during the vacations by continuing to work in the Blantyre mills.[90]

Bob Smillie, born in 1857 in Belfast, belonged to a different generation but also worked as a child piecer. He was orphaned young and raised by his grandmother in Scotland. At 9, he left school for a job as an errand boy, and by 11 he was working as a 'half time' piecer in a cotton mill. However, there were many better-paid jobs for boys in the west of Scotland, and at 15 Smillie got a job with his brother, dressing castings in a brass foundry in Glasgow. By 17, he had a highly paid job in Summerlee Colliery, Larkhall, earning 42s a week, and he began his rise through the Labour movement.[91]

However, other autobiographers spent many years working in the cotton industry. The weaver/poet William Thom was born in 1798, brought up in poverty by his widowed mother, and crippled in a childhood accident. At 10 he was apprenticed to cotton manufacturers in Aberdeen, and when the firm went bankrupt four years later, he entered the hand loom weaving factory of Gordon, Barron and Burns in School Hill, Aberdeen, where he worked for 17 years.[92]

Women workers were more likely to spend many years working in the cotton industry. Janet Hamilton, born in 1795, was brought up in Old Monkland, Lanarkshire, where her mother taught her to spin and then to work the tambour frame. She married her father's assistant in 1809 and they had 10 children together. She combined tambouring work at home with bringing up a large family. Janet was a great reader who joined the village library, although she had to read in secret because of prejudice against women reading, and learned to write only in her fifties. She continued to work at tambouring until she went blind at 55, a year after her first poetry was published.[93] Another working-class poet, Ellen Johnston, born in Hamilton, Lanarkshire in the 1830s, lost her stone-mason father, who had emigrated to America, when she was 8. At 11, her stepfather took her into a power loom factory in Bishop Street, Anderston, Glasgow to learn weaving. Here, she was the victim of sexual abuse, probably at the hands of the stepfather. She had an illegitimate child in 1852, but put the child into her mother's care and lived an itinerant life, working in factories in Glasgow, Manchester, Belfast and Dundee.[94]

Weaving

In 1791, there were 15,000 hand looms employed by Glasgow manufacturers in a 20 to 30 mile radius round the city. Each weaver employed an average of nine people, including women and children, in different stages of manufacture, from picking the cotton until the goods were brought to market, making a total of 135,000 people employed by the Glasgow market. Earnings reflected skills, age and gender. Adult hand loom weavers earned from 12s to 14s a week, some of the most skilled earning from 14s to 18s and even 20s a week. Women and girls earned about 4s a week from winding yarn and tambouring. Other groups, such as children and older men, earned from 6s to 8s a week, preparing raw cotton for spinning and yarn for weaving.[95]

During the 'Golden Age' of hand loom weaving, from 1785–1800, weavers were said to be able to earn as much as 30s to 40s a week, but this was only for the most highly skilled type of 'fancy' weaving, centred in and around Paisley.[96] The Paisley weaver William Taylor explained in 1809 that weavers' earnings were often exaggerated, as 'the fancy trade is very precarious'. The weaver could take 'from five days to six weeks in mounting his web, before he could produce an ell of cloth', the price of weaving had been declining since 1793, and average earnings for even the most skilled weavers were in the region of 12s a week.[97]

In the late eighteenth and early nineteenth centuries, the division between manufacturing and agriculture was not the gulf it came to be later. Hand loom weavers, particularly, alternated between the two areas, particularly at harvest time and in times of trade depression.[98] At William McCormick's cotton mills at Kirkintilloch, two weavers received a shilling each in August 1792 'for the time they wrought at the hay'.[99] In Perth, the depression year of 1819 saw many hand loom weavers, employed by Glasgow cotton merchants, driven to agricultural work – 'the harvest is drawing to a close and the weavers who were employed in cutting it down are returning to their homes – no work, many destitute'.[100] By December 1819, unemployed workers from Stanley cotton mills were engaged in trenching, paid for by the Duke of Atholl.[101] In the same year, the Glasgow magistrates 'placed 340 unemployed weavers, under Mr. Cleland's superintendence, at Spade work in the Public Green'. This was a token gesture, as an estimated 5,256 hand loom weavers in Glasgow were unemployed.[102]

A Glasgow hand loom weaver remembered the depression of 1826, when 'there were several hundred breaking stones' and he took on spade labour at a shilling a day until shearing began, when he and his wife found work at 1s 6d a day. It was a particularly difficult year, as not only was there depression in the cotton industry but also drought and harvest failure, and the family had to pick haws off the hedgerows to survive. This led to several hundred weaving families in the west of Scotland joining emigration societies and petitioning to go to Canada.[103] In the depression year of 1841, weavers at Carstairs were as often found 'handling implements of manual labour in the field as on the loom board', whilst Paisley weavers were engaged in harvest work in the autumn of that year. Part-time weavers were to be found in East Mains, Lanarkshire in the 1850s and in Strathvathen as late as 1872.[104]

By the late 1830s, some two-thirds of hand loom weavers in the west of

Scotland were adult males, the rest being women and children. Journeyman weavers made up some 20% of the workforce in Glasgow and Airdrie in the late 1830s and early 1840s.[105] Male weavers were hostile to the influx of women and children into hand loom weaving, as a threat to their living standards and a challenge to social norms. William Taylor described his horrified reaction to the appearance of female hand loom weavers in Paisley in the early 1800s:

> From the cheap manner of taking apprentices results another bad consequence, that is the feminine assuming the masculine. When I enter a work shop and behold two or three blooming young women, whose shuttles sound louder than their tongues, in them I see two deficiencies, the want of a beard and a pair of breeches, in order to constitute them young women. It is high time that a check is put on these abuses.[106]

There was a strong culture of self-help and self-improvement amongst the Paisley 'fancy' weavers. Clubs of from 30 to 50 weavers met once a week on Saturday evenings in 'every decent public house'. Members paid 6d a week and the clubs operated as friendly societies and as 'the academies of the fancy work and the tribunals to which imposition trembles to appeal. What the merchant or manufacturer is on the 'change, so is the operative in the club.' However, there were limits to self-improvement – 'one teacher of dancing will have more scholars in his evening class than three teachers of the useful branches of education can boast of'.[107]

Paisley weavers were famed for their poetry. Leonard identified 68 working-class poets who were born or lived in Renfrewshire, mainly in Paisley, during the period from the French Revolution to the outbreak of the First World War. Of these, 29% had worked as a weaver or a weaver's drawboy (assistant). This radical literary culture was sustained by a network of clubs and societies such as the Literary and Political Club, founded in 1803 by a group including the weaver-poet Robert Tannahill, or the Paisley Literary and Convivial Club of 1814, whose members included James Yool, a weaver, poet and trade unionist.[108]

When power looms were introduced into Scotland, they were overwhelmingly staffed by women, as in Lancashire. This was because employers saw a chance to keep wages low, but also because of male prejudice against working on power looms. Female power loom weavers in Glasgow organised themselves into a trade union early on. By the early 1830s, almost all the women at John Sommerville's power loom factory in Glasgow belonged to the Association of Female Weavers, 'to provide for one another when thrown out of work by a strike etc'.[109] The women weavers at Dougall Macphail's power loom factory in William Street, Glasgow belonged to the same union, paying a penny a week, although a weaver called Margaret Watson, who had taken charge of the funds, had been dismissed by the company.[110]

Table 20 Estimated weekly wages for selected occupational groups in Scotland, 1836–1856

Occupational group	1836–1837	1841–1842	1846	1851	1856
Mule spinners (cotton)	20s to 35s	25s	26s	21s	20s to 35s
Power weavers (cotton)	6s to 11s	7s	8s	7s 3d	8s 3d
Hand loom weavers	6s	6s	7s	–	–
Coal miners	30s	25s	15s to 20s	–	–
Bricklayers	18s to 21s	21s	24s	–	–
Masons	22s	15s	22s 6d	–	–

Sources: L. C. Wright, *Scottish Chartism* (Edinburgh, 1953), 216 and G. Macgregor, *The History of Glasgow* (Glasgow, 1881), 442–443.

Female power loom weavers were paid much less than male mule spinners, something like a third of their earnings, on average. In the 1830s and 1840s, their earnings, shown in Table 20, were similar to those of hand loom weavers and much less than male colliers, bricklayers or masons. At Mather's factory in Tureen Street, Glasgow, female weavers as young as 13 earned 7s a week in 1833, but had to produce a minimum number of yards of cloth every fortnight or face dismissal.[111] In 1846, out of 35,116 people working in cotton factories in Scotland, no fewer than 74% were women, compared to 55% in England.[112]

By 1896, 'the great feature which differentiates the textile industries of Scotland from those of England is that while in the latter country they are followed by both sexes, in this they are practically *women's* industries'. In both countries power loom weaving was dominated by women, and in Scotland, 'a rooted prejudice exists among the working classes of Scotland against the employment of men on the power loom'. A manager claimed that he introduced men to power looms but after four weeks they gave up, 'being unable to stand the ridicule to which they were daily exposed for taking up women's work'.[113] However, in late nineteenth-century Scotland women dominated mule spinning, where it still existed, contrasting with Lancashire, where mule spinning was regarded as 'men's work'.[114]

The finishing trades

The size of the workforce was increasing in the bleachfields and printfields too. In 1791, three printfields at Bonhill in the Vale of Leven,

9 Female power loom weavers with male overseer, 1890s, Colinslee Works, Paisley Co-Operative Manufacturing Company

Dunbartonshire, employed a total of 993 people, of whom 51% were female. The average workforce in each printfield was a substantial 331 people.[115] These were 'proto factories', where skilled male journeymen printers could earn up to 18s a week on piece work. Significantly, it was this well-paid group of workmen that was engaged in a fierce struggle with employers regarding entry to the trade, wage regulation and workplace control. At Cordale Printworks in Dunbartonshire, there were complaints in 1791 about 'illegal combinations' amongst printworkers, who had 'appointed a committee of their number, from the different printfields in the West of Scotland, to meet and regulate the prices, which they were to oblige their masters to give for the different pieces of work'. Like the mule spinners, the male printworkers restricted entry to their trade by high entry fees and apprenticeships for their sons and other male relatives, and the issue was seen as ultimately one of workplace control: 'one of the parties must be in complete subjection to the other, before the trade can be upon a proper or sure footing'.[116]

Employers were particularly worried by the degree of national organisation amongst printfield workers. At Ruthven printworks, near Perth, the firm of Young, Ross, Richardson and Co., who employed some 600 people, complained about British-wide combinations 'among the operative calico

Table 21 Average weekly wages of Scottish printfield workers, 1793 (Campsie, Stirlingshire) and 1868 (Cordale, Dunbartonshire)

Occupation	Nos employed, 1793	Wages, 1793	Wages, 1868
Block printers	36	18s to 22s	25s to 40s
Copperplate printers	22	17s to 21s	
Machine printers			30s to 40s
Pencillers (girls)	160	4s to 6s	
Tearing boys	34	2s	
Bleachers	26	8s	
Engravers	16	18s to 22s	
Mill wrights	2	12s	
Labourers	6	7s	
Furnace men	8	7s	
Excise officers	2	£50 a year	
Total	312		

Sources: OSA, 1978, Vol. IX, 246 and D. Bremner, *The Industries of Scotland*, 1869, 304.

printers in all three kingdoms, the objects of which are to raise the price of work'.[117]

Cordale Printworks in the Vale of Leven was the largest printworks in Scotland. In 1792 it employed 876 people, of whom 49% were children – 300 girl pencillers and 130 boys aged from 8 to 15.[118] A major attraction to employers was that Scottish wages were lower than in England. In 1831, journeyman's wages in calico printing in Scotland were 40% to 50% lower than England, and larger numbers of low-paid women were employed in Scotland. By the 1830s, it was becoming more difficult to attract young men into the industry, which paid less than the 'new' industries of iron and steel, coal mining and heavy engineering. As a result, entry fees for apprentices in the Glasgow area were reduced from 7 guineas in 1795, to £5 in 1833 and £2 in 1840.[119] By 1868, Cordale employed fewer workers – 500 men, women and children. Calico printing was still a high-wage industry, at least for adult males. In 1868, as shown in Table 21, machine printers earned from 30s to 40s a week, small block printers 25s to 30s, large block printers 30s to 40s and boys 4s to 7s.[120]

The United Turkey Red Company in the Vale of Leven, a combination of four firms, continued to be a major employer, employing 2,600 people in 1914, and strongly anti-union. In 1911, over 1,000 women went on strike against the United Turkey Red Company to gain general wage increases, improvements in working conditions and union recognition.[121]

Trade unions and workforce control

Organised resistance to employers and a sense of solidarity amongst workers and their local communities appeared early amongst textile workers in the west of Scotland. As early as 1768, a 'female combination' was formed in Paisley by young women in the linen trade employed 'in clipping of lawns who refuse to work unless on higher wages'. The strike had a festival or theatrical flavour, as the women, numbering two or three hundred, 'mostly clothed in white, drew up this day in Maxwelltown and marched in procession four in a rank to this place and proceeded through the streets'. Significantly, they received support from 'great crowds of journeymen weavers and others'. The Paisley authorities reacted by jailing three of the women for a month for their part in the 'riotous proceedings'.[122] Accounts of trade union demonstrations by female workers in this period are rare, although women and children took an active role in food riots. E. P. Thompson argued that in England it was the period from 1815 to 1835 that saw 'the first indications of independent trade union action among women workers'.[123]

Although most cotton workers were not employed in factories, the concentration of occupations in well-defined geographical areas of towns led to a strong communal and occupational identity amongst hand loom weavers in places like Paisley or the industrial suburbs of Glasgow. By the late 1780s, hand loom weavers in Calton, Glasgow were taking action against wage cuts by destroying the work of weavers who worked at the reduced rates. Again, there was a theatrical element to their protest, as the weavers 'very unanimously, hindered the few from working at the reduced prices, cut many webs out of the looms, and carried the yarn home to the owners, and at last came the length of burning them'. This went on through the summer of 1787 and eventually, on 3 September, the Glasgow magistrates called in the military, who fired on the crowd, killing six of them. The rioters enjoyed an extraordinary degree of community support and 6,000, men, women and children, attended the Calton funeral of three of those killed.[124]

This community support or coercion continued amongst Glasgow weavers, when 40,000 went on strike in December 1812. In January 1813, 'In Govan, Anderston etc., the village drummers have been ordered by the managers of the weavers to alter the hours of beating their drums. This they did at 8 o'clock and it was candidly avowed that any person continuing to work after that hour ran a great risk of getting his windows destroyed.' An English visitor claimed that the weavers had the support of 'the commonalty of Glasgow and of the landed interest'.[125]

As manufacturing industries began to develop, there were fears that large numbers of workers in one workplace, or in one district, would lead to radical views on economics and politics spreading more easily amongst the lower orders. In the late eighteenth century, the language of class was not fully developed and middle-class observers used phrases like 'servants', 'lower ranks' or 'lower orders' to describe the labouring poor. At Neilston, Renfrewshire, the Rev. John Monteith complained in 1791 that 'the rapid increase of manufactures is neither friendly to the health, nor morals of the people' and that 'the lower ranks of mankind . . . when collected and confined together, are too apt to corrupt one other; and when assembled in such promiscuous crowds, are probably often not exposed to the best examples'.[126]

At Deanston in Perthshire, Alexander MacGibbon believed that:

> So many people collected in one house refined each other in all manner of wickedness. The duties of the family were neglected; the Sabbath was profaned; the instruction of youth was forgotten; and a looseness and corruption of manners spread, like a fatal contagion, everywhere around. The advancement of high wages at this work raised the price of all other kinds of labour; and what was worst of all, servants became insolent, disobedient and careless.[127]

The relationships between labour and capital in the cotton industry began to change as larger industrial units appeared in spinning and finishing and greater divisions emerged between employers and workers. There were tensions between the older, paternalistic society, where concepts of fairness and state regulation of wages still lingered, and the 'new', individualistic, capitalist society, where regulation was anathema and wages were set by the market. This conflict was seen at its height in the Scottish cotton industry in the early nineteenth century. An Association of Operative Cotton Spinners was established in the west of Scotland in 1810 to establish a closed shop in mule spinning. Entry to the trade was restricted by family ties and high entry fees: 'the object of the society is to limit the business of spinning to members and their sons, so that they may be able, as far as possible, to keep the wages to the standards that they fix, by preventing the possibility of the mill owners procuring spinners from any other quarter'.[128]

Remnants of the 'old' paternalism still lingered amongst the landed classes, who provided the majority of Justices of the Peace. In July 1810, Lanarkshire JPs recognised the constitution of the new union as a friendly society, to the disgust of the employers, who claimed that the society was operating outside its remit by supporting unemployed cotton spinners, rather than widows and orphans. They also believed the union was behind attacks on workers who had stayed in work or replaced strikers. The employers retaliated by forming the Association of Master Cotton Spinners on 12 October 1810. They levied members according to the number of spindles they owned and offered a reward of 20 guineas to those giving evidence on the assaults. The employers also took advice from the Lord Advocate on the legality of the new union.

He advised that the Operatives' Society was acting illegally in trying to keep earnings high and restrict entry to the trade.[129]

The employers' association agreed to notify each other of strikes, to decide whether to operate a general lock-out or a blacklist, and to fine employers £50 per 1,000 spindles if they broke the agreement. They also invited Paisley employers to a joint meeting to collect information about regulations 'relative to truancy amongst operative spinners'. Workers in each mill were presented with a 'deed of obligation', an agreement not to join the union, on pain of a fine of £20. The union petitioned the Lanarkshire JPs again. On 18 January 1811, the employers resolved that the new association was still illegal and made their position clear by 'dismissing their servants and putting a stop to their works'. The employers also claimed that their deeds of obligation had been oversubscribed by their employees, that their interests would be represented at 'ensuing trials' and a levy of 10s per 1,000 spindles would be made on employers.[130]

The union launched a highly targeted campaign of violence against non-union, female and blackleg labour employed by the most prominent members of the Association of Master Cotton Spinners. On 21 December 1810, two male spinners from the Barrowfield Mill, Glasgow were attacked by 'several Persons armed with bludgeons and other weapons' because they were not union members. This was followed by attacks on two female workers at Crombie and Carnegie's mill in Anderston, Glasgow, and on the house of an employer, James Dunlop. Henry Houldsworth's mills in Anderston were a particular target. On 28 December, a group of women and children was attacked by three men with sticks, including Gavin Simson, 'a Member of the United Society of Operative Cotton Spinners'. On the same night, Peter McAuley, a male spinner, was attacked at the Duntocher cotton mills, Dunbartonshire and a young female worker at Barrowfield Mill was attacked by two men 'who tore her cloak to pieces, knocked her down and kicked her on the breast'.[131]

Industrial unrest overlapped with political unrest. The context of the Radical War of 1820 was the depression following the end of the French Wars. It was part of increasing social and political unrest on both sides of the border, including Peterloo in 1819 and the Cato Street conspiracy of 1820. A general strike was called in the west of Scotland and was supported by colliers and cotton spinners, who closed spinning mills in Glasgow and Paisley.[132] James Paterson, then a 13-year-old printer's apprentice in Kilmarnock, remembered attending radical meetings at the house of Willie Semple, a cobbler. The other members of the club were weavers, and newspapers such as the *Black Dwarf* and the *Glasgow Chronicle* were read aloud and discussed three times a week. The weavers were 'all . . . keen Reformers; some carried their notions so far as to come under the denominations of Blacknebs, which latter were understood to stop at nothing less than an absolute and bona fide division of property'.[133]

Middle-class reactions can be gauged from the views of contemporaries such as the Glasgow minister Rev. Thomas Chalmers, who blamed 'well paid workmen of cotton mills and other manufactories where there has been little or no decline in wages', although he noted that weavers, who had been badly affected by the depression, were also involved. Chalmers believed that some of the weavers had acquired organisational skills through their membership of dissenting congregations, but generally thought that radicalism was 'an aspect of infidelity and irreligion'.[134]

Rev. Henry Duncan, of Ruthwell in Dumfrieshire, was another evangelical Christian with a well-developed fear of irreligion and disaffection amongst the lower orders. In 1821 he published *The Young South Country Weaver; or A Journey to Glasgow: A Tale for the Radicals*, 'with the view of fighting Disaffection with their own weapons' and to 'counteract some of the prejudices prevalent among the middle and lower classes and to convey moral and religious instruction through the alluring mechanism of a tale'. The central character of the novel is William Webster, a young Dumfrieshire weaver, who travels to his uncle's house in the Calton, Glasgow in December 1819. His uncle Daniel is a Radical weaver and wants to know whether his nephew is for the government or the people – red or green. When his son runs away from home after a violent quarrel with his father, father and nephew search for him in Glasgow pubs and attend a Radical Reform meeting attended by 'the very lowest of the rabble', where the speaker is Thistlethorn, an Englishman who declaims on liberty and equality. Thistlethorn stands on a platform flanked by a green flag emblazoned with the words 'Liberty or Death'.[135] The name invokes Arthur Thistlewood, the English republican, who was convicted and hanged in 1820 for his part in the Cato Street conspiracy.[136]

Strikers enjoyed considerable community support for their actions, enforced by a variety of sanctions against strike-breakers. In 1824, Neil Snodgrass, owner of the Mile End Mills in Calton, Glasgow sacked his existing spinners and replaced them by others. This provoked a mass reaction as 'several hundreds of persons, supposed cotton spinners, assembled in front of the Mill and broke a number of panes of glass'.[137] The following year, John Graham, a cotton spinner at Dunlop's mill at Broomward, Calton was attacked while going home from work by two men from amongst a large crowd. Graham was shot in the back and his home was besieged afterwards by a crowd who denounced him as a 'nob' (strike-breaker) and 'continued to utter oaths and sing songs, prepared for the occasion, which they, as the glorious termination of a nob as they called it, continued to do, until dispersed by the military'.[138] 'Nob songs', sung by women and childen inside and outside the mills, reflected hostility towards employers and strike-breakers.[139] Indeed, women and children played a prominent role in intimidating opponents in industrial disputes, as acknowledged in a passage from *The Young South Country Weaver* stating that 'women and bairns are aye the best at a mob'.[140]

However, the union presented itself in a different light when it came to its official image. A metal tea tray preserved at the Peoples' Palace, Glasgow, dating from c. 1825, displays the symbols of the Friendly Association of Cotton Spinners (Plate 1). A male mule spinner stands in front of his machine, with a girl piecer to one side. The iconography is British, rather than Scottish; loyalist and royalist, rather than republican. The tableau is surmounted by a crown, with the words 'Britain's Glory, Live and Let Live'. To either side are pictures of a cotton plant with the words 'Success to the Cotton Tree' and a sailing ship with the words 'Success to Commerce'. At the bottom are the words 'Success to the Friendly Association of Cotton Spinners' and the slogan 'United we Stand, Divided we Fall'. This is the very model of a 'respectable' skilled male craft union.

Robert Thomson, a Glasgow mill manager, blamed the repetitive nature of factory work for growing class consciousness and discontent amongst the working class: 'there is a general tendency to discontent and sourness of feeling amongst the whole working class in this country, arising from the necessity of constant and unremitting labour'. The manager of cotton mills in Neilston, Renfrewshire complained in 1837 that 'the management of them has been found a much more difficult task for two or three years past than it wont to be; and that a spirit of insubordination and dissatisfaction seems to be spreading rapidly amongst the working classes'.[141]

The struggle for control of the workplace extended to workers taking time off for political demonstrations and holidays. At Bogle's spinning works in Bridgeton, Glasgow in the early 1830s, 'upon two occasions, when reform processions took place, the workers got leave to attend them on condition of making up the lost time', and this was echoed by comments from the Barrowfield Cotton Works, Glasgow. At Blantyre cotton works in Lanarkshire, the work routine had been disrupted by 'several exceptions last year, chiefly arising from reform processions'. Elsewhere, traditional and religious holidays were observed, as at Bartholomew's spinning and weaving mills in Glasgow, where 'at New Year's Day and the annual city fair two or three holidays are always allowed, and there are also three sacramental fast days yearly, during which we shut our works'. At Orr's spinning mills in Paisley, holidays included 'two sacramental fast days, two days idle at New Years Day, one on the race course and probably two others', whilst Brown, Malloch and Co's spinning mills in Johnstone, Renfrewshire, were closed for 'religious fasts, three days; Horn Fair, three days; and at New Year, two days'. Workers clearly exerted pressure to gain additional holidays. At Kerrs' spinning mills in Paisley, 'there are two town fasts in the year when we cannot work, and there is three or four other days which is not wrought by almost any person', whilst at Crums' spinning and weaving works at Thornliebank, Renfrewshire, time was lost 'when the workers wished to have a holiday at fairs or at the New Year'.[142]

The Glasgow Cotton Spinners' Strike of 1837 marked the peak of union activity. A bad harvest in 1836 was followed by a commercial crisis in the USA, which prompted employers to reduce wages, resulting in a strike by 'the sawyers, the carpenters, the masons, the iron moulders, the dyers'. The Cotton Spinners' Strike in April 1837, involving some 32,000 workers, was followed by a strike of 16,000 Lanarkshire colliers. The Glasgow authorities were alarmed by the scale of the unrest, 'bands of 600 or 800 or 1,000 men traversed the streets, with banners flying and drums beating' and the cotton mills were 'beset by crowds' in the evenings. The strike was highly organised and run by a committee of delegates from 38 different cotton firms in and around Glasgow. It lasted three months, by which time the cotton workers were on the breadline and union funds exhausted. On 22 July 1837, John Smith, a strike-breaker, was shot in the back and killed. The inner circle (16 members) of the union committee were arrested in the Black Boy Tavern, Gallowgate on 29 July, and two days later the spinners voted to go back to work.[143]

The 1837 strike showed how class issues could be blurred by separation along gender and religious divides. Although there were armed attacks on employers by strikers, violent attacks on strike-breakers or blacklegs were common, including attacks on young women. The violence of the Cotton Spinners' Strike was frequently blamed on the large numbers of Irish employed in the cotton industry, who had brought with them from Ireland traditions of direct action in support of their economic, social and political grievances. The use of violence in strikes has been linked by Fraser to heavy alcohol consumption by working men.[144] However, this generally happened towards the end of a strike, when personal and union funds were exhausted and families were facing hardship.

In working-class communities, both sexes resorted to violence on occasion, although using different methods and for different purposes. Sulphuric acid or vitriol was a readily available bleaching material and was a favoured and deadly weapon for throwing in the faces of opponents, leading to blindness or disfigurement. Vitriol was used by both sexes; assault by sticks or guns was confined to men. Men used violence against both sexes, in strikes, in political demonstrations, in crime or in the domestic setting. Women used violence against other women, usually in a domestic or workplace situation. Walter Freer, the son of a radical Glasgow hand loom weaver, recalled how his father and two companions were meeting in a Glasgow pub during the Radical War period, when their conversation was interrupted by a known informer. One of his father's companions threw vitriol into the face of the informer, who lost both eyes as a result. Freer added, 'in these wild days vitriol throwing was a frequent means whereby many a jealous lass in her vengeful rage sought to disfigure her rival in love'.[145]

Fraser has claimed that after the defeat of the Cotton Spinners' Union in 1837 and the depression years that followed, 'the struggle over authority in the factories had been won decisively by the employers'.[146] However, throughout the 1850s and 1860s, the highest-paid male spinners were still earning 5s 4d to 6s 6d a day, comparable with crafts such as printing. By 1866, male self-acting minders on higher counts of cotton were earning as much as 26s a week and female minders as much as 19s to 19s 6d a week.[147]

Alcohol and workforce control

Violence in the workplace and in the home was often associated with alcohol abuse, and middle-class observers also linked radical activities amongst the working classes with their use of pubs. *The Young South Country Weaver* (1821) denounced Glasgow pubs as 'hotbeds of sedition and infidelity'[148], whilst in New Monkland, Lanarkshire, union activities were linked to heavy drinking amongst colliers and weavers in the late 1830s:

> The frequent associations and combinations which prevail here and are connected with similar combinations in different parts of the country to raise the price of labour, are very hurtful . . . These combinations arise most amongst the colliers and the weavers. The great number of inns, alehouses and spirit shops that abound in Airdrie and other parts of the parish afford great temptation to idleness and dissipation, which involve many families in poverty and misery.[149]

If nineteenth-century cities can be seen as 'places of order', with the factory as a microcosm and symbol of regulation and authority, then the urban pub was the polar opposite. Pubs were male, working-class spaces, largely removed from the control of the authorities. Union activists met in pubs during the Radical War of 1820, and in 1837, the leaders of the Cotton Spinners' Strike were arrested (in a secret room) in the Black Boy Tavern in Glasgow, after which the strike collapsed.[150]

There were fears that this atmosphere might be re-created in the workplace, with drink being smuggled into work and used in workplace rituals. Employers tried to shield themselves from the consequences of this type of behaviour through devices like apprenticeship indentures. At the Spinningdale cotton mills in Sutherland, in 1793, Andrew McPherson was bound as an apprentice cotton weaver for three years to learn the skills of the trade, during which time 'he shall abstain from all riotous and debauched company and from playing at idle and expensive games'.[151]

In the 1830s, a Paisley thread manufacturer reported: 'I heard a master spinner say that it was his conviction that half of all their [cotton spinners'] earnings was spent in whisky'.[152] Nor was this behaviour confined to spinners. James Thompson, a Glasgow cotton manufacturer, linked heavy drinking to increasing poverty and demoralisation amongst hand loom weavers: 'The practice of spirit drinking has increased in Glasgow among the weavers, in proportion to the depreciation of wages.'[153] In Neilston, Renfrewshire, the local minister complained in 1837 about the high wages paid to workmen in the local cotton mills, bleachfields and printworks and 'the vast sums they spending in drinking'.[154]

Certainly the scale of the problem was considerable. The annual average spirits consumption in Scotland in 1838 was an estimated 23 pints a head, compared to 7 in England and 13 in Ireland.[155] In the 1840s, Edinburgh had 555 pubs, one for every 30 families and Dundee one for every 24 families.[156] Even by 1850, after 20 years of temperance agitation, Glasgow still had 2,000 licensed premises, one for every 160 people.[157]

With this background, it was unsurprising that drink played an important part in workplace culture.[158] William Thom, remembering his unhappy youth in the School Wynd hand loom weaving factory in Aberdeen, described how children were used to smuggle drink into work: 'Weaving commenced gradually on Wednesday; then were little children pirn fillers, and such were taught to steal warily past the gate keeper, concealing the bottle.'[159]

In the Dalsholm Printfield in Maryhill, apprentices paid a high entry fee (13 guineas in 1818), which was spent 'in a guzzle with lots of drink, setting some of the more thoughtless members on a spree for a day or two or even longer'. The work rituals and initiations were marked by drink: 'If a block printer, he had to pay a pint of whisky when he printed his first handkerchief and grounded it; another for his first garment pieces; for his first furniture piece; another for his first shave; for his first long tailed coat; and for other reasons which must be nameless.' This was a highly communal and ritualised activity: 'every day at 12 o'clock the biggest of the tear boys was sent down to the store for a quantity of whisky in a piggin (a small pail or bowl); this was brought up to the printing shop; a quantity of sugar was put in and well stirred, then all the men gathered round the table on which stood the piggin of whisky, and each got his bucket, crackit a wee, an' awa' tae the work again'.[160]

This is the opposite of the strictly disciplined factory workplace where working life was regulated by the machine and a mainly female workforce was subject to close male supervision. It shows the survival of traditional modes of work well into the nineteenth century, where male workers worked 'in relatively small workplaces but retained much control'.[161] Sometimes, employers connived with this workplace culture. During the Radical War of 1820, the workers at Dalsholm were thanked for their lack of involvement by their manager, 'who afterwards entertained them with a case of Highland whisky'.[162]

Productivity

As working hours shortened in Britain, new work regimes were introduced from the 1880s, characterised by 'regularity, a curtailment of worker independence, closer and more direct management control, intensification of work pace and shorter working hours'. The speeding up of work in cotton factories impacted particularly on women. Some 75% of disputes in the British cotton industry between 1900 and 1914 were about 'bad material' causing breakages and loss of work.[163] In Scotland, this 'new' regime met with passive resistance by cotton workers in the form of low productivity and resistance to new technology and to supervising a larger number of machines. In power loom weaving, for example, there was a striking contrast between Scotland, where, in 1886, 79% of weavers minded two looms, and Lancashire, where three or four looms per weaver was the norm.[164]

Amongst foreign competitors, the differences were even more marked. By the 1850s, the New England cotton industry had much higher productivity than Britain's. In Lowell, Massachusetts, employers succeeded in speeding up machinery, in getting workers to mind more machines and in establishing a premium system, where bonuses were paid to overseers whose workers produced the greatest amount. Between 1840 and 1854, the workload of spinners and weavers at the Hamilton Company in Lowell more than doubled, with no increase in wages. The average number of spindles per worker increased from 129 to 294, whilst the number of looms per weaver went up from 1.3 to 2.9. In four textile mills in the Waltham–Lowell area of Massachusetts, between 1836 and 1850, output per worker rose by 49%, whilst wages increased by only 4%. At eight cotton firms in Lowell, between 1840 and 1850, spindle capacity more than doubled from 155,000 to 330,000; the size of the workforce only increased by 30%, whilst the average number of spindles per operative rose by 64%.[165]

The contrasts between the productivity of the English and Scottish cotton industries in the late nineteenth century are striking. In 1883, a factory inspector claimed that 'Even though lower wages may be paid in Scotland, it is doubtful if the cost of production is not even greater.' This was because the English cotton industry produced an average 87.5lbs of yarn per worker per week in 1867, compared to only 56lbs in Scotland. By 1907, the lead had grown, with England producing 132.4lbs of yarn per worker per week, whilst Scotland averaged only 64lbs.[166] In weaving, the picture was similar. The Chief Factory Inspector claimed in 1890:

> There are no operatives of whom I have ever had an experience who work with so much energy as the Lancashire people, and the contrast between a Scotch and a Lancashire weaving factory in this respect is very remarkable. The Lancashire weaver works with a will, she earns a high wage (on average double that of her Scotch sister on the same class of work) and is anxious to maintain it. She will take charge of four power looms without hesitation; and indeed, her energetic industry is not unfrequently an embarrassment to the inspector, for it makes her indifferent to the provisions of the Act of Parliament, which has been passed for her protection. She has practically to be driven from her work . . . In Scotland . . . it is common to find weavers of long experience with only two power looms, and it is with difficulty that they can be persuaded to take a third. Such is the recognised contrast between the two classes of cotton operatives.[167]

These differences in attitude and productivity between the cotton workers of Scotland, England and the USA cannot be solely explained by blaming the workers – management clearly shared a good deal of the responsibility. The nature of management and mill ownership in Scotland is explored in the next chapter.

Notes

1. E. P Thompson, *The Making of the English Working Class* (London, 1963), 12 and 939.
2. See C. W. J. Withers, *Urban Highlanders: Highland–Lowland Migration and Urban Gaelic Culture* (East Linton, 1998); and M. J. Mitchell, *The Irish in the West of Scotland, 1797–1848* (Edinburgh, 1998).
3. See C. A. Whatley, 'The Experience of Work', in T. M. Devine and R. Mitchison (eds), *People and Society in Scotland. Volume I, 1760–1830* (Edinburgh, 1988); and W. W. Knox, *Industrial Nation: Work, Culture and Society in Scotland, 1800–Present* (Edinburgh, 1999).
4. Sir J. Sinclair (ed.) *[Old] Statistical Account of Scotland* (*OSA*) (Wakefield, 1973–1983), 1973, VII, 133 and 142.
5. *OSA*, 1973, VII, 191; and 1982, VI, 15.
6. *OSA*, 1982, VI, 72 and 114–15.
7. *OSA*, 1978, IX, 283.
8. *OSA*, 1978, IX, 362.
9. *OSA*, 1979, XVIII, 153.
10. *OSA*, 1977, XII, 813.
11. *Glasgow Courier*, 16 June 1792.
12. *OSA*, 1972, VII, 466; and E. Richards, *The Highland Clearances* (Edinburgh, 2000), 86–104.
13. Quoted in R. S. Fitton, *The Arkwrights, Spinners of Fortune* (Manchester, 1989), 205.
14. Blair Castle, Perthshire, Atholl Mss, Box 55, 11/3, fol. 14, Letter from John, fourth Duke of Atholl, November 1786.

15. *OSA*, 1977, XII, 411.
16. P. Graham, *General View of the Agriculture of Stirlingshire* (Edinburgh, 1812), 349.
17. P. Morgan, *Annals of Woodside and Newhills* (Aberdeen, 1886), 254.
18. *Dundee, Perth and Cupar Advertiser*, 6 December 1806. I am grateful to Dr Douglas Lockhart of Keele University for this reference.
19. D. Landes, *The Unbound Prometheus* (Cambridge, 1969), 87.
20. Atholl Mss, Box 25, 11/3, fols 92–4, Robert Owen to James Craig, 7 January 1808.
21. *OSA*, 1973, VII, 855.
22. Report on the State of the Irish Poor in Great Britain, 1835, *Parliamentary Papers* (*PP*), 1836, XXXIV, Appendix G, Scotland, 109.
23. Mitchell, *The Irish*, 1.
24. *OSA*, 1973, VII, 350.
25. C. G. Brown, 'Religion', in A. J. Cooke et al. (eds), *Modern Scottish History, 1707 to the Present. Volume I, The Transformation of Scotland, 1707–1850*, 80.
26. G. Walker, 'The Protestant Irish in Scotland', in T. M. Devine (ed.), *Irish Immigrants and Scottish Society in the Nineteenth and Twentieth Centuries* (Edinburgh, 1991), 46; and Mitchell, *The Irish*, 1–2.
27. *PP*, 1836, XXXIV, G, 113.
28. Mitchell, *The Irish*.
29. Walker, 'Protestant Irish', 49–50.
30. *PP*, 1836, XXXIV, G, 107–8.
31. W. Hammond, *Recollections of a Glasgow Handloom Weaver* (Glasgow, 1904), 19–20.
32. *PP*, 1836, XXXIV, G, 132–3.
33. *Ibid.*, 107.
34. *Ibid.*, 133.
35. *Ibid.*, 108.
36. *Ibid.*, 151.
37. *Ibid.*, 107 and 111.
38. *Ibid.*, 109 and 113.
39. Factory Inquiry Commission Reports, *PP*, 1833, XX, A1, 207–8, Evidence of Patrick Magowan; and Mitchell, *The Irish*, 26–9.
40. W. W. Knox, *Hanging by a Thread: The Scottish Cotton Industry, c. 1850–1914* (Preston, 1995), 124.
41. W. Sloan, 'Employment Opportunities and Migrant Group Assimilation: The Highlanders and Irish in Glasgow, 1840–1860', in A. J. G. Cummings and T. M. Devine (eds), *Industry, Business and Society in Scotland since 1700* (Edinburgh, 1994), 199–202.
42. W. Gordon, *Mill Girls and Strangers: Single Women's Independent Migration in England, Scotland and the United States, 1850–1881* (New York, 2002), 106 and 122.
43. T. Dublin, *Women at Work: The Transformation of Work and Community in Lowell, Massachusetts, 1826–1860* (New York, 1979), 26–7.

44. Sloan, 'Employment'; and Withers, *Urban Highlanders*, 141–5.
45. M. Anderson, *Family Structure in Nineteenth Century Lancashire* (Cambridge, 1971), 25 and 34–9.
46. Gordon, *Mill Girls*, 11.
47. *Ibid.*
48. Dublin, *Women at Work*, 138–9.
49. A. Brown, *A History of Glasgow and of Paisley, Greenock and Port Glasgow* (Glasgow, 1795), Vol. III, 239–44. These figures are summarised in Table 4.
50. *OSA*, 1977, XII, 34.
51. See E. Gordon, *Women and the Labour Movement in Scotland, 1850–1914* (Oxford, 1991) and K. Honeyman, *Women, Gender and Industrialisation in England, 1700–1870* (London, 2000).
52. Report of Select Committee on State of Children Employed in Manufactures, *Parliamentary Papers* (*PP*), 1816, Vol. III, 236–7 and 240–1.
53. Select Committee on the Bill to Regulate the Labour of Children in Factories, *PP*, 1831–2, XV, 236.
54. *PP*, 1831–2, XV, 25–6.
55. D. Bremner, *The Industries of Scotland: Their Rise, Progress and Present Condition* (Edinburgh, 1869), 291.
56. Knox, *Hanging by a Thread*, 21–5.
57. National Archives of Scotland, Edinburgh (NAS), CS 96/1370, Kirkintilloch Wages Book.
58. J. Butt, 'Labour and Industrial Relations in the Scottish Cotton Industry during the Industrial Revolution', in J. Butt and K. Ponting (eds), *Scottish Textile History* (Aberdeen, 1987), 144.
59. Signet Library, Edinburgh (SL), CS 290/18, Robert Barr to John McIllwham, 22 December 1797.
60. Glasgow University Archives (GUA), Records of James Finlay and Co., UGD, 91/1/5/2/6/1/1, List of People Employed at Catrine Works, 1813–1833.
61. Dublin, *Women at Work*, 60, 70 and 184.
62. Whatley, 'Experience of Work', 240.
63. A. J. S. Gibson and T. C. Smout, *Prices, Food and Wages in Scotland, 1550–1780* (Cambridge, 1995), 349–56.
64. W. Taylor, *An Answer to Mr. Carlile's Sketches of Paisley* (Paisley, 1809).
65. Honeyman, *Women, Gender and Industrialisation*, 108–10.
66. *PP*, 1836, XXXIV, G, 133.
67. W. Cobbett, *A Tour in Scotland* (1833; Aberdeen, 1984), 21.
68. *OSA*, 1973, VII, 24.
69. Morgan, *Annals of Woodside*, 24.
70. A. Ure, *The Philosophy of Manufactures*, (1835; London, 1861), 393.
71. Brown, *History of Glasgow*, III, 233–8.
72. *OSA*, 1977, XX, 88–9.
73. *OSA*, 1973, VII, 850–1.
74. *OSA*, 1973, VII, 7.
75. *OSA*, 1973, VII, 852.

76. *OSA*, 1973, VII, 7.
77. See B. Collins, 'Sewing and Social Structure: The Flowerers of Scotland and Ireland', in R. Mitchison and P. Roebuck (eds), *Economy and Society in Scotland and Ireland, 1500–1939* (Edinburgh, 1988).
78. Brown, *History of Glasgow*, III, 239–44.
79. *OSA*, 1973, VII, 250.
80. J. Galt, *Annals of the Parish, 1821* (London, 1919), 179.
81. Taylor, *Answer to Mr Carlile*, 20–1.
82. Collins, 'Sewing and Social Structure'.
83. *OSA*, 1978, IX, 503, 536–7 and 619.
84. *OSA*, 1982, VI, 42 and 71; and 1973, VII, 526.
85. Bremner, *Industries of Scotland*.
86. S. Pollard, *The Genesis of Modern Management: A Study of the Industrial Revolution in Great Britain* (London, 1965), 165–6.
87. Factory Inquiry Commission Reports, Evidence taken by Mr. Stuart, *PP*, 1833, XX, A1, 77–9.
88. Factory Inquiry Commission Reports, *PP*, 1834, XX, 159.
89. J. Parkhill (ed.), *The Life and Opinions of Arthur Sneddon: An Autobiography* (Paisley, 1860), 27; and C. Campbell, *Memoirs of Charles Campbell at Present Prisoner in the Jail of Glasgow* (Glasgow, 1828), 1–4.
90. D. Livingstone, *Missionary Travels and Researches in South Africa* (London, 1857), 13; and D. Ross, *David Livingstone: Mission and Empire* (London, 2002).
91. R. Smillie, *My Life for Labour* (London, 1924), 13–24.
92. W. Thom, *Rhymes and Recollections of a Handloom Weaver* (Paisley, 1880), 1–37.
93. J. Hamilton, *Poems and Ballads* (Glasgow, 1868), xx–xxvii.
94. E. Johnston, *Autobiography: Poems and Songs of Ellen Johnston, the 'Factory Girl'* (Glasgow, 1867), 4–14.
95. *OSA*, 1973, VII, 296.
96. H. Hamilton, *The Industrial Revolution in Scotland* (1932, 2nd edition London, 1966) 139.
97. Taylor, *Answer to Mr. Carlile*, 24.
98. C. A. Whatley, *Scottish Society, 1707–1830: Beyond Jacobitism, Towards Industrialisation* (Manchester, 2000).
99. NAS, CS 96/1371, Account Book with Sir John Stirling of Glovat, 1792–3.
100. *Perthshire Courier*, 16 September 1819.
101. Atholl Mss 68, 9, 356, James Craig to Frederick Graham, 21 December 1819.
102. J. Sinclair, *Analysis of the Statistical Account of Scotland* (Edinburgh, 1825), 62.
103. Anon, *A Short Account of the Life and Hardships of a Glasgow Weaver* (Glasgow, 1834), 5–7.
104. N. Murray, *The Scottish Handloom Weavers, 1790–1850: A Social History* (Edinburgh, 1978), 14.
105. *Ibid.*, 28–9.
106. Taylor, *Answer to Mr. Carlile*, 60.
107. *Ibid.*, 16 and 29–30.

108. T. Leonard, *Radical Renfrew: Poetry from the French Revolution to the First World War* (Edinburgh, 1990), 38 and 63; Murray, *Handloom Weavers*, 168–72; and A. J Cooke, *From Popular Enlightenment to Lifelong Learning. A History of Adult Education in Scotland, 1707–2005* (Leicester, 2006), 65–6.
109. Evidence taken by Mr. Mackintosh, *PP*, 1833, XX, A2, 51.
110. Evidence taken by Mr. Stuart, *ibid.*, A1, 72–3.
111. *Ibid.*, 90.
112. Ure, *Philosophy of Manufactures*, 14.
113. M. B. Irwin, 'Women's Industries in Scotland', *Proceedings of the Philosophical Society of Glasgow*, 1895–6, XXVII, 72–3.
114. Gordon, *Women and the Labour Movement*, 39.
115. *OSA*, 1978, IX, 12.
116. *Ibid.*, 15.
117. A. Clow and N. Clow, *The Chemical Revolution: A Contribution to Social Technology* (London, 1952), 231.
118. *OSA*, 1978, IX, 27.
119. G. Turnbull, *A History of the Calico Printing Industry of Great Britain* (Altrincham, 1951), 193 and 93.
120. Bremner, *Industries of Scotland*, 304.
121. A. J. McIvor, 'Work, Wages and Industrial Relations in Cotton Finishing, 1880–1914', in J. A. Jowitt and A. J. McIvor (eds), *Employers and Labour in the English Textile Industries* (London, 1988), 128 and 144.
122. *Glasgow Journal*, 24 and 31 March 1768.
123. Thompson, *English Working Class*, 454.
124. Brown, *History of Glasgow*, II, 56–7; J. Cleland, *Annals of Glasgow* (Glasgow 1816), I, 37–8; Murray, *Handloom Weavers*, 185; and W. H. Fraser, *Conflict and Class: Scottish Workers, 1700–1838* (Edinburgh, 1988), 62.
125. A. Aspinall, *The Early English Trade Unions* (London, 1949), 143–56.
126. *OSA*, 1973, VII, 820–2.
127. *OSA*, 1977, XX, 88.
128. *PP*, 1833, XX, A1, 89.
129. Mitchell Library, Glasgow (ML), Minute Book of Glasgow Association of Master Cotton Spinners (GAMCS), AGN, 51/2, 1015.
130. *Ibid.*
131. *Glasgow Courier*, 29 December 1810.
132. See Fraser, *Conflict and Class*; and Whatley, *Scottish Society*.
133. J. Paterson, *Autobiographical Reminiscences: Including Recollections of the Radical Years in Kilmarnock* (Glasgow, 1871), 66.
134. Rev. Thomas Chalmers to William Wilberforce, 18 April 1820, in A. J. Cooke et al., *Modern Scottish History, 1707 to the Present. Volume V, Documents* (East Linton, 1998), 116.
135. Rev. H. Duncan, *The Young South Country Weaver; or A Journey to Glasgow: A Tale for the Radicals*, 2nd edition (Edinburgh 1821), iii–95.
136. Thompson, *English Working Class*, 769–80; and A. Briggs, *The Age of Improvement, 1783–1867*, 2nd edition (London, 2000), 187–8.

137. *Glasgow Courier*, 3 October 1824.
138. *Glasgow Courier*, 31 March 1825.
139. Whatley, *Scottish Society*, 274.
140. Duncan, *South Country Weaver*, 48.
141. *PP*, 1833, XX, A2, 49; and *New Statistical Account of Scotland* (*NSA*), VII, 338.
142. *PP*, 1834, XX, 130, 138, 142, 128, 195, 201, 212 and 216.
143. Sir A. Alison, *Some Account of my Life and Writings* (Edinburgh, 1883), 369–85; and W. H. Fraser, 'The Working Class', in W. H. Fraser and I. Maver (eds), *Glasgow. Volume II, 1830–1912* (Manchester, 1996).
144. Fraser, 'The Working Class'.
145. W. Freer, *My Life and Memories* (Glasgow, 1929), 12.
146. Fraser, 'The Working Class', 309.
147. Gordon, *Women and the Labour Movement*, 47.
148. Duncan, *South Country Weaver*, 64.
149. *NSA*, VI, 249.
150. Freer, *Life*; and Alison, *Account*, 384–5.
151. NAS, SC 9/28/1, fol. 1, Indenture between Andrew McPherson and the Balnoe Spinning Company, 9 November 1793.
152. *PP*, 1836, XXXIV, G, 133.
154. *NSA*, VII, 338.
155. Reports from the Assistant Handloom Weavers' Commissioners, South of Scotland and East of Scotland, *Parliamentary Papers*, 1838–9, reprinted 1970, IX, 51.
156. W. H. Fraser, 'Developments in Leisure', in W. H. Fraser and R. J. Morris (eds), *People and Society in Scotland, Volume II, 1830–1914* (Edinburgh, 1990), 241.
157. Fraser, 'The Working Class', 303.
158. See I. Donnachie, 'Drink and Society, 1750–1850: Some Aspects of the Scottish Experience', *Scottish Labour History Society Journal*, 1979, XIII; Knox, *Industrial Nation*; and Whatley, *Scottish Society*.
159. Thom, *Rhymes*, 3.
160. A. Thomson, *Random Notes and Rambling Recollections of Maryhill, 1750–1894* (Glasgow, 1895), 17.
161. A. J. McIvor, *A History of Work in Britain, 1880–1950* (London, 2001), 76.
162. C. A Whatley, 'Labour in the Industrialising City', in T. M. Devine and G. Jackson (eds), *Glasgow. Volume I, Beginnings to 1830* (Manchester, 1995), 367.
163. McIvor, *History of Work*, 76 and 68.
164. Irwin, 'Women's Industries'; and Knox, *Hanging by a Thread*, 89–91.
165. W. Dublin, *Women at Work*, 109–11. See also J. Greenlees, *Female Labour Power: Women Workers' Influences on Business Practices in the British and American Cotton Industries, 1780–1860* (Aldershot, 2007).
166. Knox, *Hanging by a Thread*, 89–91.
167. Quoted in *ibid.*, 69.

6

Employers

> The interest of the dealers, however, in any branch of trade or manufactures, is always in some respect different from, and even opposite to, that of the public. To widen the market and to narrow the competition, is always the interest of the dealers. (Adam Smith, *The Wealth of Nations*, 1776)

Introduction

In spite of their importance in the early industrialisation of the country, the men who established the Scottish cotton industry have been less well studied than the nation's cotton workers or many other entrepreneurial groups.[1] The Glasgow 'Tobacco Lords' were the subject of a classic study[2] but there has been no overall survey of their later successors, the cotton masters, despite the fact that the achievements of Glasgow and Paisley entrepreneurs attracted much attention in Scotland in the late nineteenth and early twentieth centuries.[3] The *Dictionary of Scottish Business Biography* only included 16 people connected with the cotton industry in its survey of 44 textile manufacturers, and because it confined itself to those who died after 1860, it excluded the founding generation of the cotton industry.[4]

The neglect of the Scottish cotton masters is also surprising when compared with the attention given to those in England, with studies of middle-class elites in both Scotland and England and with general studies of the origins of wealth in Britain.[5] This chapter draws on the wills and probate inventories of Scottish cotton merchants and manufacturers, together with business records and biographical studies. Its purpose is to examine the backgrounds and careers of a group who played a major role in the early industrialisation of Scotland; to see in what ways, if any, they differed from their counterparts in the North and Midlands of England; to explore how they fitted into the Scottish enterprise system in terms of how far they diversified into other areas such as coal mining, iron and steel manufacture, railways, shipping and landholding; and to link this with an explanation for the early decline of the cotton industry in Scotland.

Like their Lancashire counterparts, the Scottish cotton masters were a heterogeneous group socially, economically and culturally. They ranged from great magnates like the Dennistouns, Dunlops, Finlays and Buchanans, who dominated the trade and whose interests ranged from manufacturing to overseas trade with places like India and China, to much smaller operators struggling to make a living with a small spinning or weaving factory in Paisley or in the industrial suburbs of Glasgow such as Anderston or the Calton. A third and interlocking group consisted of cotton merchants and brokers.[6]

To analyse the Scottish cotton masters, I examined the wills and probate inventories of 52 men who died between 1787 and 1912 and were active in the Scottish cotton industry, including the finishing trades. Wills and probate inventories have to be used with caution but they do give some indication of the range of business interests of the group studied and of how wealth and shareholdings at death changed over time. There are obvious difficulties in deciding who should be included in such an analysis. I have used a modified version of R. H. Trainor's analysis of the Glasgow 'elite', defined either by position or by reputation. The 'positional' definition includes those who held key posts in public life, such as in the Glasgow Chamber of Commerce or the Glasgow Association of Master Cotton Spinners, employers who gave evidence to the Factory Commissioners in 1816 and 1833–1834, and those who held senior positions in large firms or who served as Lord Provosts, Provosts or Members of Parliament. The 'reputational' definition includes those who featured in key biographical directories in the nineteenth century, including *Memoirs and Portraits of 100 Glasgow Men* (1886) and the modern *Dictionary of Scottish Business Biography.*

By any definition, this is an unrepresentative group, consisting of the cotton 'elite', as only 12% of Scottish adults dying in 1881 left a will.[7] A major weakness of this type of study, as both Honeyman and Payne have pointed out, is that it is biased towards the successful entrepreneur, to the neglect of business failure.[8] Wills and probate inventories are also likely to underestimate wealth, and sometimes to leave out entirely the principal business that the deceased founded. This happened with Henry Houldsworth, whose 1853 probate inventory included agricultural rentals and arrears from his Coltness estate in Lanarkshire but not his interests in Coltness Ironworks or his cotton mills in Anderston, Glasgow.[9]

The Scottish cotton masters generally shared a similarly well-established merchant or manufacturing background with their English counterparts. Few of them conformed to the Smilesian myth of the self-made man. Many of the wealthier Scots had highly diversified interests and their wills and probate inventories describe them as merchants rather than as cotton spinners or manufacturers. Out of 52 Scottish wills and probate inventories of

Scottish cotton masters cited in the Appendix, 34 individuals are described by occupation. Of these, 20 (59%) are described as 'merchants', the dominant group being 'merchants in Glasgow' (16, or 47%), with Paisley and Perth contributing two each. In Glasgow, 'merchants and ship owners were commonly linked by family or economic interest with the industrialists' to form 'an exceedingly experienced and well connected elite'.[10]

Well-established mercantile backgrounds also characterised the cotton manufacturers of the English Midlands and the North of England. A survey by S. D. Chapman of the occupations of the principal partners in 43 leading cotton spinning firms in the North of England revealed that the trade was dominated by Manchester fustian merchants, who headed 12 firms with an insured capital of £255,960, some 33% of total capital, and calico printers and merchants, owners of only 4 cotton firms, but which accounted for an insured capital of £234,590, about 31% of the total. Another study by Chapman of the principals of cotton firms established in the Midlands from 1769 to 1800 showed that the dominant group here was merchant hosiers, accounting for 15 (36%) of the 42 firms surveyed.[11] Katrina Honeyman's study of the social origins of early cotton spinners, lead miners and lace manufacturers in England challenged the theory that 'entrepreneurs emerged from diverse social origins' and concluded that 'the evidence for this is sparse'.[12] Another analysis of social mobility in Britain in this period, by Crouzet, argued that 'most people who benefited from it rose from within the middle class, from its lower stratum (in some cases on the fringe of the working class) to a new stratum of wealthy, or at least well to do industrialists'.[13]. These arguments can equally be applied to this survey of the Scottish cotton masters.

Multiple partnerships

One significant difference between firms in Scotland and England was the prevalence of multiple partnerships in Scotland. This enabled Scottish entrepreneurs to spread risks and to recruit partners with different skills and assets, including commercial and technical skills, access to capital or to land and water rights. An example of a multiple partnership, dated 1788, was for two cotton mills at Johnstone and Lochwinnoch in Renfrewshire. The partners were William McDowall of Garthland, George Houston of Johnstone and Robert Burns, a cotton manufacturer at Johnstone. Houston and McDowall, who supplied the capital, both came from Glasgow merchant families who had made money in the Atlantic trade and invested some of it in country estates. Robert Burns provided the technical expertise and was given 'the whole trouble of overseeing and erecting the machinery and ordering the works'. The partners agreed to invest £6,000 in the mill at Lochwinnoch and £12,000 in the mill at Johnstone.[14]

At Stanley in Perthshire, a partnership contract was drawn up in January 1787. The company's capital was £7,000, with seven partners holding a £1,000 share each. They included Richard Arkwright, two local landowners, three Perth linen merchants and the Perthshire bleacher William Sandeman.[15] Further north, at Woodside on the River Don on the edge of Aberdeen, Gordon, Barron and Co. entered an agreement with Richard Arkwright in the early 1780s to build a cotton spinning mill and to train workers at Cromford. On 1 January 1784, the capital stock of the company was £18,333, held in 11 equal shares by eight Aberdeen merchants, including the Provost of Aberdeen, William Cruden.[16]

Multiple partnerships had their risks, in that it could be difficult to monitor and keep track of investments. This happened to David Dale, a multiple partner on a large scale. On his death in 1806 his will, which has not been previously published in detail, recorded a modest estate of £11,433, with his share of the capital stock of the Royal Bank of Scotland valued at £5,683. However, Dale's business affairs were so complicated that a further, more detailed inventory had to be drawn up on 9 January 1811. This showed an upwardly revised estate of £64,684, mainly due to his unresolved holdings in several Scottish cotton mills. The Dale/Alexander partnership at Ballochmyle (Catrine) was valued at £6,666, of which Dale's share was half, or £3,333. Unresolved debts owed to Dale included £6,378 from Sir William Douglas at Newton Stewart, Kirkcudbrightshire and £8,199 from Claude Alexander at Ballochmyle, Ayrshire. The largest debts involved Stanley Mills, Perthshire, where Dale's stock in the company with James Craig, 'Cotton Spinner at Stanley', was valued at £22,370, written down to £10,000. The dispute over the unresolved debts at Stanley rumbled on, ending in an acrimonious court case between the Royal Bank of Scotland and the Stanley company, which revealed debts of over £40,000 owing to the Royal Bank, due to Craig's mismanagement of Stanley.[17]

Sources of capital and the early entrepreneurs

The early cotton industry in Scotland developed on water-powered sites outside the major urban centres. The first water-powered spinning mills were at Penicuik in Midlothian and Rothesay on the Isle of Bute. Thereafter, Renfrewshire became a major centre of cotton manufacture, using water power from the Black and White Cart and the Levern.[18] In this context, the involvement of local landowners, who controlled access to water rights, was crucial. However, with the development of steam-powered mills in Glasgow and Paisley from 1800 onwards, the importance of Glasgow and Paisley capital, which had always controlled large numbers of outworkers in the surrounding counties, began to assert itself. By 1837, Factory Commissioner

Leonard Horner reported that there were 134 cotton mills in Scotland and that 'with the exception of some large establishments at Aberdeen and one at Stanley, near Perth, the cotton manufacture is almost confined to Glasgow and the country immediately adjoining, to a distance of about 15 miles radius; and all these cotton mills, even including the great house at Stanley, are connected with Glasgow houses, or in the Glasgow Trade'.[19]

Glasgow overseas merchants made an important contribution to the early cotton industry in Scotland. Tom Devine identified seven early cotton spinning firms in Scotland with a combined insurance valuation of £50,800, in which Glasgow colonial merchants held between 33% and 50% of the capital.[20] Many Scottish cotton merchants and manufacturers boasted impressive transatlantic networks, based on kinship and nationality. James Neilson, a Paisley cotton manufacturer, dealt in gauze, lappet, muslins, piquet and shawls. Between 1806 and 1811, during difficult wartime conditions, his customers included merchants in London, Manchester, Rio de Janeiro and St Kitts. One of his regular contacts was William Smith, a Scottish merchant based in Rio de Janeiro.[21] Another Scottish overseas merchant was George Yuille, partner in a Glasgow cotton manufacturing and merchant firm and in companies in London, Liverpool, Manchester, Virginia and New York. In April 1817, he wrote: 'This Market has been very lately sweeped of the Kind of Cotton Cloth which you wrote for to be shipped to the British Settlements in North America.'[22] William Kelly, manager of New Lanark in the 1790s, ran cotton mills in Busby, Renfrewshire and the Gorbals, Glasgow by 1831 and traded in cotton yarn to Cartagena (South America), New York and India. He had debtors in New York, Savannah (Georgia), Belfast, Dublin, Liverpool and London[23] Similarly, the estate of Henry Dunlop, who died in 1867 and owned cotton mills at Barrhead, Renfrewshire, recorded debts from foreign houses in Calcutta, Batavia, Singapore, Valparaiso, Rangoon, Rio de Janeiro, Buenos Aires and Colombo.[24]

The role of linen weavers and merchants and of landowners in the Scottish cotton industry has been discussed in Chapter 3. The agricultural sector provided further capital for the cotton industry through activities such as cattle dealing. The Birtwhistle family, who owned two cotton mills at Gatehouse of Fleet, were Yorkshire cattle dealers who had established economic links with the Galloway area by purchasing cattle there.[25] Another cotton spinner with roots in Borders cattle dealing was William Johnston of Glasgow, who in 1793 was owed debts by cattle dealers from Kirkby Lonsdale in Westmorland, and from Lockerbie and Ecclefechan in Dumfrieshire. Johnston's own debts included money owing to farmers from Langholm, Lockerbie, Ecclefechan, Dumfries and Galloway.[26] Similarly, Archibald Campbell of Jura, who was an unwitting investor in the Stanley company when his money on deposit with David Dale at the Royal Bank of Scotland got diverted into the deeply unprofitable Stanley cotton spinning operation, had made much of his fortune out of the sale of black cattle.[27]

Early managers, managing partners and their remuneration

Most of the wealthier cotton masters did not involve themselves in the day-to-day running of their factories, hiring managers or family members to do this for them. David Dale spent little time at New Lanark, delegating most of the day-to-day duties to managers such as William Kelly and his half-brother James Dale. Even Dale's son-in-law and successor, Robert Owen, who boasted of his 'hands on' approach to management, spent a good deal of time away from New Lanark, travelling frequently to Lancashire. The day-to-day running of New Lanark was carried on by Robert Humphreys, whom Owen had brought from Bank Top Mills, Manchester.[28] An exception was Archibald Buchanan, resident and managing partner at Catrine, Ayrshire, who in 1833 was described as 'a gentleman of the greatest respectability, the oldest cotton spinner in Scotland, originally educated in the cotton spinning business with Sir Richard Arkwright [at Cromford] and afterwards having successively led the management of the works at Ballindalloch, Deanston and Catrine'.[29] By this time Buchanan had spent nearly 50 years in the industry.

The remuneration of managers varied greatly according to the size and profitability of the mills they were managing and whether they were salaried managers or managing partners with a share in the business. In 1788, Robert Burns, 'a native of Paisley', was appointed as Managing Partner of cotton spinning mills at Johnstone and Lochwinnoch in Renfrewshire and was required to live at the works, where he would 'be accommodated with a house and garden at the expense of the Company' and be paid £150 a year for four years. In return for this he would have 'the whole trouble of overseeing and erecting the machinery and conducting the works'.[30]

Another Paisley-born manager was Robert Barr, a muslin manufacturer. In 1791, Barr was persuaded to give up his own business and become the managing partner of cotton spinning mills at Crosslee in Renfrewshire, contributing a third share of the capital stock of £5,000. His partners were the Glasgow merchants John and James M'Ilwham, who held a third share between them, and Alex Speirs, a merchant from Kilbarchan, Renfrewshire. Barr received £100 a year and a free house but in 1798 was forced out of the business by the other partners, who installed another manager in his place.[31] By December 1804, Barr had been recruited by Robert Owen as a manager for Stanley, Perthshire. Barr asked for a salary of £100 a year, a free house, coal and candle, or an interest in the firm adequate to it. However, by April 1805 he had fallen out with the Stanley workforce.[32] Those with experience in the Paisley cotton industry were much in demand. In 1809, it was reported that Glasgow cotton manufacturers 'get their foremen from Paisley. Likewise, they have upwards of twenty agents here.'[33]

Managers and partners varied greatly in their skills, temperaments and probity. William McAlpine and Co. was involved in manufacturing, bleaching and printing linen and cotton cloth, with bases in Glasgow and at Dalquharn printfield. In 1781 two of the partners, William McAlpine and William Fleming, entered into a partnership with James Kenyon, owner of the Rothesay Mills on Bute. However, McAlpine, 'whose speculative, enterprising and irregular genius is pretty widely known', was said to have nearly ruined the company by his 'wild schemes'. His successor as manager, William Fleming, was accused of 'incapacity and irregular habits', whilst a later manager, David Orr, 'would soon have ruined the business'. McAlpine later lost the enormous sum of £280,000 when he set up a printfield at Cromwellpark, near Perth.[34]

Historians such as Payne and Honeyman have argued that most surveys of firms and businessmen highlight the successful, long-lived and prudent firms and individuals at the expense of those, possibly more typical, who were none of these things. However, court records, such as the Session Papers of the Court of Session, give an insight into an alternative business world. This is a world of squabbling and litigious business partners, incompetent or feckless managers and questionable business practices and behaviour. They reveal that by no means all businesses were motivated by a tireless drive for efficiency, by probity or even by the immediate pursuit of profit. The Court of Session papers provide claims that partners were deliberately withholding raw cotton supplies from spinning mills to create losses, to drive down the valuation of the mills and the subsequent price at auction.[35] Other examples are claims of partners drawing heavily on a cotton spinning business for their personal use, without the knowledge or approval of the other partners.[36] This serves as a timely reminder that by no means all Scottish businessmen were the heroic figures of Smilesian mythology.

Andrew Keay, managing partner at Stanley, Perthshire in 1787, held one seventh of the total share capital of £7,000 and took a seventh share of the profits. His role included signing all bills, orders, letters etc.[37] At Woodside Mills, Aberdeen, James Young, 'sometimes of Glasgow, now of Aberdeen, merchant', who had managed the Woodside bleachfield and printworks since 1779, was admitted as a partner to the new cotton mills in 1785. He held 3 shares out of a total of 11 in a share capital of £18,333.[38] Sandeman, Ross, Turnbull and Co. was formed in 1812 at Luncarty bleachfield, Perthshire, after the credit crisis of 1810. The total share capital of this company was £30,000 and William Turnbull, who held a 10% stake, was appointed manager on a salary of £400 a year with a free house and a riding horse. His son William was made assistant to his father and clerk to the company at a salary of £100 a year and a riding horse. However, the firm went bankrupt shortly afterwards.[39]

These were modest rewards compared to the salaries paid to managers at New Lanark. Robert Humphreys was recruited as Under Manager at New Lanark by Robert Owen from Peter Drinkwater's mill in Manchester and offered a 20-year contract at a salary of £350 a year and 2.5% of the profits. By 1811, Humphreys had tired of this arrangement and wanted a salary of £700 a year in return for giving up his share of the profits. Even this was modest compared to Robert Owen's earnings from cotton spinning. As a callow youth of 19 he had had the self-confidence to demand and receive a salary of £300 a year for managing Drinkwater's mill in Manchester. Owen was so successful that Drinkwater offered him a four-year contract amounting to £400 for the second year, £500 for the third and a partnership in the fourth year. When Owen and his English partners took over New Lanark in 1801 he took one ninth of the share capital of £60,000 and was paid £1,000 a year for managing the mills.[40]

Another highly profitable cotton firm, the thread manufacturers J. and P. Coats, started in a modest way. In 1830, James and Peter Coats took over their father's thread mill in Paisley. They paid him £500 a year rent and themselves an annual salary of £70, rising to £100 in the second year, £120 in the third. Over the next 50 years, the profits of the firm averaged 20% per annum but were ploughed back into the business, which became the largest manufacturing concern in the UK. The rate of return on capital was a modest 7.5% in the 1830s, of which 75% was reinvested. The rate of return rose to 21% in the 1850s and 1870s, of which 43% was reinvested in the 1870s.[41]

Early management systems and methods

The management systems adopted in Scottish cotton mills were heavily influenced at first by Richard Arkwright, who had trained Archibald Buchanan, Andrew Keay from Stanley and the managers of the Woodside Mills, Aberdeen at his mills in Cromford, Derbyshire. At Deanston, Perthshire:

> The general order of management of the Deanston Works is very much on the principle of Arkwright – a proof of the talents of that eminent person. There is a head or superintendent to each department – everyone has his own allotted part – and in most cases they are paid by the piece – not in weekly wages . . . They have all the privilege of leaving any moment they choose, without previous warning; and we were informed that this is found to insure a more steady, agreeable, and lengthened service than could be obtained by the firmest indenture. There is no fine or punishment, excepting for damage to the works through evident carelessness. The order of the establishment is preserved by the dismissal of offending individuals or their banishment for a limited period.

> By 'stopping the supplies' every member of the family is interested in the good conduct of the whole, and a banished child, man or friend, finds no rest at home.[42]

James Smith, Managing Partner at Deanston in 1833, confirmed this: 'Every overlooker is allowed to select his own workers, and on the other hand, every worker is allowed to engage with the overlooker he may like best.'[43]

Similar principles operated at the Catrine cotton mills, Ayrshire, which Kirkman Finlay bought in 1801. He installed Archibald Buchanan as manager, who recounted in 1839 how he had reorganised the mills along Arkwright lines:

> In the works there are 21 different rooms or departments; in each of these the master or overlooker is at liberty to choose his own hands; and in like manner, the workers have it in their power to change at the end of every week, and to go to any room within the establishment, where the master of that room can employ them, upon giving six days' previous notice to the master they leave . . . The master, as well as all the workers, with the exception of learners and extra hands, are paid by piece work; of course it is in his interest to have the best workers he can get, and, should a worker not be able to obtain employment from any master, it is pretty evident that the fault lies with the individual, who must choose some other employment.[44]

David Dale adopted similar methods at New Lanark, although his son-in-law, Robert Owen, not always the most reliable witness, claimed that Dale 'knew little about cotton spinning, having always left the management of his various mills (for he had other cotton mills besides New Lanark) to such managers as he could procure'.[45] Owen was able to build on these methods when he took over New Lanark. He developed a thoroughgoing system of checks on the quality of the product and the productivity of the workforce: 'my previous habits had prepared me for great nicety and exactness of action, and for a degree of perfection in operations to which parties then employed in cotton spinning were little accustomed'. He introduced checks to stop theft at New Lanark and 'had also a daily return presented to me each morning of the preceding day's operations, and frequent balances in every department'.[46]

Owen used similar methods in his unsuccessful attempts to turn the cotton mills at Stanley, Perthshire into profitability. In February 1804, Owen wrote to James Craig that he had not had time to investigate the Stanley account for the last month but would do so in a few days. In May of the same year, Owen commented that weekly returns would be useful and that Craig would then be able to see which parts of the works required most attention.[47]

Owen found 'the most efficient check upon inferior conduct' at New Lanark to be the 'silent monitor':

> This consisted of a four sided piece of wood, about two inches long and one broad, each side coloured, – one side black, another blue, the third yellow, and the fourth white, tapered at the top and finished with wire eyes, to hang upon a hook with either side to the front. One of these was suspended in a conspicuous place near to each of the persons employed and the colour at the front told the conduct of the individual during the preceding day, to four degrees of comparison. Bad, denoted by black and No. 4 – indifferent by blue, and No. 3 – good by yellow and No. 2 – and excellent by white and No. 1.[48]

The silent monitor was reinforced by 'books of character' for each department into which the daily conduct of each worker was entered. Owen claimed that this Orwellian style of management was highly effective. 'At the commencement of this new method of recording character, the great majority were black, many blue and a few yellow; gradually the black diminished and were succeeded by the blue and the blue was gradually succeeded by the yellow, and some, but at first very few, were white.'[49] However, Owen's encouragement of education and discouragement of drunkenness amongst the workforce was nothing new in Scottish cotton mills.

The Scottish cotton masters – origins and education

Of 52 Scottish cotton masters, the 13 who died before 1840, with one or two exceptions, have left fairly scant evidence behind them, other than the details of their estate at death. More detailed evidence is available for the 39 who died between 1840 and 1912, including in many cases year of birth, place of birth, father's occupation, education, religious and political affiliation, and public offices held. From this it is possible to trace a picture of the origins, social formation and social and political influence of a group who played a key role in Scottish business and public life. Their origins and education are summarised in Table 22.

An analysis by A. Slaven of 381 entrepreneurs from all sectors in the *Dictionary of Scottish Business Biography* (1986) revealed that they shared a number of common characteristics. The dominant form of business was the family firm. Over the period from 1860 to 1960, 42% founded their own firm and 80% either founded or inherited the firms they controlled. One in three had no education beyond elementary level, although some 40% had received some form of higher education in universities or technical colleges. More important than school or university education, however, was practical or apprenticeship training in the industry itself, where 56% had received apprenticeship training and 36% training on the job. The group shared a well-defined religious background, with just over a third belonging to the Church of Scotland, and another third to various dissenting Presbyterian churches.[50]

Table 22 Scottish cotton masters, 1840–1912: origins and education of 39 leading manufacturers/merchants

Year of birth	Place of birth	Father's occupation	Education
Pre-1780: 8	Glasgow: 12	Manufacturer: 7	Parish school: 2
1780–1799: 5	Paisley: 6	Merchant/ manufacturer: 4	Glasgow High: 5
1800–1819: 6	Renfrewshire: 3	Merchant: 3	Paisley Grammar: 1
1820–1840: 9	Govan: 1	Merchant/ landowner: 1	Ayr Academy: 1
Unknown: 11	Ayrshire: 2	Farmer: 5	Glasgow University: 10
	Argyll: 1	Weaver: 1	Edinburgh University: 3
	Stirlingshire: 2	Dyer: 3	Andersonian Institution: 2
	Perth: 1	Cotton spinner: 1	Unknown: 22
	England: 1	Chemical manufacturer: 2	
	Unknown: 10	Cotton trader: 1	
		Unknown: 11	
Total: 39	Total: 39	Total: 39	Total: 39

Sources: National Archives of Scotland, Edinburgh, Wills and Probate Inventories; J. Maclehose, *Memoirs and Portraits of 100 Glasgow Men* (Glasgow, 1886); A. Slaven and S. G. Checkland (eds), *Dictionary of Scottish Business Biography* (Aberdeen, 1986).

These characteristics are mirrored by my own group of 52 Scottish cotton entrepreneurs, covering men born in the 1760s, who were in their 20s at the outbreak of the French Revolution, to those born after the 1832 Reform Act. This was a highly localised elite, and the geographical origins of the group were restricted. Out of 29 whose place of birth is known, 13 (45%) were born in Glasgow or the adjoining burgh of Govan. A further nine (31%) were born in Renfrewshire, including Paisley. Only one, the Nottinghamshire-born Henry Houldsworth, was born outside Scotland. This echoes other surveys such as Miskell's analysis of 30 Dundee textile manufacturers active between 1820 and 1870, which revealed that of the 26 whose birthplace was known, 13 (50%) were born in Dundee. Similarly, Howe found that out of 330 Lancashire cotton masters active between 1830 and 1860, 265 (80%) were born in Lancashire.[51]

The Scottish cotton masters were born into a relatively privileged background – the fathers of most of them were employers, as merchants, manufacturers and farmers. Of the 28 whose paternal background is known, eight (28%) had fathers described as 'merchants' or variations on this, seven (25%) as 'manufacturers', and five (18%) as 'farmers'. The rarity of self-made men amongst this group is confirmed by the fact that only one father was described as a weaver. Howe discovered that out of 230 Lancashire cotton masters active between 1830 and 1860 whose parental background is known, 193 (84%) had fathers who were textile employers.[52] Of 52 Scottish cotton masters, 46% founded their own firm and 42% inherited it, reflecting the dominance of the family firm in Scotland.

Only 2 of the 39 men in Table 22 are known to have attended a parish school, although most would have attended a local school before practical training in industry. The Glasgow mercantile elite generally sent their children to prestigious local day-schools, such as Glasgow High School, and then on to Glasgow University. Of the 17 whose educational background is known, 10 (58%) had attended Glasgow University and a further 3 had studied at Edinburgh University. Glasgow University, founded in 1451, was situated in the heart of the industrial city until its move to Gilmorehill in the western suburbs in 1870. Furthermore, unlike its English equivalents, its curriculum, available relatively cheaply on a part-time basis, was seen as 'useful' by the local middle classes.[53] By contrast, university education amongst Lancashire cotton masters was a rarity. Out of 105 cotton masters in Howe's study active between 1830 and 1860, and whose educational background is known, only 16 (15%) had attended university.[54]

Formal education was generally supplemented by practical training in industry, sometimes outside Scotland. Walter Crum of Thornliebank, Renfrewshire (1796–1867), dyer and calico printer, attended Glasgow University, followed by an industrial placement in Clitheroe, Lancashire. His eldest son, Alexander (1828–1893), was also educated at Glasgow University and received an industrial training in Germany.[55] Frank Stewart Sandeman (1838–1898), who owned the cotton mills at Stanley, Perthshire, had a scientific education at Edinburgh University followed by practical training in the Lancashire bleaching industry.[56] This was in line with experience elsewhere in Scotland, where Slaven and Kim showed that most early industrialists received practical training in their industry, whilst later in the nineteenth century formal apprenticeships became the norm.[57]

Religion and politics

The Scottish cotton masters shared an overwhelmgly Presbyterian background, in line with their counterparts in the rest of Scottish industry. However, of the 16 individuals in Table 23 whose religious affiliation is known, only 4 (25%) were members of the established (Presbyterian) Church of Scotland, the rest (11, or 69%) were members of dissenting Presbyterian

10 The mill owner as country gentleman: Frank Stewart Sandeman, Stanley Mills, Perthshire, c. 1890

Table 23 Scottish cotton masters, 1840–1912: religious, political and community affiliations of 39 leading manufacturers/merchants

Religion	**Politics**	**Offices held**
Church of Scotland 4	Whig 3	Lord Provost, Glasgow 5
Free Church 5	Tory 1	Provost, other burghs 3
UP Church 4	Liberal 8	Member of Parliament 9
UF Church 2	Lib/Unionist 2	Office holder GCC 6
Baptist 1	Conservative 4	Member GAMCS 6
Unknown 23	Unknown 21	Witness to Parliamentary Commisson 5
Total 39	Total 39	Total 39

Source: As for Table 22, plus Records of Glasgow Association of Master Cotton Spinners (Mitchell Library, Glasgow); and *Parliamentary Papers*, 1816, Vol. III and 1834, Vol. XX, Part II.

churches, and one was Baptist. In many ways, this simply reflected the contemporary religious context in Glasgow and Paisley. In Glasgow, for example, Presbyterian dissent accounted for 57% of church attendances in 1851, compared with the Church of Scotland's 20% of attendances.[58]

In Paisley, the dissenting Presbyterian churches – the Free Church formed after the Disruption in 1843 and the United Presbyterian Church formed in 1847 by an amalgamation of most of the old secession churches – were equally strong. In March 1844, just after the Disruption, the Paisley thread manufacturer James Clark (1782–1865) wrote that 'as for myself, I have long belonged to the Relief Church and see no cause to change. I am voluntary through and through and my creed is let every man support his own religion.'[59] In Dundee, out of 22 textile manufacturers active between 1820 and 1870, the proportion of those belonging to the Church of Scotland was higher – 7, or 32%, with 6 (27%) affiliated to the Congregational Church.[60] The Scottish figures contrast with Lancashire, where Howe showed that out of 292 cotton masters active between 1830 and 1860 whose religious background is known, half (145 or 49.7%) were members of the Church of England, the next largest group being 55 Unitarians (18%), followed by 27 Wesleyan Methodists (9%) and 27 Independents/Congregationalists (9%).[61]

Unlike Manchester, late eighteenth-century Glasgow was a long-established burgh with its own civic life, its own Lord Provost and a share of parliamentary representation in the unreformed parliament. Again unlike Manchester, Glasgow had a number of institutions founded before 1700 such as the University, the Faculty of Procurators, the Trades House and the Merchants' House. Between 1780 and 1830, the city also established or transformed a number of key institutions, such as the Glasgow Chamber of Commerce (1783), the first of its kind in the world, the Royal Infirmary, and its own specialised trade and employers' associations, including the Glasgow Association of Master Cotton Spinners. After the 1832 Reform Act, Glasgow acquired its own two MPs.[62]

The politics of the Scottish cotton masters reflect the strength of the Liberal Party in Scotland after 1832. Of the 18 whose political affiliation is known, the largest group – eight, or 44% were Liberals. This reflects the political position from 1832 until the late 1880s, when Liberal Unionism and Conservatism began to provide more of a challenge and 'Scotland was no longer a one party State'.[63] After the 1832 Reform Act, the Liberal hegemony in Glasgow was such that, apart from the Conservative dyer James Ewing, elected MP in 1832 with the Liberal James Oswald, all 21 Glasgow MPs elected between 1832 and 1859 were Liberals.[64] These figures are similar to the political allegiances of Dundee manufacturers between 1820 and 1870, surveyed by Miskell, where, of the 18 whose politics were known, no fewer than 16 (89%) were Liberals.[65] They are also similar to Lancashire, where, in spite of the strength of Toryism in boroughs such as Blackburn, Howe's survey of Lancashire MPs between 1832 and 1860 revealed that of the 31 described as 'textile masters', 25 (80%) were Liberals.[66]

The 39 Scottish cotton masters who died between 1840 and 1912 provided five Lord Provosts of Glasgow (Kirkman Finlay, Henry Monteith, James Ewing, Henry Dunlop and Sir John Muir), together with three Provosts of smaller burghs (Henry Houldsworth at Anderston, Henry Birkmyre at Greenock and Thomas Reid in Govan). There were nine Members of

Parliament (23% of the total), including four Glasgow MPs (Kirkman Finlay, James Ewing, John Dennistoun and Sir Charles Tennant, who was MP for Glasgow 1877–1880 and for Peebleshire 1880–1886), two for Dunbartonshire (Alexander Dennistoun and John Orr Ewing), and one each for Linlithgow (Henry Monteith, who was later MP for Saltash), Renfrewshire (Alexander Crum) and Stirlingshire (Sir Archibald Orr Ewing). Kirkman Finlay made the political breakthrough for the business community in 1812, when he was elected MP for the Clyde burghs, the first Lord Provost of Glasgow to be elected MP in over a hundred years.[67] This was a highly influential group, often linked through family, business ties and religious affiliations, which was experienced and successful in lobbying on behalf of business interests.

Business networks – Glasgow Chamber of Commerce

Whilst the Scottish business community in the late eighteenth and early nineteenth centuries was highly competitive and individualistic, it was also mutually supportive through a network of clubs, societies, churches, professional institutions, employers' organisations and business networks. An example of the latter is Glasgow Chamber of Commerce, which included cotton merchants and manufacturers such as Henry Houldsworth, David Dale and Kirkman Finlay amongst its early membership. However, its membership was dominated by Glasgow merchants rather than manufacturers. On its foundation, the Chamber had 216 individual members. Of these, 130 were Glasgow merchants, 38 Glasgow manufacturers, 23 Paisley merchants and manufacturers, 16 Greenock merchants and manufacturers, 7 Port Glasgow merchants and manufacturers and 2 Kilbarchan manufacturers.[68] The membership figures reveal that the Chamber represented not only the city of Glasgow but its surrounding region, with Renfrewshire supplying 22% of individual members. Kirkman Finlay played a fleeting role on the national political stage when he headed the campaign by Glasgow Chamber of Commerce to challenge the monopoly of the East India Company in 1813, which was partly successful. After a second challenge in 1830, the Chinese monopoly was seceded in 1834. However, Finlay's support for laissez-faire and unrestricted competition was not unwavering. As President of Glasgow Chamber of Commerce, he supported the Corn Laws and was defeated when he stood again for Parliament in 1831.[69]

Employers' organisations – the Glasgow Association of Master Cotton Spinners

This successful experience of political lobbying and mutual business support was utilised by the Glasgow cotton masters, who by 1810 had formed a specialised trade organisation to protect and advance their interests. In Lancashire, formalised employers' associations began slightly later – the Preston Masters' Association seems to date from the industrial conflict of 1836.[70] The Glasgow Association of Master Cotton Spinners was founded in 1810 to combat the activities of combinations of cotton workers. It reflected a commonality of interests amongst cotton employers in the west of Scotland faced by labour disputes, as Paisley employers were also involved. The events of 1810 have been described in Chapter 5. Here, it is enough to note that certain employers were much more active in the Association than others, and they were the ones whose mills were targeted by workers. The committee consisted of employers such as Henry Houldsworth, Adam Bogle of Henry Monteith, Bogle and Co., William Dunn of Duntocher, William Stevenson of Todd and Stevenson and James Dunlop of James Dunlop and Co.[71]

The Glasgow Association of Master Cotton Spinners resurfaced in 1816, when Parliament set up a Select Committee on the State of Children Employed in Manufactures. Robert Owen had instigated a motion to Parliament to restrict working hours for children and introduce schools paid for by mill owners. He gave evidence to the Committee that his profits and productivity at New Lanark had not been affected by his humane treatment of the workforce; in fact, as a result of the schooling provided at New Lanark, parents were willing 'to work at much lower wages'. Owen criticised the regime of his predecessor and father-in-law, David Dale, for producing children who appeared 'to a superficial observer, healthy in their countenances; yet their limbs were very generally deformed, their growth was stunted and . . . in general they made a very slow progress even in learning the common alphabet'.[72]

Henry Houldsworth, of the Glasgow Association of Master Cotton Spinners, appeared in person before the Select Committee and testified that he and two Scottish colleagues had sat in on its deliberations for six weeks before being called to give evidence. Houldsworth took a determinedly laissez-faire attitude towards factory regulation, believing that 'any interference in the regulation of free labour never fails to excite a spirit of restlessness and insubordination, inimical to the habits of sobriety and industry amongst the operatives, by raising expectations which cannot be fulfilled'.[73]

Another member of the Glasgow Association who gave evidence to the Select Committee was Adam Bogle, a partner in Henry Monteith, Bogle and Company, who owned cotton spinning mills and dyeworks at Blantyre and weaving factories in Lanarkshire. Bogle, who incidentally also employed parish apprentices, including some from London, criticised Robert Owen by contrasting Blantyre, where the company had controlled the sale of liquor by closing down taverns and strictly regulating the one surviving public house, with New Lanark, where, he claimed, it was easy to get liquor. Bogle's travel expenses to London were paid by the Association. He died in 1817, and his will recorded a substantial payment of £120 owing to him by the cotton spinners in Glasgow and neighbourhood 'for going to London to promote the bill for regulating hours of work in cotton mills in 1816'.[74]

Similar lobbying techniques were used by Scottish cotton employers in their evidence before the Parliamentary Commissioners in the 1830s. George Macleroy, of the Barrowfield Cotton Works, Glasgow testified in 1834 that 'the interference of the legislature in restricting or limiting the power of production in a manufacturing community must be looked upon as a serious evil, except such interference is rendered necessary by the existence of abuses which the partners themselves are unable or unwilling to rectify'.[75] However, Henry Dunlop, who owned spinning mills in Calton, Glasgow, conceded that 'the law should be rendered as simple as possible, that it should merely regulate the hours of work for children, and the earliest age at which they should be employed; and that agents should be employed by government in various districts to see that the law was carried into effect'.[76] Similarly James Coats Junior, giving evidence on behalf of J. and P. Coats, Paisley, claimed: 'while we contemn the disgusting cant about the miseries of factory children, the evidence elicited regarding their treatment in the north of Scotland imperiously demands the interference of the legislature for the protection of this interesting class from the possibility of such inhuman treatment as they there were subjected to'.[77] Eventually, it was Dunlop's formula of 'light touch' legislation, aimed at regulating child labour and enforced by government inspection, that was adopted by Parliament.

The continuation of some form of employers' association was demonstrated by their effective opposition to the Glasgow Cotton Spinners' Strike of 1837. The strike began in October 1836 at William Dunn's Duntocher Mills in Dunbartonshire but was broken in February 1837. Six weeks after this, a meeting of Glasgow employers chaired by Henry Dunlop and including William Hussey, Peter Bogle, Daniel McPhail, William Houldsworth, Patrick McNaught and William Kelly agreed to a cut in wages. Dunlop and Houldsworth were singled out by the Cotton Spinners' Union for confrontational attitudes and actions towards trades unions. The strike had been precipitated by a commercial crisis in the USA, leading to employer attempts to cut wages, but eventually revolved as much around issues of workplace control, where highly paid mule spinners hired and paid their own support workers and controlled entry to the trade through kinship ties and high entry fees.[78]

Diversification and the changing economy of the west of Scotland

From 1840 onwards, an increasing amount of the wealth of Glasgow and Paisley cotton manufacturers and merchants, as revealed in their wills and probate inventories, was invested in areas other than cotton manufacturing, such as railways, roads, canals, docks, coal mines, iron works, shipping companies and overseas interests.

The growth in wealth can be seen by contrasting the first generation of cotton merchants and manufacturers (1787–1839), whose 13 estates averaged a modest £11,809 a head, with the third generation (1880–1912), whose 12 estates averaged a staggering £797,159, a 70-fold increase. Among the owners of the latter estates were two Paisley thread millionaires, Thomas and Archibald Coats, the millionaire dyer Sir Archibald Orr Ewing and the third-generation chemical manufacturer Sir Charles Tennant, MP (1823–1906), who left an estate of over £3 million. The largest fortunes were made not in the spinning and weaving industries but in 'fringe' industries like the cotton thread trade, Turkey red dyeing and chemical manufacture. They were associated with the formation of limited liability companies from the 1880s onwards and with the growth of cartels in the 1890s to fix prices and corner a larger share of national or international markets. Examples are provided by the combination of dyeing firms in the Vale of Leven, Dunbartonshire in 1898 into the United Turkey Red Company, of calico printing firms such as Crums of Thornliebank, Renfrewshire in 1899 into the (Manchester-based) Calico Printers' Association and of cotton thread firms in 1896 into J. and P. Coats.

The informal ties between Scottish cotton masters created by family, business links, religion and civic associations, mentioned earlier in this chapter, were strengthened by multiple and interlocking directorships on the boards of banks, railways, shipping companies and public utilities. By 1905, 85% of the 108 top Scottish companies across all sectors were linked through interlocking directorships.[79] Of the 39 men identified in Table 24 who died after 1840, 8 left estates containing banking shares worth on average £51,004. Cotton masters played an active role in Scottish banks. Henry Dunlop (1799–1867) served as a director of the City of Glasgow Bank, Alexander Dennistoun (1790–1874) and Alexander Crum of Thornliebank (1823–1893) as directors of the Union Bank of Scotland.[80] In the same group of 39, 12 estates contained railway shares worth on average £27,647. Railways were a key to the success or survival of many cotton enterprises and a number of cotton masters took an active role in their management. Henry Dunlop served as Deputy Chairman of the Edinburgh and Glasgow Railway Company and John Orr Ewing (1809–1878) as a director. Orr Ewing was also a director of the Caledonian and Dumbartonshire Railway, 'the existence of which was of great value to the Vale of Leven dyeing industry'. Alexander Crum, of Thornliebank calico printers, was Chairman of the Caledonian Railway Company.[81] At Stanley, Perthshire, the owner, George Buchanan, held £4,000 in shares in the Scottish Midland Junction Railway Company, which brought raw cotton from Glasgow to Stanley, and served as its Deputy Chairman.[82]

Table 24 Wealth at death of 52 Scottish cotton manufacturers, merchants and partners in printfields, dyeworks and chemical works, 1787–1912

Years	**Number**	**Average probate value**	**Number of estates over £0.5m**	**Average probate value omitting estates over £0.5m**
1787–1819	5	£20,247	–	£20,247
1820–1839	8	£5,285	–	£5,285
1840–1859	17	£60,423	–	£60,423
1860–1879	10	£118,712	–	£118,712
1880–1899	6	£447,844	3	£83,854
1900–1912	6	£1,026,439	3	£259,519
Total	52	£229,495	6	£73,868

Sources: National Archives of Scotland, Wills and Probate Inventories, 1787–1912; J. Maclehose, *Memoirs and Portraits of 100 Glasgow Men*, Glasgow, 1886; and A. Slaven and S. G. Checkland (eds), *Dictionary of Scottish Business Biography. Vol. 1. The Staple Industries*, Aberdeen University Press, 1986. For full details see Appendix.

11 The mill owner as patriarch: Thomas Coats of Ferguslie, Paisley and family, early 1880s

As the century progressed, the investments of the cotton masters diversified into shipping, shipbuilding and heavy engineering, reflecting the changing economy of the west of Scotland. Four Scottish estates between 1883 and 1900 had shares in ships, shipping lines and shipbuilding companies at an average value of £64,166. The dyer Thomas Reid (1831–1900) left an estate of £186,180, including a share of 17 ships at £23,820 and shares worth £15,437 in the London and Glasgow Engineering and Iron Shipbuilding Co. Ltd. Reid was Chairman of the company in the 1880s and of Nobel Explosives Ltd from 1884. Similarly, Henry Birkmyre (1832–1900), of the Gourock Ropework Co. and the Lanark Spinning Co., left an estate of £435,883, with shares in shipping worth £51,876. Birkmyre's daughter married William Todd Lithgow of the Port Glasgow shipbuilding firm, Russell and Co.[83] These changing investments reflected how the rapid growth of heavy industries in the west of Scotland coincided with the decline of the cotton industry in the same period.

Landownership, conspicuous consumption and cultural activities

The growing wealth and self-confidence of the Scottish cotton masters was reflected in their private and cultural life, particularly in their houses, house contents and estates. The Dickensian caricature of Lancashire cotton manufacturers as uncultured self-made men on the Josiah Bounderby model is belied by modern research, such as Howe's study of the English cotton masters, which concluded that, as a group, they possessed 'literacy, a combination of classical and "useful" knowledge, some science, much religion and not a little gentility'.[84] In Scotland, wills and probate inventories list the libraries and art collections of men such as Kirkman Finlay, who died at Castle Toward, Bute in March 1842, leaving his wife a life rent of 'three hundred of such of my Books as she may select'.[85] Sir Peter Coats, of the Paisley cotton thread dynasty, left an estate of £127,957 at his death in 1890, including his pictures in Paisley Free Library and Museum valued at £797. Two paintings – *The Crucifixion* and *Moses on Mount Hebron* – were left to Paisley Museum. Another art collector was the millionaire Sir Charles Tennant, owner of the St Rollox chemical works, Glasgow. His paintings 'included works by Reynolds, Gainsborough, Constable, Turner, Cotman and others' and he served as a trustee of the National Galleries in London.[86] These libraries and art collections were displayed in the increasingly imposing country houses that the cotton masters began to acquire.

There was a well-marked social hierarchy amongst the Glasgow merchant and manufacturing classes. When Archibald Alison moved from Edinburgh to become Sheriff of Lanarkshire in 1835, he found that middle-class society in the west of Scotland was made up of distinct 'coteries'. Top of the hierarchy was the 'Sugar Aristocracy' of West India merchants, consisting of five or six families, who kept to themselves socially. Next came the cotton magnates, of whom Kirkman Finlay was the undisputed leader, and after them a small group of calico printers. Last of all came the iron and coal masters, often wealthier than the others but regarded as socially inferior. In this context, social status was determined by the length of time that wealth had been created. Like antique furniture, wealth acquired a desirable patina with age. Alison believed that 'it takes three generations to make a gentleman' and that 'it is because so few of them remain in trade to the third generation that good society is so limited and access is guarded with so much jealousy'.[87] Landownership was one way of addressing these status concerns.

Property in the form of buildings and land was an important indicator of the growing wealth, confidence and changing aspirations of the Scottish cotton magnates. Land ownership was inextricably linked to social status and often provided the entry ticket to political office. The move to country houses and estates outside Glasgow and Paisley, which had begun as early as 1800, accelerated after 1840, reflecting greater wealth and the development of faster and more reliable transport links by rail and steamships. Table 25 reveals a widely dispersed geographical pattern of landownership amongst Scottish cotton masters in 1872, with 21 estates ranging from Stirlingshire to Argyll and the Isle of Bute, and from Peebleshire to Perthshire. Of these 21 estates, the average size of holding was a substantial 2,594 acres, with an average annual rental of £3,835.

However, the business elite generally retained a residence in Glasgow or Paisley, where the family lived during the winter and the paterfamilias stayed during the week in the summer, returning to the country retreat at the weekend.[88] The Paisley thread manufacturer James Clark boasted in 1844 that he could reach his country house in Dunoon from Paisley by rail and ferry in 1 hour and 35 minutes for the modest sum of 6d.[89] In 1884, the prolific Glasgow novelist Sarah Tytler (Henrietta Keddie) published her novel *St. Mungo's City*, whose central character was Tam Drysdale, a calico printer and dyer. She wrote of the Glasgow business elite: 'these thrice fortunate individuals bought more of the estates which the old country gentry saw themselves compelled to bring under the hammer; rented the best deer forests, extended and enlarged ranges of conservatories and picture galleries; had visions of entering Parliament or going on the turf – if only the men had leisure'.[90]

Wiener and other historians have seen this retreat by second- and third-generation industrialists to country estates as evidence of an anti-industrial bias in British culture and linked it to long-term economic decline.[91] However, in Scotland 'gentlemanly capitalism' had its limits. Not only did many Scottish cotton masters combine country living with a town house in Glasgow or Paisley for business activities during the week, but some carried

Table 25 Landownership by Scottish cotton masters, calico printers, bleachers, dyers and chemical manufacturers, 1872 (includes 24 companies)

County	No. of land-owners	Size of holding (acres)	Average size (acres)	Annual rental	Average rental
Argyllshire	2	24,434	12,217	£5,749	£2,874
Ayrshire[a]	2	170	85	£2,633	£1,316
Bute	1	300	300	£672	£672
Dunbartonshire[b]	6	9,713	1,618	£12,583	£2,097
Glasgow[c]	11	302	27	£29,550	£2,686
Lanarkshire[d]	3	9,572	3,190	£44,068	£14,689
Paisley[e]	3	334	111	£3,087	£1,029
Peebleshire	1	3,500	3,500	£897	£897
Perthshire[f]	2	219	109	£3,460	£1,730
Renfrewshire[g]	11	2,194	199	£12,207	£1,109
Stirlingshire[h]	3	4,576	1,525	£4,558	£1,519
Total	45	55,314	1,229	£119,464	£2,654
Total (excluding 24 companies)	21	54,480	2,594	£80,550	£3,835

Notes:

[a] Includes James Finlay and Co., Catrine Works.

[b] Includes John Orr Ewing and Co., Alexandria.

[c] Includes 9 Glasgow cotton companies.

[d] Includes Walker and Co., New Lanark.

[e] Includes Carlile and Co., Kerr and Co.

[f] Includes Trustees of Samuel Howard, Stanley and James Finlay and Co., Deanston.

[g] Includes 6 Renfrewshire cotton companies.

[h] Includes Hurlet and Campsie Alum Co. and Culcreuch Spinning Co.)

Source: Parliamentary Papers, 1874, LXXII, Part III, Returns of Owners of Land: Scotland, 1872–3.

out manufacturing activities on their estates. Henry Houldsworth established the Coltness Ironworks on his Lanarkshire estate and by 1872 the gross annual value of the minerals on the estate was £21,239, almost double the £11,498 for agricultural activities.[92] William Dunn, who by the time of his death in 1849 had amassed a landed estate of over 2,000 acres in Dumbartonshire, founded the Duntocher Cotton Mills on his estate.[93] Charles Macintosh (1766–1843) had estates at Dunchattan on the edge of Glasgow and at Campsie in Stirlingshire, bringing in a rental income of £1,049 a year. However, the Campsie estate contained valuable deposits of alum, the basis of a profitable business, the Hurlet and Campsie Alum Company, valued at £8,868 (11% of his estate). The largest portion of Macintosh's estate of £77,186 was his 'share and interest in the hot blast patent', valued at no less than £45,000 (58% of the estate).[94]

The decline of the family firm and the growth of limited liability companies and cartels

The American Civil War and the Cotton Famine of the early 1860s brought hardship to the British cotton industry north and south of the border. Both industries subsequently recovered, but the Scottish industry, despite the success of the Paisley cotton thread industry, went into long-term decline from 1890. From the 1880s onwards, as Payne has shown, cotton businesses and other Scottish manufacturing firms began to move away from family partnerships and towards limited liability companies, as discussed in Chapter 3.[95] This resulted in a gradual loss of family control and the slow emergence of the professional manager.

This was accompanied by another trend, whereby a small core of dominant companies emerged towards the end of the nineteenth century in most of the leading sectors in Scotland, often surrounded by a number of smaller firms acting as their suppliers. Slaven has linked this to the emergence of 'industrial clusters' in the Scottish economy, notably in the shipbuilding and iron and steel trades, but also in the links between the production of cotton piece goods and printing and dyeing. These clusters had a regional and geographical dimension, such as the cluster in the Renfrewshire/Dunbartonshire area of firms concerned with the dyeing and printing of cotton cloth and yarn.[96]

There was an increasing move towards mergers and takeovers in Scottish industry, sometimes leading to a loss of Scottish control. These mergers have been discussed in Chapter 3. Here, it is enough to mention the amalgamation of the Paisley thread firms and most of their English competitors into the giant J. and P. Coats Company in 1896, the combination of the Vale of Leven dyeing firms in Dumbartonshire into the United Turkey Red Company in 1898 and the formation of the United Alkali Company in 1890 out of 45 firms, including the St Rollox chemical plant in Glasgow. Similarly in 1899, the Thornliebank Company Ltd, Renfrewshire, the largest printworks in Britain, became part of the Manchester-based Calico Printers Association.

In spite of their increasing wealth and growing representation in Parliament, the Scottish cotton masters remained a largely localised elite, with a relatively modest impact on the national stage. In this they were similar to the Lancashire cotton masters. An exception was Sir Charles Tennant, MP (1823–1906), the millionaire owner of the St Rollox Chemical Works, Glasgow, which had begun by manufacturing chemicals for the textile industry such as bleaching powder, mordants and dyes. Tennant diversified by forming the Tharsis Sulphur and Copper Co. to exploit pyrites mines in Spain in 1862. Ten years later he formed the Steel Company of Scotland and served as its Chairman until forced to step down in 1895. He was also prominent in the foundation of Nobel Explosives Ltd in 1876. Tennant 'was one of the first of the great regional men to metropolitanise himself'. At the age of 29, he bought a 3,500 acre estate in Peebleshire and he also owned a house in Grosvenor Square, London, where his 'three scintillating daughters' presided over a glittering social scene. Tennant switched from Liberalism to Liberal Unionism in 1895 and his son became the first Lord Glenconner.[97]

Hudson has queried the role of merchant capital in the industrial transformation of the Yorkshire woollen industry and emphasised the sale and mortgage of land as a major source of industrial finance in the West Riding.[98] By contrast, Chapman has argued that in the later Victorian period 'the British textile industry was dominated by merchants'.[99] In Scotland, the importance of merchant capital in the cotton industry is unambiguous. Many of the Scottish cotton masters came from merchant families who were active in overseas trade or in linen dealing and manufacturing. The majority (58%) of men whose wills and probate inventories contained self-descriptions identified themselves as 'merchants' and their estates at death reveal an increasing diversity of investments outside cotton manufacturing from the 1840s. Their experiences reflect changes taking place in the economy of the west of Scotland from the 1830s onwards, and the determination of Scottish cotton entrepreneurs to keep pace by moving into iron and steel production, railways, shipping, shipbuilding, overseas investment etc. that offered higher rates of return on capital than cotton spinning, weaving, calico printing or dyeing. The Glasgow and Paisley cotton masters made a major contribution to the economic development of the west of Scotland. As a German traveller observed in the 1840s, 'It is to the cotton lords and their enterprising speculations, that Glasgow chiefly owes its prosperity.'[100]

Notes

1. This is a revised and expanded version of an article that appeared in *Textile History*, 2009, XL, 1, 29–50, under the title 'The Scottish Cotton Masters, 1780–1914'. I am grateful to the editor, Professor Katrina Honeyman, Professor Stanley Chapman and an anonymous referee for their comments on earlier drafts.
2. T. M. Devine, *The Tobacco Lords: A Study of the Tobacco Merchants of Glasgow and their Trading Activities c. 1740–1790* (Edinburgh, 1990).
3. See, for example, R. Reid (Senex), *Glasgow Past and Present*, 3 vols (Glasgow, 1884); R. Reid, *Old Glasgow and Its Environs* (Glasgow, 1864); J. Maclehose, *The Old Country Houses of the Old Glasgow Gentry* (Glasgow, 1878); G. Macgregor,

The History of Glasgow (Glasgow, 1881); J. Maclehose, *Memoirs and Portraits of 100 Glasgow Men*, 2 vols (Glasgow, 1886); and J. O. Mitchell, *Old Glasgow Essays* (Glasgow, 1905). On Paisley see J. Parkhill, *The History of Paisley* (Paisley, 1857); and R. Brown, *The History of Paisley*, 2 vols (Paisley, 1886).

4. A. Slaven and S. G. Checkland (eds), *Dictionary of Scottish Business Biography. Volume 1, The Staple Industries* (*DSBB*) (Aberdeen, 1986).
5. On the English cotton masters, see A. Howe, *The Cotton Masters, 1830–1860* (Oxford, 1984) and the same author's 'The Business Community', in M. B. Rose (ed.), *The Lancashire Cotton Industry: A History since 1700* (Preston, 1996), 94–121. See also S. D. Chapman, *Merchant Enterprise in Britain: From the Industrial Revolution to World War I* (Cambridge, 1992) and the same author's 'The Commercial Sector', in Rose (ed.), *The Lancashire Cotton Industry*, 63–94. For more general studies see K. Honeyman, *Origins of Enterprise: Business Leadership in the Industrial Revolution* (Manchester, 1982); and F. Crouzet, *The First Industrialists: The Problem of Origins* (Cambridge, 1985). On the Scottish middle classes see S. Nenadic, 'The Rise of the Urban Middle Classes', in T. M. Devine and R. Mitchison (eds), *People and Society in Scotland. Volume I, 1760–1830* (Edinburgh, 1988), 109–26; N. Morgan and R. H. Trainor, 'The Dominant Classes', in W. H. Fraser and R. J. Morris (eds), *People and Society in Scotland, Voume. II, 1830–1914* (Edinburgh, 1990), 103–37; R. H. Trainor, 'The Elite', S. Nenadic, 'The Victorian Middle Classes' and I. Maver, 'Glasgow's Civic Government', all in W. H. Fraser and I. Maver (eds), *Glasgow. Volume II, 1830–1912* (Manchester, 1996), 227–64, 265–99 and 441–85. See also L. Miskell, 'Civic Leadership and the Manufacturing Elite: Dundee, 1820–1870', in L. Miskell, C. A. Whatley and B. Harris (eds), *Victorian Dundee: Images and Realities* (East Linton, 2000), 51–69. For political connections see G. Teviotdale, 'The Glasgow Parliamentary Constituency, 1832–1846', B. Litt. thesis, University of Glasgow, 1963. For studies of the English provincial middle classes see T. Koditschek, *Class Formation and Urban Industrial Society, Bradford, 1750–1850* (Cambridge 1990); R. J. Morris, *Class, Sect and Party: The Making of the British Middle Class, Leeds, 1820–1850* (Manchester 1990); and R. Trainor, *Black Country Elites: The Exercise of Authority in an Industrialised Area, 1830–1900* (Oxford, 1993). For a general survey of wealth accumulation in Britain see W. D. Rubinstein, *Men of Property: The Very Wealthy in Britain since the Industrial Revolution* (London, 1981).
6. C. Brogan, *James Finlay and Company Ltd., 1750–1850* (Glasgow, 1951).
7. Morgan and Trainor, 'The Dominant Classes', 113.
8. Honeyman, *Origins of Enterprise*, 1982, 169; and P. L. Payne, *British Entrepreneurship in the Nineteenth Century*, 2nd edition (London, 1988), 22.
9. National Archives of Scotland, Edinburgh (NAS), Sheriff Court of Glasgow, SC 36/48/40, Probate Inventory of Henry Houldsworth, Coltness House, Lanarkshire, 12 November 1853.
10. J. Butt, 'The Industries of Glasgow', in W. H. Fraser and I. Maver (eds), *Glasgow. Volume II, 1830–1912* (Manchester 1996), 97.
11. S. D. Chapman, 'Fixed Capital Formation in the British Cotton Manufacturing

Industry', in J. P. P. Higgins and S. D. Chapman (eds), *Aspects of Capital Investment in Great Britain, 1750–1850* (London, 1971), 72; and S. D. Chapman, *The Early Factory Masters* (Newton Abbot, 1967), 78.

12. Honeyman, *Origins of Enterprise*, 1982, 7.
13. Crouzet, *The First Industrialists*, 1985, 142.
14. Mitchell Library, Glasgow (ML), Houston of Johnstone Papers, TD 263/194, Contract of Co Partnery between William McDowall, George Houston and Robert Burns for a cotton mill, February 1788.
15. NAS, Sheriff Court of Perthshire, Register of Deeds, SC 49/48/104, Contract of Co-Partnery, Stanley Mills, 1 January 1787.
16. P. Morgan, *Annals of Woodside and Newhills* (Aberdeen, 1886), 19–23.
17. NAS, Sheriff Court of Glasgow, SC 36/48/1, Will of David Dale, 4 August 1806 and SC 36/48/3 fol. 412, Additional Inventory of Estate of Dale, 9 January 1811. For the Stanley debts see A. J. Robertson, 'Robert Owen and the Campbell Debt', *Business History*, 1969, XI; and A. J. Cooke, 'Robert Owen and the Stanley Mills, 1802–1811', *Business History*, 1979, XXI (1).
18. J. Shaw, *Water Power in Scotland, 1550–1870* (Edinburgh, 1984); C. A. Whatley, *Scottish Society, 1707–1830: Beyond Jacobitism, Towards Industrialisation* (Manchester, 2000), 219–29; and S. M. Nisbet, 'The Rise of the Cotton Factory in Eighteenth Century Renfrewshire' (PhD thesis, University of the West of Scotland, 2003), 17.
19. Quoted in J. Cleland, *An Account of the Present State of Glasgow* (Glasgow, 1836), 34.
20. Devine, *Tobacco Lords*, 45.
21. NAS, Court of Session Papers, CS 96/630.
22. NAS, CS 96/2233, fol. 1.
23. NAS, CS 96/4722–3.
24. NAS, Sheriff Court of Paisley, SC 58/42/34, Will of Henry Dunlop, 4 September 1867.
25. Shaw, *Water Power*, 323.
26. NAS, CS 96/3339.
27. Robertson, 'Robert Owen'; and Cooke, 'Robert Owen'.
28. I. Donnachie and G. Hewitt, *Historic New Lanark: The Dale and Owen Industrial Community since 1785* (Edinburgh, 1993), 65.
29. Factory Inquiry Commission Reports, *Parliamentary Papers* (*PP*), 1833, Vol. XX, Evidence of Archibald Buchanan.
30. ML, Houston of Johnstone Papers, TD 263/194, Partnership Contract, 1788.
31. Signet Library, Edinburgh (SL), Court of Session Papers (CS), 290/18.
32. Blair Castle, Perthshire, Atholl Mss, 25, XI, 3, fols 48–51 and 67–70.
33. W. Taylor, *An Answer to Mr Carlile's Sketches of Paisley* (Paisley 1809), 17.
34. SL, CS 290/34, 3 and CS 411/62, 29.
35. SL, CS 209/43, Rothesay Mills, Bute.
36. SL, CS 264/2, Cartside Mills, Renfrewshire.
37. NAS, Sheriff Court of Perthshire, SC 49/48/104, fols 1–5, Stanley Partnership Contract, January 1787.

38. Morgan, *Annals of Woodside*, 20–3.
39. Contract of Co Partnery, Luncarty Bleachfield, Perthshire, 9 November 1812 (document formerly in the possession of the late John Culbert, Stanley).
40. J. Butt, 'Robert Owen as a Businessman', in J. Butt (ed.), *Robert Owen, Prince of Cotton Spinners* (Newton Abbot, 1971), 183–4; I. Donnachie, *Robert Owen. Owen of New Lanark and Harmony* (East Linton, 2000), 79; and J. Butt (ed.), *The Life of Robert Owen Written by Himself* (London, 1971), 27, 31 and 171–2.
41. A. K. Cairncross and J. B. K Hunter, 'The Early Growth of Messrs J. and P. Coats, 1830–83', *Business History*, 1987, XXIX, 157 and 169.
42. *New Statistical Account of Scotland* (*NSA*), Vol. X, Perthshire (Edinburgh, 1845), 1253.
43. Factory Inquiry Commission Report, Employment of Children, Supplementary Report, *PP*, 1834, Vol. XX, 171.
44. R.S. Fitton, *The Arkwrights, Spinners of Fortune* (Manchester, 1989), 206.
45. Butt (ed.), *Robert Owen, Prince of Cotton Spinners*, 59.
46. *Ibid.*, 29 and 80.
47. Atholl Mss, 25, IX, 3, Letter Book of Robert Owen, 1802–1819, fols 52–5 and 59–60.
48. Butt (ed.), *Robert Owen, Prince of Cotton Spinners*, 80–1.
49. *Ibid.*
50. A. Slaven, 'Entrepreneurs and Business Success and Business Failure in Scotland', in D. H. Aldcroft and A. Slaven (eds), *Enterprise and Management: Essays in Honour of Peter L. Payne* (Aldershot, 1995), 59–92.
51. Miskell, 'Civic Leadership', 59; and Howe, *The Cotton Masters*, 51.
52. Howe, *The Cotton Masters*, 54.
53. A. Bannatyne, *Memoir of Dugald Bannatyne and Agnes Stirling, his Wife* (Glasgow, 1896), 28. See also A. J. Cooke, *From Popular Enlightenment to Lifelong Learning: A History of Adult Education in Scotland, 1707–2005* (Leicester, 2006), 32–3.
54. Howe, *The Cotton Masters*, 55.
55. Maclehose, *100 Glasgow Men*.
56. *Dundee Advertiser*, 8 November 1898.
57. A. Slaven and D. W. Kim, 'The Origins and Economic and Social Roles of Scottish Business Leaders, 1860–1960', in T. M. Devine (ed.), *Scottish Elites* (Edinburgh, 1994), 159–60; and Slaven, 'Entrepreneurs'.
58. Trainor, *Black Country Elites*, 243.
59. P. King-Clark (ed.), *The John Caldwell Letters from Canada, 1821–1837* (Paisley, 1991), 39.
60. Miskell, 'Civic Leadership', 60.
61. Howe, *The Cotton Masters*, 62.
62. Trainor, *Black Country Elites*, 231.
63. T. M. Devine, *The Scottish Nation, 1700–2000* (London, 2000), 302.
64. J. F. McCaffrey, 'Political Issues and Developments', in W. H. Fraser and I. Maver (eds), *Glasgow. Volume II, 1830–1912* (Manchester, 1996), 192.
65. Miskell, 'Civic Leadership', 59.

66. Howe, *The Cotton Masters*, 212 and 96.
67. I. Maver, *Glasgow* (Edinburgh, 2000) 61–2.
68. Anon, 'The First Years of Glasgow Chamber of Commerce', *Glasgow Chamber of Commerce Journal*, June 1970, 298–301.
69. Anon, 'Kirkman Finlay 1773–1842', *Glasgow Chamber of Commerce Journal*, April 1969, 210–11.
70. Howe, *The Cotton Masters*, 164–5.
71. ML, Glasgow Association of Master Cotton Spinners (GACMS), 1810–1835, AGN, Vol. 51/52, 1015, TMJ 99.
72. Report of the Select Committee on the State of Children Employed in Manufactures, *PP*, 1816, III, Evidence of Robert Owen, 20–2; and ML, GACMS, Sederunt Book, 1816, TMJ 100, Letter from Robert Lyon in Edinburgh, 16 April 1816.
73. *PP*, 1816, III, Evidence of Henry Houldsworth, 245.
74. *PP*, 1816, III, Evidence of Adam Bogle, 162–8; and NAS, Sheriff Court of Glasgow, SC 36/48/13/531, Inventory of Adam Bogle, merchant in Glasgow, died 1817.
75. Factory Inquiry Commission Reports, *PP*, 1834, XX, Part II, Factory Inquiry Commission Report, Employment of Children in Factories, Evidence of George Macleroy, 140.
76. *PP*, 1834, XX, Evidence of Henry Dunlop, 146.
77. *PP*, 1834, XX, Evidence of James Coats Junior, 200.
78. Sir A. Alison, *Some Account of my Life and Writings* (Edinburgh, 1883), 369–85; and W. H. Fraser, 'The Glasgow Cotton Spinners, 1837', in J. Butt and J. T. Ward (eds), *Scottish Themes* (Edinburgh, 1976), 90.
79. R. Johnston, *Clydeside Capital, 1870–1920: A Social History of Employers* (East Linton, 2000), 13.
80. Maclehose, *100 Glasgow Men*.
81. *DSBB*, I, 357.
82. A. J. Cooke, *Stanley: From Arkwright Village to Commuter Suburb, 1784–2003* (Perth, 2003), *106*.
83. NAS, Wills and Probate Inventories (see Appendix).
84. Howe, *The Cotton Masters*, 59. See also J. Wolff and J. Seed (eds), *The Culture of Capital: Art, Power and the Nineteenth-Century Middle Class* (Manchester, 1988).
85. NAS, Sheriff Court of Dunoon, SC 51/32/5, Will of Kirkman Finlay, 8 April 1842.
86. NAS, Sheriff Court of Ayr, SC 6/44/52/64 and SC 6/46/21/393, Will and Inventory of Sir Peter Coats, 1890. For Tennant see *DSBB*, I, 288.
87. Alison, *Account*, 344–8.
88. Nenadic, 'Victorian Middle Classes', 283.
89. King-Clark, *John Caldwell Letters*, 38.
90. S. Tytler, *St. Mungo's City*, 3 vols (London, 1884), II, 113.
91. M. A. Wiener, *English Culture and the Decline of the Industrial Spirit, 1850–1980* (London, 1981).

92. Return of Owners of Land, Scotland, 1872–3, *PP*, 1874, LXXII, Part III.
93. *NSA*, VIII, 26.
94. NAS, SC 36/48/30/555, Inventory of Charles Macintosh, 19 July 1844. See also G. Macintosh, *Biographical Memoir of the late Charles Macintosh, FRS* (Glasgow, 1847) and A. Clow and N. Clow, *The Chemical Revolution: A Contribution to Social Technology* (London, 1952), 246–53.
95. P. L. Payne, *The Early Scottish Limited Companies, 1856–1895* (Edinburgh, 1980).
96. Slaven, 'Entrepreneurs', 63–4.
97. *DSBB*, I, 285–9.
98. P. Hudson, *The Genesis of Industrial Capital: A Study of the West Riding Wool Textile Industry, c. 1750–1850* (Cambridge, 1986), 260.
99. Chapman, *Early Factory Masters*, 181.
100. J. G. Kohl, *Scotland* (London, 1844), 9.

Conclusion

The Scottish cotton industry was totally dependent on overseas trade for its raw material and heavily dependent on overseas markets for its finished products. In this it resembled the earlier Glasgow tobacco trade, which was similarly based on a slave-grown, colonial raw material, traded on to overseas (in this case European) markets. The cotton industry also exhibited many of the characteristics of early manufacturing industries, displaying a combination of modernity and tradition in its adoption of new technologies, working practices and methods of organisation. Whereas some processes in the industry, such as carding and spinning cotton, were quickly organised into water- and steam-powered factories, others, such as picking cotton, pirn winding, the tambouring of muslin or hand loom weaving, remained labour intensive, heavily dependent on the labour of women and children, on hand power and on the division of labour, rather than on labour-saving machinery.

Even in cotton, the most 'advanced' manufacturing industry, traditional modes of work remained in certain processes well into the nineteenth century, with the male artisan having a considerable degree of control over the timing and pace of his work. This was true of hand loom weaving and of more prosperous trades such as calico printing. It was even found in the spinning mills, with the male mule spinner hiring and firing his own piecers, enjoying high earnings and generally aspiring to the image and lifestyle of the skilled artisan. The Glasgow Cotton Spinners' Strike of 1837 represented a turning point in attempts by male mule spinners to retain their high wages and a degree of workforce control. By contrast, women and children acted as the 'shock troops' of early industrialisation, subject either to poorly paid outwork at much lower rates than men, or to the strictly disciplined regime of the factory, with the pace of work regulated by the machine, fixed working hours and close (male) supervision.

This began to change with the decline of hand loom weaving in the 1840s and the collapse of the sewed muslin trade in the late 1850s. By the 1880s, as working hours shortened, new work regimes were introduced with less worker independence, closer management control and an intensification of the work rate, as machines speeded up and workers were required to mind more machines. Again, this impacted particularly on women. In Scotland, there was a good deal of passive resistance by cotton workers to these new work regimes, which were introduced more successfully in Lancashire and even more so in the United States, leading to a relative loss of productivity in Scotland, as compared to its rivals. This provides part of the explanation for the industry's early decline in Scotland.

From the 1830s, capital from the cotton industry was channelled into coal mining and iron and steel manufacture by industrialists such as William Dunn of Duntocher or Henry Houldsworth of Coltness. In the west of Scotland, these offered more profitable investment opportunities than cotton. Margaret Irwin, an astute observer, who had been Assistant Commissioner on the Royal Commission of Labour, noted in 1895 that whilst the cotton industry was the major outlet for manufacturing energy in Lancashire, in Scotland it was only one of many outlets.[1] Whilst historians such as Payne have been relatively kind to the Victorian entrepreneur, as compared with earlier historians,[2] well-informed contemporaries were critical of the second and third generation of Scottish cotton masters. For example, Archibald Alison, who became Sheriff of Lanarkshire in 1834, remarked on the tendency of successful Glasgow businessmen to sever their links with the city and retreat to estates in the country.[3] Similar comments were made by W. O. Mitchell in his Introduction to Maclehose's *The Old Country Houses of the Old Glasgow Gentry*, published in 1870: 'Nowadays, our leading merchant has too often ceased to be a citizen. Glasgow is the place where he has his office, and which is always wanting subscriptions from him. But he lives as far from it as he can. He cultivates other society. Outside of his own business the circle of his acquaintances here is gradually narrowing.' Mitchell was particularly critical of the second and third generation, 'who come back from their English schools strangers, knowing nothing and caring nothing about Glasgow or Glasgow folk, and rather ashamed of having anything to do with that big, smoky town'.[4] Margaret Irwin held similar views and believed the decline of the Scottish cotton industry was due to the large fortunes made by mill owners and the next generation being 'lacking in commercial enterprise'.[5]

However, these contemporary views need to be balanced by the findings of Nenadic, who has shown that many Glasgow businessmen, even if they lived in the country, kept an office and a residence in Glasgow, where they lived during the week.[6] My own research on wills and probate inventories suggests that many businessmen, even those with country estates, kept strong links with Glasgow organisations and charities, as shown by their legacies to Glasgow churches, charities and organisations such as the Trades House.

By the late nineteenth century, the nature of large manufacturing firms in

Britain was changing, as increasing numbers of family firms became limited liability companies. Sometimes, as in the case of J. and P. Coats, family members retained a controlling share of the company, but in other cases, it meant a decline in family influence and the rise of professional managers from outside the founding family. This was typified by the emergence of the German-born Otto O. Phillippi as the driving force in the giant Coats company.[7] This was accompanied by an increasing number of mergers and groupings, such as the combination of dyeing firms into the United Turkey Red Company, of chemical firms into United Alkali, of calico printing firms into the Calico Printers' Association and of cotton thread firms into J. and P. Coats.

Another explanation for decline is the dependence of the Scottish cotton industry on the production of a relatively small number of highly specialised fashion goods – the Paisley shawl, embroidered muslins and brightly coloured Turkey red dyed fabrics for the Indian market. This left the industry vulnerable to changes of fashion, foreign competition or overseas tariffs, as production was so highly geared to export markets. The very success and efficiency of the industry could create problems, as middle-class women stopped buying fashion items such as Paisley shawls and embroidered muslins once overproduction and falling prices brought them within the reach of the working-class consumer. By the 1890s, the bulk of the plain calico weaving trade had practically disappeared from Glasgow, and the Scottish weaving industry was confined to 'fancy' goods with short production runs, as compared to the mass production of plain goods by the Lancashire industry.[8]

I have argued in this book that the cotton industry was the 'secret spring' behind the early industrialisation of Scotland, building on the earlier linen industry, which declined in the west of Scotland but continued to expand in the east. Cotton manufacturing had a powerful influence over the later development of manufacturing industry in the west of Scotland. It created an expanding market for the manufacture of steam engines and machinery, including cotton manufacturing machinery, produced in places like the iron foundries at Houldsworth's cotton mills in Anderston, Glasgow. It also gave a boost to the construction industry, including the manufacture of bricks, and to the development of transport systems, such as railways and ports. Perhaps most importantly, the cotton industry continued to strengthen the Scottish tradition of worldwide networks of trade, shipping and credit that would stand the west of Scotland in good stead in its next phase of export-led development in iron and steel manufacture, coal mining, heavy engineering and shipbuilding.

Many gaps remain in our understanding of the industry in Scotland. Few records remain of individual firms, and the industry was secretive and mistrustful of sharing information, so that there is little regional data about it, compared to Lancashire. One obvious gap is the absence of a modern history of Paisley, along the lines of recent work on Aberdeen, Dundee, Edinburgh or Glasgow. Paisley was a mini-Lancashire in its social and economic structure, with a heavily feminised workforce and overreliance on a staple industry. The place in Scotland it most resembled was Dundee, another textile town with a largely female workforce, which has been better studied. There is also no modern history of the giant cotton thread firm of J. and P. Coats, one of Britain's largest manufacturing concerns, which has extensive surviving records. Another gap, shared with the historiography of the English cotton industry, is the neglect of the finishing trades of bleaching, dyeing and calico printing, which played a particularly important role in Scotland and where records survive for the United Turkey Red Company. The centre of the Scottish industry was the Vale of Leven in Dunbartonshire, which again deserves a modern history.

I end with the words of an anonymous Paisley weaver/poet, celebrating the wide range of fabrics the Scottish textile industry produced and revealing a wry humour and the craftsman's pride in his work:

> There's shirtings, sheetings, corduroys, nankeens,
> There's sacking, canvass, osnaburgs and jean,
> There's ticking, broad cloths, cassimere and checks,
> There's velvets, bombazines and bombasets,
> There's plaiding, duffle, flannel, serge and crepe,
> There's gauze, lace, ribbons, sarsenets and tape,
> There's many other fabrics coarse and fine,
> Whose names prosaic will not respond to rhyme,
> And some few more which metre very well,
> I could pronounce them but I cannot spell.[9]

Notes

1. M. H. Irwin, 'Women's Industries in Scotland', *Proceedings of the Philosophical Society of Glasgow*, XXVII, 1895–6, 73–4.
2. See P. Payne, *British Entrepreneurship in the Nineteenth Century*, 2nd edition (London, 1988).
3. A. Alison, *Some Account of my Life and Writings* (Edinburgh, 1883), 348.
4. J. Maclehose, *The Old Country Houses of the Old Glasgow Gentry* (Glasgow 1878), Introduction.
5. Irwin, 'Women's Industries in Scotland', 78.
6. S. Nenadic, 'The Victorian Middle Classes', in W. H. Fraser and I. Maver (eds), *Glasgow. Volume II, 1830–1912* (Manchester, 1996), 265–99.
7. A. Slaven and S. G. Checkland (eds), *Dictionary of Scottish Business Biography. Volume I, The Staple Industries* (*DSBB*) (Aberdeen, 1986), I, 330–1.
8. Irwin, 'Women's Industries in Scotland', 73.
9. *Weavers' Magazine and Literary Companion*, 1818–1819, I, 272.

Appendix: wills and probate inventories of Scottish cotton merchants and manufacturers/partners in Scottish cotton mills, bleachfields and printworks, dyeworks and chemical works, 1787–1912

Abbreviations

B	Shares in banking companies
Bl	Bleacher
C	Charitable bequests in will
CC	Commissary Court
Ch	Chemical manufacturer
Cp	Calico printer
Cs	Cotton spinner
D	Dyer
E	Value of total estate
FM	Former manager
GAMCS	Glasgow Association of Master Cotton Spinners
I	Insurance policies
LP	Lord Provost of Glasgow
ManP	Managing partner
MP	Member of Parliament
P	Partner
PP	Principal partner
Pw	Power loom weaver
R	Shares in railway companies
SC	Sheriff Court
Tm	Thread manufacturer

Note: Dates refer to the date of the will/probate inventory

28 October 1787, Andrew Keay, Cs, Stanley, Perthshire, E £1,260, B £160, CC8/8/127/1187.

4 August 1806, David Dale, Glasgow, PP New Lanark, P, Catrine, Ayr, Newton Stewart, Kirkcudbrightshire, E £64,684, B £5,683, SC36/48/1 and SC36/48/3/412.

22 December 1809, David McVicar, Cs and FM Stanley, Perthshire, E £3,316, B £640, CC20/7/5/526.

1817, Adam Bogle, Cs and Pw, Blantyre, Lanarkshire, GAMCS, E £28,875, SC36/48/13/531.

1818, George Dempster, MP, Perth Burghs, P Stanley, Perthshire, E £3,101, CC3/5/5/220.

25 July 1826, William Stevenson, Cs Crosslee, Renfrewshire, GAMCS, E £22,106, SC36/48/21/104.

5 February 1830, William Carlile, Cs Paisley, E £1,719, B £1,110, SC58/42/4/31.

5 November 1831, James Neilson, Cs Paisley, E £6,779, C £220, SC58/42/5/231.

4 July 1835, Robert Freeland, Cs Paisley, GAMCS, E £12,671, SC58/42/8/275.

1835, Peter Kerr, Tm Paisley, E £3,255, B £1,040, SC58/42/8/421.

18 October 1837, Robert Dick, Cs Glasgow, E £4,594, I £1,030, SC36/48/28/185.

15 June 1839, William Kelly, Snr, Cs Glasgow, E £2,326, SC36/48/32/177.

15 December 1839, James Craig, Cs and FM Stanley, Perth, E £1,049, SC49/44/30.

7 January 1840, Charles Tennant, Bl and Ch St Rollox, Glasgow, E £94,237, R £3,187, I £100, SC36/48/27/625.

6 February 1841, Archibald Buchanan, Cs and ManP, Catrine, Ayrshire, E £39,001, SC6/44/10.

17 October 1841, John Orr, Cs Paisley, E £21,954, B £1,100, SC58/42/13/113.

8 April 1842, Kirkman Finlay, Castle Toward, Argyll, Cs Ballindalloch, Catrine and Deanston, E £90,240, B £5,980, I £15,698, R £31,028, Lord Provost of Glasgow, and MP, Glasgow, SC51/32/5.

25 July 1843, Charles Macintosh, D and Ch Campsie, Stirlingshire, E £77,186, SC36/48/30/555.

27 January 1847, John Finlay, Cs Glasgow, E £54,273, SC36/48/34/358.

14 December 1847, Robert Thom, Ascog, Argyll, Cs Rothesay, Bute, E £2,669, SC8/35/5/107.

14 December 1848, Henry Monteith, Carstairs, Lanarkshire, Lord Provost of Glasgow and Tory MP, Linlithgow Burghs, Cs, D and Pw, Blantyre and Barrowfield, E £53,571, R £1,092, SC36/48/35.

11 January 1849, George Buchanan, ManP and Cs Stanley, Perthshire, E £33,770, R £3,108, SC49/31/47/27.

4 October 1849, William Dunn, Cs Duntocher, Dunbartonshire, GAMCS, E £88,004, SC65/34/6/117.

7 October 1852, Charles Dunlop, Cs Paisley, E £15,776, I £150, SC58/42/19/702.

26 July 1853, Peter Bogle, Cs Glasgow, E £21,371, SC36/48/40/575.

12 November 1853, Henry Houldsworth, Coltness, Lanarkshire, E £7,954, P, Cs Provost of Anderston, Glasgow, 1824–1831, GAMCS, SC36/48/40.

21 February 1854, James Ewing, Lord Provost of Glasgow, MP for Glasgow,

D Strathleven, Dunbartonshire, E £281,296, C £49,700, B £13,278, R £3,549, SC65/34/7/200.

27 August 1855, William Hussey, Cs Glasgow, GAMCS, E £96,657, B £26,625, R £15,157, SC36/48/41/759.

28 August 1855, Hugh Cogan, Cs Glasgow, E £42,500, I £432, R £135, SC36/48/42/683.

1857, James Coats, Snr, Tm Paisley, E £6,740, C £300, SC58/42/24/234.

23 May 1861, James Crum, Cs Busby, Renfrewshire, E £63,819, B £8,000, SC58/42/27/358.

1864, John Clark, Tm Paisley, E £18,437, SC58/42/8/421.

24 August 1867, Walter Crum, Thornliebank, Cp, E £29,914, SC 58/42/34/746.

4 September 1867, Henry Dunlop, Cs, Barrhead, Whig/Liberal Lord Provost of Glasgow, E £28,158, SC 58/42/34/800.

4 June 1871, John Dennistoun, manufacturer and merchant, E £113,308, Liberal MP for Glasgow, 1837, SC 65/34/16/524.

2 November 1874, Alexander Dennistoun, Golfhill, Glasgow, E £343,084, UP Church, Liberal MP for Dumbartonshire, 1834, SC 36/48/75/204.

6 September 1876, James Clark, cotton manufacturer (P, James Finlay) E £49,718, SC 36/48/80/730 and *DSBB*.

8 May 1877, William Stevenson, Cs Johnstone, Renfrewshire, E £816, SC58/42/45/634.

1878, John Tennant, Ch St Rollox, Glasgow, E £ £79,325, SC 36/48/85 and *DSBB*.

15 April 1878, John Orr Ewing, D, died Cannes, France, E £460,549, R £17,544, C of S., Conservative MP for Dumbartonshire, SC65/34/22/212 and *DSBB*.

15 October 1883, Thomas Coats, Tm Ferguslie, Paisley, E £1,308,734, SC58/42/51/226.

9 March 1890, Sir Peter Coats, Auchendrane, Ayr, Tm Paisley, E £123,457, C £5,500 (UP Church), SC6/44/52/64.

23 August 1893, Alexander Crum, Cp Thornliebank, E £106,603, B £2,150, R £4,541, Liberal MP, Renfrewshire 1880–1885, SC58/42/58/142 and *DSBB*.

27 November 1893, Sir Archibald Orr Ewing, D, E £1,094,771, B £53,669, R £229,904, C of S, Conservative MP, Stirlingshire, SC67/36/102 and *DSBB*.

11 April 1894, John Clark, Tm E £752,211, C £32,000, U P Church, SC 58/45/8/674 and *DSBB*.

17 August 1899, Frank Stewart Sandeman, Cs Stanley, E £21,504, Free Church, Conservative, SC 49/31/177/385.

4 May 1900, Henry Birkmyre, Springbank, Kilmalcolm, Cs New Lanark and Gourock Ropework Company, E £435,883, Liberal/Liberal Unionist, Provost of Greenock, UP Church, SC53/41/10/394 and *DSBB*.

5 July 1900, Thomas Reid, D, E £207,234, R £5,761, Provost of Govan, 1869–1872, SC65/34/47/508 and *DSBB*.

6 August 1903, Sir John Muir, Deanston, Senior partner, James Finlay and Co., E £862,972, Liberal, Lord Provost of Glasgow, 1889–1892, *DSBB*.

1906, Sir Charles Tennant, Ch St Rollox, Glasgow, E £3,151,974, Liberal MP, Peebleshire, SC 42/20/16 and *DSBB*.

6 September 1907, James Paterson, Cs Glasgow, E £135,440, *DSBB*.
11 May 1912, Archibald Coats, Tm Paisley, E £1,365,132, *DSBB*.

Sources: NAS, Commissary and Sheriff Court records; J. Maclehose, *Memoirs and Portraits of 100 Glasgow Men*, Glasgow, 1886; and A. Slaven and S. G. Checkland (eds), *Dictionary of Scottish Business Biography. Volume 1, The Staple Industries* (Aberdeen, 1986), cited as *DSBB*.

Bibliography

Manuscript sources

A. K. Bell Library, Perth
F. S. Sandeman Papers

Blair Castle, Blair Atholl, Perthshire
Atholl Papers

Dornoch Heritage Society, Dornoch, Sutherland
Gilchrist of Ospidale Mss

Dundee University Library
Sidlaw Industries (some of F. S. Sandeman papers now missing)

Edinburgh University Library
Laing Papers

Glasgow University Archives
David and John Anderson Ltd., Atlantic Mills, Bridgeton, Glasgow, 1862–1949
J. and P. Coats Ltd., Coats Paton plc, cotton thread manufacturers, Glasgow and Paisley, 1821–1972
James Finlay and Co., textile manufacturers and merchants, Glasgow, 1789–1914
Lancaster, Duncan and Company, calico printers and merchants, Glasgow
John Lean and Sons, muslin manufacturers, Glasgow, 1852–1958
United Turkey Red Company, Alexandria, Dumbartonshire

Guildhall Library, London
Sun Fire Office Policies

Mitchell Library, Glasgow
Dale-Alexander Correspondence, 1787–1797
Glasgow Chamber of Commerce Correspondence, 1783 onwards
Glasgow Master Cotton Spinners' Association, Minute Book, 1810–1825

Houston of Johnstone Papers
Lennox of Woodhead Estate Papers
Mackinnon Mss, Letters of John Mackinnon, Carnbroe Ironworks, Glasgow to his son James
Monteith Correspondence, Letters to Lord Provost Henry Monteith of Carstairs, 1820
Letter from William Murdoch, Glasgow to Boulton and Watt, Birmingham, 18 August 1802 (Boulton and Watt Papers, Birmingham Reference Library)
Pettigrew and Dickie, cotton weavers, Glasgow, 1800–1843

National Archives, London
Board of Trade Papers

National Archives of Scotland, Edinburgh
Campbell of Jura Muniments
Census Enumerators' Returns 1841 and 1851
Court of Session Records
Cunningham Grahame Muniments
Graham of Fintry Papers
Sheriff Court of Perthshire Register of Deeds
Sheriff Court Records for Argyll, Ayrshire, Buteshire, Glasgow, Lanarkshire, Paisley, Perthshire and Commissary Court Records for Edinburgh and St Andrews (Wills and Probate Inventories of Glasgow, Paisley and Perth cotton merchants and manufacturers, from 1787 (Andrew Keay) to 1912 (Archibald Coats))
Sinclair of Ulbster Muniments (microfilm)

National Library of Scotland, Edinburgh
Account Book of Milton Printworks, Dumbarton
Melville Papers
Saltoun Manuscripts

Signet Library, Edinburgh
Court of Session Papers

Stanley Mills, Stanley, Perthshire
Stanley Mills (Scotland) Ltd. Papers (now missing)

Printed sources

Books and articles

Aldcroft, D. and Slaven, A. (eds) (1995), *Enterprise and Management: Essays in Honour of Peter L. Payne*, Aldershot, Scolar Press.
Alison, Sir A. (1883), *Some Account of my Life and Writings*, Edinburgh, Blackwood.
Anderson, M. (1971), *Family Structure in Nineteenth Century Lancashire*, Cambridge, Cambridge University Press.

Anon (1834), *A Short Account of the Life and Hardships of a Glasgow Weaver*, Glasgow, W. R. McPhin.
Anon (1838), *The Case of the Cotton Spinners Considered: A Report of a Meeting at Paisley 29 January 1838 in the Old Low Church*, Glasgow, Liberator Office.
Anon (1883), *Biographical Sketches of Lord Provosts of Glasgow*, Glasgow, John Tweed.
Anon (1952), *Famous Fabrics 1822–1952: David and John Anderson, Atlantic Mills, Bridgeton, Glasgow*, Glasgow.
Anon (1969), 'Kirkman Finlay 1773–1842', *Glasgow Chamber of Commerce Journal*, April, 210–11.
Anon (1970), 'The First Years of Glasgow Chamber of Commerce', *Glasgow Chamber of Commerce Journal*, June, 298–301.
Anon (1980), *Coats the Threadmakers, 1830–1980, 150th Anniversary Exhibition*, Paisley, Paisley Museum and Art Galleries.
Anon (1996), *Six Cord Thread: The Story of Coats and Clarks Paisley Thread Mills*, Paisley, Paisley Project Team.
Aspinall, A. (1949), *The Early English Trade Unions*, London, Bletchworth Press.
Baines, E. (1835), *History of the Cotton Manufacture in Great Britain*, reprinted 1966, London, Frank Cass.
Bannatyne, A. (1896), *Memoir of Dugald Bannatyne and Agnes Stirling, his Wife*, Glasgow, William Hodge.
Berg, M. (1994, 2nd edition), *The Age of Manufactures, 1700–1820: Industry, Innovation and Work in Britain*, London and New York, Routledge.
Berg, M. (1994), 'Factories, Workshops and Industrial Organisation', in Floud and McCloskey, Vol. I, 1700–1860, 123–50.
Blair, M. (1907), *The Paisley Thread Industry*, Paisley, Alexander Cook, reprinted 2004, Glasgow, Grimshaw Press.
Blake, G. (1963), *The Gourock: A History of the Gourock Ropework Company*, Glasgow, Pillans and Wilson.
Bolin-Hort, P. (1989), *Work, State and the Family: Child Labour and the Organisation of Production in the British Cotton Industry, 1780–1920*, Lund, Lund University Press.
Bolin-Hort, P. (1994), 'Managerial Strategies and Worker Responses: A New Perspective on the Decline of the Scottish Cotton Industry', *Journal of the Scottish Labour History Society*, XXIX, 63–83.
Bremner, D. (1869), *The Industries of Scotland: Their Rise, Progress and Present Condition*, reprinted 1969, Newton Abbot, David and Charles.
Briggs, A. (2000), *The Age of Improvement, 1783–1867*, 2nd edition, London, Longman.
Brogan, C. (1951), *James Finlay and Company Ltd., 1750–1950*, Glasgow, Jackson Son and Company.
Brown, A. (1795 and 1797), *A History of Glasgow and of Paisley, Greenock and Port Glasgow*, 3 vols, Glasgow, William Paton.
Brown, C. G. (1981), 'The Sunday School Movement in Scotland', *Records of the Scottish Church History Society*, XXI.

Brown, C. G. (1998), 'Religion', in Cooke, Donnachie, MacSween and Whatley, Vol. 1, 63–85.

Brown, R. (1886), *The History of Paisley*, 2 vols, Paisley, J. and J. Cook.

Butt, J. (ed.) (1971a), *Robert Owen, Prince of Cotton-Spinners*, Newton Abbot, David and Charles.

Butt, J. (1971b), 'Robert Owen as a Businessman', in Butt (ed.), *Robert Owen, Prince of Cotton-Spinners*, 168–213.

Butt, J. (ed.) (1971c), *The Life of Robert Owen Written by Himself*, London, Charles Knight.

Butt, J. (1976), 'Capital and Enterprise in the Scottish Iron Industry, 1780–1840', in Butt, J. and Ward, J. T., *Scottish Themes*, Edinburgh, Scottish Academic Press, 67–79.

Butt, J. (1977), 'The Scottish Cotton Industry during the Industrial Revolution 1780–1840', in Cullen, L. M., and Smout, T. C. (eds), *Comparative Aspects of Scottish and Irish Social and Economic History, 1600–1900*, Edinburgh, John Donald, 116–28.

Butt, J. (1987), 'Labour and Industrial Relations in the Scottish Cotton Industry during the Industrial Revolution', in Butt and Ponting, 139–60.

Butt, J. (1996), 'The Industries of Glasgow', in Fraser, and Maver, 96–140.

Butt, J. and Ponting, K. (eds) (1987), *Scottish Textile History*, Aberdeen, Aberdeen University Press.

Bythell, D. (1969), *The Handloom Weavers: A Study in the English Cotton Industry during the Industrial Revolution*, Cambridge, Cambridge University Press.

Cairncross, A. K. and Hunter, J. B. K. (1987), 'The Early Growth of Messrs J. and P. Coats, 1830–83', *Business History*, XXIX, 157–77.

Campbell, C. (1828), *Memoirs of Charles Campbell at Present Prisoner in the Jail of Glasgow*, Glasgow, James Duncan.

Campbell, R. H. (1965), *Scotland since 1707: The Rise of an Industrial Society*, reprinted 1971, Oxford, Blackwell.

Campbell, R. H. (1980), *The Rise and Fall of Scottish Industry, 1707–1939*, Edinburgh, John Donald.

Campbell, R. H. (1995), 'The Making of the Industrial City', in Devine and Jackson, 184–213.

Carlile, W. (1787), *A New Description of Paisley*, Paisley, n.p.

Carlile, W. (1806), 'Sketches of Paisley', *Scots Magazine and Edinburgh Literary Miscellany*, July.

Carnegie, A. (1920), *Autobiography*, London, John Constable.

Carvel, J. L. (1948), *The Coltness Iron Company: A Study in Private Enterprise*, Edinburgh, T. and A. Constable.

Catling, H. (1986), *The Spinning Mule*, Preston, Lancashire Libraries.

Chaloner, W. H. (1954), 'Robert Owen, Peter Drinkwater and the Early Factory System in Manchester, 1788–1800', *Bulletin of the John Rylands Library*, XXXVII, 78–102

Chapman, S. D. (1967), *The Early Factory Masters*, Newton Abbot, David and Charles.

Chapman, S. D. (1970), 'Fixed Capital Formation in the British Cotton Industry, 1770–1815', *Economic History Review*, 2nd series, XXIII, 235–66.

Chapman, S. D. (1971), 'Fixed Capital Formation in the British Cotton Manufacturing Industry', in Higgins, J. P. P. and Chapman, S. D. (eds), *Aspects of Capital Formation in Great Britain, 1750–1850*, London, Methuen, 57–119.
Chapman, S. D. (1987, 2nd edition), *The Cotton Industry in the Industrial Revolution*, London, Macmillan.
Chapman, S. D. (1992), *Merchant Enterprise in Britain: From the Industrial Revolution to World War I*, Cambridge, Cambridge University Press.
Chapman, S. D. (1996), 'The Commercial Sector', in Rose, 63–93.
Chapman, S. D. and Butt, J. (1988), 'The Cotton Industry, 1775–1880', in Feinstein and Pollard, 105–25.
Chapman, S. D. and Chassagne, S. G. (1981), *European Textile Printers in the Eighteenth Century: A Study of Peel and Oberkampf*, London, Heinemann.
Checkland, O. and Checkland, S. G. (1989, 2nd edition), *Industry and Ethos. Scotland 1832–1914*, Edinburgh, Edinburgh University Press.
Checkland, S. G. (1975), *Scottish Banking: A History, 1695–1973*, Glasgow and London, Collins.
Clark, A. (1995), *The Struggle for the Breeches: Gender and the Making of the British Working Class*, Berkeley, CA, University of California Press.
Clarke, T. and Dickson, T. (1982), 'Class and Class Consciousness in Early Industrial Capitalism, Paisley, 1770–1850', in Dickson, 10–55.
Clarkson, L. A. (1990), 'Proto-Industrialisation: The First Phase of Industrialisation?', in Clarkson, L. A. (ed.), *The Industrial Revolution: A Compendium*, London, MacMillan, 149–209.
Cleland, J. (1816), *Annals of Glasgow*, 2 vols, Glasgow, James Hedderwick.
Cleland, J. (1831), *Enumeration of the Inhabitants of the City of Glasgow and County of Lanark*, Glasgow, Edward Kull.
Cleland, J. (1836), *An Account of the Present State of Glasgow*, Glasgow, Glasgow and Clydesdale Statistical Society.
Clow, A. and Clow, N. (1952), *The Chemical Revolution: A Contribution to Social Technology*, London, Batchworth Press.
Cobbett, W. (1833), *A Tour in Scotland*, 1984 edition, Aberdeen, Aberdeen University Press.
Collins, B. (1988), 'Sewing and Social Structure: The Flowerers of Scotland and Ireland', in Mitchison, R. and Roebuck, P. (eds), *Economy and Society in Scotland and Ireland, 1500–1939*, Edinburgh, John Donald, 242–54.
Collins, B. (1991), 'The Origins of Irish Immigration to Scotland in the Nineteenth and Twentieth Centuries', in Devine, 1–18.
Colville, J. (ed.) (1904), *Letters of John Cockburn of Ormiston to his Gardener, 1727–1744*, Edinburgh, Scottish History Society.
Cooke, A. J. (ed.) (1977), *Stanley, Its History and Development*, Dundee, University of Dundee.
Cooke, A. J. (1979a), 'Richard Arkwright and the Scottish Cotton Industry', *Textile History*, X, 196–202.
Cooke A. J. (1979b), 'Robert Owen and the Stanley Mills, 1802–1811', *Business History*, XXI (1), 107–11.

Cooke, A. J. (1980), *Baxters of Dundee*, Dundee, University of Dundee.

Cooke, A. J. (ed.) (1984), *A History of Redgorton Parish*, Dundee, University of Dundee.

Cooke, A. J. (1995), 'Cotton and the Scottish Highland Clearances – Spinningdale, 1791–1806', *Textile History*, XXVI, 1, 89–94.

Cooke, A. J. (2003), *Stanley. From Arkwright Village to Commuter Suburb, 1784–2003*, Perth, Perth and Kinross Libraries.

Cooke, A. J. (2006), *From Popular Enlightenment to Lifelong Learning: A History of Adult Education in Scotland, 1707–2005*, Leicester, National Institute of Adult and Continuing Education.

Cooke, A. J. (2009), 'The Scottish Cotton Masters, 1780–1914', *Textile History*, XL, 1, 29–50.

Cooke, A. J. and Donnachie, I. (1998), 'Aspects of Industrialisation in Scotland before 1850', in Cooke, Donnachie, MacSween and Whatley, Vol. I, 130–54.

Cooke, A. J., Donnachie, I., MacSween, A. and Whatley, C. A. (eds) (1998), *Modern Scottish History, 1707 to the Present*, 5 volumes, East Linton, Tuckwell Press.

Crafts, N. F. R. (1985), *British Economic Growth during the Industrial Revolution*, Oxford, Clarendon Press.

Crafts, N. F. R. (1994), 'The Industrial Revolution', in Floud, R. and McCloskey, D. (eds), 44–59.

Crathorne, N. (1973), *Tennants Stalk: The Story of Tennants of the Glen*, London, Macmillan.

Crawford, G. (revised Semple, W.) (1782), *The History of the Shire of Renfrewshire*, Paisley (reprinted Paisley, 1991).

Crouzet, F. (ed.) (1972), *Capital Formation in the Industrial Revolution*, London, Methuen.

Crouzet, F. (1985), *The First Industrialists: The Problem of Origins*, Cambridge, Cambridge University Press.

Cummings, A. J. G. and Devine T. M. (eds) (1994), *Industry, Business and Society in Scotland since 1700*, Edinburgh, John Donald.

Daniels, G. W. (1920), *The Early English Cotton Industry with Some Unpublished Letters of Samuel Crompton*, Manchester, Manchester University Press.

Deane, P. (1979, 2nd edition), *The First Industrial Revolution*, Cambridge, Cambridge University Press.

Deane, P. and Cole, W. A., *British Economic Growth 1688–1959*, Cambridge, Cambridge University Press.

Defoe, D. (1724–6), *A Tour Through the Whole Island of Great Britain*, London, Penguin (reprinted 1971).

Devine, T. M. (1976), 'The Colonial Trades and Industrial Investment in Scotland c. 1700–1815', *Economic History Review*, 2nd series, XXIX, 1–13.

Devine, T. M. (1990 edition), *The Tobacco Lords: A Study of the Tobacco Merchants of Glasgow and their Trading Activities c. 1740–1790*, Edinburgh, Edinburgh University Press.

Devine, T. M. (ed.) (1991), *Irish Immigrants and Scottish Society in the Nineteenth and Twentieth Centuries*, Edinburgh, John Donald.

Devine, T. M. (ed.) (1994), *Scottish Elites*, Edinburgh, John Donald.

Devine, T. M. (2000), *The Scottish Nation, 1700–2000*, London, Penguin.
Devine, T. M. (2004), *Scotland's Empire, 1600–1615*, London, Penguin.
Devine, T. M. (2005), 'Industrialisation', in Devine, Lee and Peden.
Devine, T. M. and Jackson, G. (eds) (1995), *Glasgow. Volume 1: Beginnings to 1830*, Manchester, Manchester University Press.
Devine, T. M. and Mitchison, R. (eds) (1988), *People and Society in Scotland. Volume 1, 1760–1830*, Edinburgh, John Donald.
Devine, T. M., Lee, C. H. and Peden, G. C. (eds) (2005), *The Transformation of Scotland*, Edinburgh, Edinburgh University Press.
Dickson, A. and Treble, J. H. (1992), *People and Society in Scotland. Volume III, 1914–1990*, Edinburgh, John Donald.
Dickson, D. (1977), 'Aspects of the Rise and Decline of the Irish Cotton Industry', in Cullen, L. M. and Smout, T. C. (eds), *Comparative Aspects of Scottish and Irish Economic and Social History*, Edinburgh, John Donald, 100–15.
Dickson, T. (ed.) (1982), *Capital and Class in Scotland*, Edinburgh, John Donald.
Donnachie, I. (1979), 'Drink and Society, 1750–1850: Some Aspects of the Scottish Experience', *Scottish Labour History Society Journal*, 13, 5–22.
Donnachie, I. (1987), 'The Textile Industry in South West Scotland, 1750–1914', in Butt and Ponting, 19–36.
Donnachie, I. (1994), 'A Tour of the Works: Early Scottish Industry Observed, 1790–1825', in Cummings and Devine, 43–57.
Donnachie, I. (1995), '"The Darker Side": A Speculative Survey of Scottish Crime during the first half of the Nineteenth Century', *Scottish Economic and Social History*, XV, 5–24.
Donnachie, I. (2000), *Robert Owen: Owen of New Lanark and New Harmony*, East Linton, Tuckwell Press.
Donnachie, I. and Hewitt, G. (1993), *Historic New Lanark. The Dale and Owen Industrial Community since 1785*, Edinburgh, Edinburgh University Press.
Dublin, T. (1979), *Women at Work. The Transformation of Work and Community in Lowell, Massachusetts, 1826–1860*, New York, Columbia University Press.
Duncan, Rev. H. (1821), *The Young South Country Weaver: or A Journey to Glasgow: A Tale for the Radicals*, 2nd edition, Edinburgh, Waugh and Innes.
Durie, A. J. (1979), *The Scottish Linen Industry in the Eighteenth Century*, Edinburgh, John Donald.
Durie, A. J. (ed.) (1996), *The British Linen Company 1745–1775*, Edinburgh, Scottish History Society.
Edwards, M. M. (1967), *The Growth of the British Cotton Trade 1780–1815*, Manchester, Manchester University Press.
Eyre-Todd, G. (1909), *Who's Who in Glasgow in 1909. Biographical Dictionary of 500 Living Glasgow Citizens and those who have died since 1 January 1907*, Glasgow, Gowans and Gray.
Eyre-Todd, G. (1934), *History of Glasgow. Volume III, From the Reformation to the Passing of the Reform Acts 1832–33*, Glasgow, Jackson Wylie.
Farnie, D. A. (1979), *The English Cotton Industry and the World Market 1815–1896*, Oxford, Clarendon Press.

Feinstein, C. H. and Pollard, S. (eds) (1988), *Studies in Capital Formation in the United Kingdom, 1750–1920*, Oxford, Oxford University Press.

Fergusson, J. (ed.) (1934), *Letters of George Dempster to Sir Adam Fergusson, 1756–1813*, London, Macmillan.

Fitton, R. S. (1989), *The Arkwrights, Spinners of Fortune*, Manchester, Manchester, Manchester University Press.

Fitton, R. S., and Wadsworth, A. P. (1958), *The Strutts and the Arkwrights 1758–1830*, Manchester, Manchester, Manchester University Press.

Floud, R. and McLoskey, D. (eds) (1994), *The Economic History of Britain since 1700, Volume I, 1700–1860*, 2nd edition, Cambridge, Cambridge University Press.

Foster, J. (1974), *Class Struggle and the Industrial Revolution*, London, Methuen.

Foster, J. (1998), 'Class', in Cooke, Donnachie, MacSween and Whatley, vol. II, 210–34.

Fraser, W. H. (1976), 'The Glasgow Cotton Spinners, 1837', in Butt, J. and Ward, J. T., *Scottish Themes*, Edinburgh, Scottish Academic Press, 80–97.

Fraser, W. H. (1988a), 'Patterns of Protest', in Devine, and Mitchison, vol. I, 268–91.

Fraser, W. H. (1988b), *Conflict and Class: Scottish Workers, 1700–1838*, Edinburgh, John Donald.

Fraser, W. H. (1990) 'Developments in Leisure', in Fraser and Morris, 236–64.

Fraser, W. H. (1996), 'The Working Class', in Fraser and Maver, vol. II, 300–51.

Fraser, W. H. (1998), 'Social Class', in Cooke, Donnackie, MacSween and Whatley, vol. I, 203–29.

Fraser, W. H. and Maver, I. (eds) (1996), *Glasgow. Volume II, 1830–1912*, Manchester, Manchester University Press.

Fraser, W. H., and Morris, R. J. (eds) (1990), *People and Society in Scotland, Volume II, 1830–1914*, Edinburgh, John Donald.

Freer, W. (1929), *My Life and Memories*, Glasgow, Civic Press.

Freifeld, M. (1986), 'Technological Change and the "Self Acting" Mule: A Study of Skill and the Sexual Division of Labour', *Social History*, XI, 319–43.

French, G. J. (1859), *The Life and Times of Samuel Crompton*, reprinted 1971, Bath, Adams and Dart.

Gallagher, T. (1991), 'The Catholic Irish in Scotland: In Search of Identity', in Devine, 19–43.

Galt, J. (1919 edition), *Annals of the Parish*, London and Edinburgh, T. N. Foulis.

Gibson, A. J. S. and Smout, T. C. (1995), *Prices, Food and Wages in Scotland, 1550–1780*, Cambridge, Cambridge University Press.

Gibson, J. (1777), *The History of Glasgow*, Glasgow, Chapman and Duncan.

Gilmour, D. (1876), *Paisley Weavers of other Days: The Pen Folk*, Paisley, Alexander Gardner.

Gold, G. F. (1978), *Chartism and Paisley*, Glasgow, Jordanhill College.

Gordon, E. (1991), *Women and the Labour Movement in Scotland, 1850–1914*, Oxford, Clarendon Press.

Gordon, W. (2002), *Mill Girls and Strangers: Single Women's Independent Migration in England, Scotland and the United States, 1850–1881*, New York, State University of New York Press.

Graham, P. (1812), *General View of the Agriculture of Stirlingshire*, Edinburgh, W. Creech and A. Constable.

Greenlees, J. (2007), *Female Labour Power: Women Workers' Influence on Business Practices in the British and American Cotton Industries, 1780–1860*, Aldershot, Ashgate.

Gunn, S. (1988), 'The "Failure" of the Victorian Middle Class: A Critique', in Wolff and Seed, 17–44.

Hamilton, H. (1932), *The Industrial Revolution in Scotland*, 2nd edition, 1966, London, Frank Cass.

Hamilton, H. (1963), *An Economic History of Scotland in the Eighteenth Century*, Oxford, Clarendon Press.

Hamilton, J. (1868), *Poems and Ballads*, Glasgow, James Maclehose.

Hammond, W. (1904), *Recollections of a Glasgow Handloom Weaver*, Glasgow, Citizen Press.

Handley, J. (1945), *The Irish in Scotland, 1798–1845*, Cork, Cork University Press.

Harding, A. W. (1991), *Pullars of Perth*, Perth, Perth and Kinross District Libraries.

Henderson, W. O. (1969, 2nd edition), *The Lancashire Cotton Famine, 1861–1865*, Manchester, Manchester University Press.

Heron, R. (1799), *Scotland Delineated*, reprinted 1975, Edinburgh, James Thin.

Hills, R. L. (1970), *Power in the Industrial Revolution*, Manchester, Manchester University Press.

Hills, R. L. (1989), *Power from Steam: A History of the Stationary Steam Engine*, Cambridge, Cambridge University Press.

Hobsbawm, E. J. (1969), *Industry and Empire. From 1750 to the Present Day*, London, Penguin.

Honeyman, K. (1982), *Origins of Enterprise: Business Leadership in the Industrial Revolution*, Manchester, Manchester University Press.

Honeyman, K. (2000), *Women, Gender and Industrialisation in England, 1700–1870*, London, Macmillan.

Howe, A. C. (1984), *The Cotton Masters, 1830–1860*, Oxford, Clarendon Press.

Howe, A. C. (1996), 'The Business Community', in Rose, 94–120.

Hudson, J. W. (1851), *The History of Adult Education*, reprinted 1969, London, Woburn Press.

Hudson, P. (1986), *The Genesis of Industrial Capital: A Study of the West Riding Wool Textile Industry, c. 1750–1850*, Cambridge, Cambridge University Press.

Hudson, P. (ed.) (1989), *Regions and Industries: A Perspective on the Industrial Revolution in Britain*, Cambridge, Cambridge University Press.

Hudson, P. (1992), *The Industrial Revolution*, London, Edward Arnold.

Hume, J. R. (1971), 'The Industrial Archaeology of New Lanark', in Butt (ed.), *Robert Owen, Prince of Cotton Spinners*, 215–53.

Hume, J. R. (1974), *Industrial Archaeology of Glasgow*, Glasgow and London, Batsford.

Hume, J. R. (1976–7), *The Industrial Archaeology of Scotland*, 2 vols, London, Batsford.

Irwin, M. H. (1895–6), 'Women's Industries in Scotland', *Proceedings of the Philosophical Society of Glasgow*, XXVII, 70–91.

Jackson, G. (1981), 'Scottish Shipping, 1775–1805', in Cottrell, P. L. and Aldcroft, D. H. (eds), *Shipping, Trade and Commerce: Essays in Memory of Ralph Davis*, Leicester, Leicester University Press, 117–36.

Jeremy, D. J. (1996), 'Lancashire and the International Diffusion of Technology', in Rose, 210–37.

Johnston, E. (1867), *Autobiography: Poems and Songs of Ellen Johnston, the 'Factory Girl'*, Glasgow, William Love.

Johnston, R. (2000), *Clydeside Capital, 1870–1920: A Social History of Employers*, East Linton, Tuckwell Press.

Jowitt, J. A. and McIvor, A. J. (eds) (1988), *Employers and Labour in the English Textile Industries, 1850–1939*, London, Routledge.

Joyce, P. (1980), *Work, Society and Politics: The Culture of the Factory in later Victorian England*, London, Methuen.

King-Clark (ed.) (1991), *The John Caldwell Letters from Canada, 1821–1837*, Paisley, PDC Copyprint.

Kirby, R. G. and Musson, A. E. (1975), *The Voice of the People, John Doherty, Trade Unionist, Radical and Factory Reformer, 1798–1854*, Manchester, Manchester University Press.

Kirkwood, D. (1935), *My Life of Revolt*, London, Harrap.

Knox, W. W. (1990), 'The Political and Workplace Culture of the Scottish Working Class 1832–1914', in Fraser and Morris, Vol. II, 138–66.

Knox, W. W. (1995), *Hanging by a Thread: The Scottish Cotton Industry, c. 1850–1914*, Preston, Carnegie Publishing.

Knox, W. W. (1999), *Industrial Nation. Work, Culture and Society in Scotland, 1800–Present*, Edinburgh, Edinburgh University Press.

Koditschek, T. (1990), *Class Formation and Urban Industrial Society, Bradford, 1750–1850*, Cambridge, Cambridge University Press.

Kohl, J. G. (1844), *Scotland*, London, Chapman and Hall.

Landes, D. (1969), *The Unbound Prometheus*, Cambridge, Cambridge University Press.

Lang, A. M. (1998), *A Life of George Dempster, Scottish Member of Parliament of Dunnichen, 1732–1818*, Lampeter, Edwin Mellen Press.

Lazonick, W. (1979), 'Industrial Relations and Technical Change: The Case of the Self Acting Mule', *Cambridge Journal of Economics*, III, 231–62.

Lee, C. H. (1972), *A Cotton Enterprise, 1795–1840: A History of M'Connel and Kennedy, Fine Cotton Spinners*, Manchester, Manchester University Press.

Lee, C. H. (1979), *British Regional Employment Statistics, 1841–1971*, Cambridge, Cambridge University Press.

Lemire, B. (1991), *Fashion's Favourite, The Cotton Trade and the Consumer in Britain, 1660–1800*, Oxford, Oxford University Press.

Leneman, L. (1986), *Living in Atholl: A Social History of the Estates 1685–1785*, Edinburgh, Edinburgh University Press.

Lenman, B. (1977), *An Economic History of Modern Scotland, 1660–1976* London, Batsford.

Lenman, B., Lythe, C. and Gauldie, E. (1969), *Dundee and its Textile Industry 1850–1914*, Dundee, Abertay Historical Society.

Leonard, T. (1990), *Radical Renfrew: Poetry from the French Revolution to the First World War*, Edinburgh, Polygon.

Levitt, I. and Smout, C. (1979), *The State of the Scottish Working Class in 1843*, Edinburgh, Scottish Academic Press.

Levitt, S. (1996), 'Clothing', in Rose, 154–86.

Livingstone, D. (1857), *Missionary Travels and Researches in South Africa*, London, John Murray.

Lochrie, M. (1987), 'The Paisley Shawl Industry', in Butt and Ponting, 95–111.

Lockhart, D. G. (1983), 'Planned Village Development in Scotland and Ireland', in Devine, T. M. and Dickson, D. (eds), *Ireland and Scotland 1600–1850: Parallels and Contrasts in Economic and Social Development*, Edinburgh, John Donald.

Logue, K. J. (1979), *Popular Disturbances in Scotland, 1780–1815*, Edinburgh, John Donald.

Lythe, S. G. E. and Butt, J. (1975), *An Economic History of Scotland, 1100–1939*, Glasgow and London, Blackie.

McCaffrey, J. F. (1996) 'Political Issues and Developments', in Fraser and Maver, 186–226.

McCarthy, M. (1969), *A Social Geography of Paisley*, Paisley, Paisley Public Libraries.

McCloskey, D., '1780–1860: A Survey', in Floud and McCloskey, Vol. I, 242–70.

MacDougall, I. (ed.) (1978), *A Catalogue of Labour Records in Scotland*, Edinburgh, Scottish Labour History Society, VII.

Macgregor, G. (1881), *The History of Glasgow*, Glasgow, Thomas D. Morison.

Macintosh, G. (1847), *Biographical Memoir of the late Charles Macintosh, FRS by his son*, Glasgow, Blackie.

McIvor, A. J. (1988), 'Work, Wages and Industrial Relations in Cotton Finishing, 1880–1914', in Jowitt and McIvor, 127–52.

McIvor, A. J. (1996), *Organised Capital: Employers' Associations And Industrial Relations in Northern England, 1880–1939*, Cambridge, Cambridge University Press.

McIvor, A. J. (2001), *A History of Work in Britain, 1880–1950*, London, Palgrave.

McKenzie, P. (1868), *Reminiscences of Glasgow and the West of Scotland*, Glasgow, John Tweed, 3 vols.

McLain, N. E. (1970), 'Scottish Lint Mills, 1729–1770', *Textile History*, I.

McLaren, D. J. (1999), *David Dale of New Lanark, A Bright Luminary to Scotland*, Glasgow, Caring Books.

McLean, A. (ed.) (1901), *The Industries of Glasgow and the West of Scotland*, Glasgow, British Association for the Advancement of Science.

Maclehose, J. (1878), *The Old Country Houses of the Old Glasgow Gentry*, Glasgow, J. Maclehose.

Maclehose, J. (1886), *Memoirs and Portraits of 100 Glasgow Men*, 2 vols, Glasgow, J. Maclehose.

Mann, J. A. (1860), *The Cotton Trade of Great Britain*, reprinted 1968, London and Manchester, Frank Cass.

Mantoux, P. (1928), *The Industrial Revolution in the Eighteenth Century*, revised edition 1964, London, Methuen.

Marrison, A. (1996), 'Indian Summer, 1870–1914', in Rose, 238–64.

Marx, K. (1967), *Capital*, Vol. I, New York, International.

Marwick, W. H. (1924), 'The Cotton Industry and the Industrial Revolution in Scotland', *Scottish Historical Review*, XXI, 207–18.

Mathias, P. (1983, 2nd edition), *The First Industrial Nation. An Economic History of Britain 1700–1914*, London, Methuen.

Maver, I. (1996) 'Glasgow's Civic Government', in Fraser and Maver.

Maver, I. (2000), *Glasgow*, Edinburgh, Edinburgh University Press.

Minute Book of the Board of Green Cloth, 1809–1820 (1891), Glasgow, James Maclehose.

Miskell, L. (2000), 'Civic Leadership and the Manufacturing Elite: Dundee, 1820–1870', in Miskell, L., Whatley, C. A. and Harris, B. (eds), *Victorian Dundee: Image and Realities*, East Linton, Tuckwell Press, 51–69.

Mitchell, B. R. (1988), *British Historical Statistics*, Cambridge, Cambridge University Press.

Mitchell, G. M. (1925), 'The English and Scottish Cotton Industries', *Scottish Historical Review*, XXII, 101–14.

Mitchell, J. O. (1905), *Old Glasgow Essays*, Glasgow, James Maclehose and Sons.

Mitchell, M. J. (1998), *The Irish in the West of Scotland, 1797–1848*, Edinburgh, John Donald.

Mokyr, J. (ed.) (1992), *The British Industrial Revolution*, Colorado, Westview Press.

Mokyr, J. (1994), 'Technological Change, 1700–1830', in Floud and McCloskey, Vol. I, 12–43.

Montgomery, J. (1832), *The Theory and Practice of Cotton Spinning*, Glasgow, John Niven.

Morgan, N. and Trainor, R. H. (1996), 'The Dominant Classes', in Fraser and Morris, Vol. II, 103–37.

Morgan, P. (1886), *Annals of Woodside and Newhills*, Aberdeen, David Wyllie.

Morris, R. J. (ed.) (1986), *Class, Power and Social Structure in British Nineteenth Century Towns*, Leicester, Leicester University Press.

Morris, R. J. (1990), *Class, Sect and Party: The Making of the British Middle Class, Leeds, 1820–1850*, Manchester, Manchester University Press.

Munn, C. W. (1981), *The Scottish Provincial Banking Companies, 1747–1864*, Edinburgh, John Donald.

Munn, C. W. (1995), 'Banking Enterprise in North East Scotland, 1747–1787', in Aldcroft and Slaven, 129–50.

Munro, N. (1928), *The History of the Royal Bank of Scotland, 1727–1927*, Edinburgh, R. Clark.

Murray, N. (1978), *The Scottish Handloom Weavers, 1790–1850: A Social History* Edinburgh, John Donald.

Murray, N. (1994), 'The Regional Structure of Textile Employment in Scotland in the Nineteenth Century: East of Scotland Textile Weavers in the 1830s', in Cummings and Devine, 218–33.

Murphy, W. S. (1901), *Captains of Industry*, Glasgow, W. S. Murphy.

Musson, A. E. and Robinson, E. (1969), *Science and Technology in the Industrial Revolution*, Manchester, Manchester University Press.

Neal, L. (1994), 'The finance of business during the industrial revolution', in Floud and McCloskey, Vol. I, 151–81.

Nenadic, S. (1988), 'The Rise of the Urban Middle Classes', in Devine and Mitchison, Vol. I, 109–26.

Nenadic, S. (1996), 'The Victorian Middle Classes', in Fraser and Maver, Vol. II, 265–299.

New Statistical Account of Scotland (1845), Vol. VI (Lanarkshire), Vol. VII (Renfrewshire), Vol. X (Perthshire), Edinburgh, William Blackwood.

Nicolson, M. and Donnachie, I. (2003), 'The New Lanark Highlanders: Migration, Community and Language 1785–c. 1850', *Family and Community History*, VI, 1, 19–32.

O'Brien P. K., and Quinault, R. (eds) (1993), *The Industrial Revolution and British Society*, Cambridge, Cambridge University Press.

Owen, R. D. (1874), *Threading my Way*, London, Trubner and Co.

Paterson, J. (1871), *Autobiographical Reminiscences: Including Recollections of the Radical Years in Kilmarnock*, Glasgow, Maurice Ogle.

Parkhill, J. (1857), *The History of Paisley*, Paisley, Robert Stewart.

Parkhill, J. (ed.) (1860), *The Life and Opinions of Arthur Sneddon: An Autobiography*, Paisley, James Cook.

Payne, P. L. (ed.) (1967), *Studies in Scottish Business History*, London, Cass.

Payne, P. L. (1980), *The Early Scottish Limited Companies, 1856–1895*, Edinburgh, Scottish Academic Press.

Payne, P. L. (1988, 2nd edition), *British Entrepreneurship in the Nineteenth Century*, London, Macmillan.

Payne, P. L. (1992), *Growth and Contraction. Scottish Industry, c. 1860–1990*, Dundee, The Economic and Social History Society of Scotland.

Payne, P. L. (1998), 'Industrialisation and Industrial Decline', in Cooke, Donnachie, MacSween and Whatley, Vol. II, 73–94.

Pennant, T. (1769), *A Tour in Scotland*, Warrington, reprinted 1979, Perth, Melven Press.

Pennant, T. (1772), *A Tour in Scotland and Voyage to the Hebrides*, Chester, reprinted 1998, Edinburgh, Birlinn.

Penny, G. (1836), *Traditions of Perth*, reprinted 1986, Perth, Coupar Angus.

Perren, R. (1995), 'Management Style and Business Crises in the Aberdeen Textile Industry, 1825–1934', in Aldcroft and Slaven, 251–74.

Phillipson, N. and Mitchison, R. (1970), *Scotland in the Age of Improvement*, Edinburgh, Edinburgh University Press.

Pole, W. (1877), *The Life of William Fairbairn*, London, Longmans and Green.

Pollard, S. (1963), 'Factory Discipline in the Industrial Revolution', *Economic History Review*, XVI, 254–71.

Pollard, S. (1965), *The Genesis of Modern Management: A Study of the Industrial Revolution in Great Britain*, London, Edward Arnold.

Prentice, A. (1851), *Historical Sketches and Personal Recollections of Manchester*, London and Manchester, Charles Gilpin and J. T. Parkes.

Reid, R. (Senex) (1858), *Glasgow Past and Present*, Glasgow, David Robertson.

Reid, R. (Senex) (1864), *Old Glasgow and Its Environs*, Glasgow, David Robertson.
Reid, R. (Senex) (1884), *Glasgow Past and Present*, 3 vols, Glasgow, David Robertson.
Reilly, V. (1996), *The Paisley Shawl*, Glasgow, Richard Drew.
Richards, E. (1993), 'Margins of the Industrial Revolution', in O'Brien and Quinault, 203–28.
Richards, E. (2000), *The Highland Clearances*, Edinburgh, Birlinn.
Robertson A. J. (1969), 'Robert Owen and the Campbell Debt, 1810–1822', *Business History*, XI (1), 23–30.
Robertson, A. J. (1970), 'The Decline of the Scottish Cotton Industry, 1860–1914', *Business History*, XII (2), 116–28.
Robertson, R. (1799), *General View of the Agriculture in the County of Perth*, Edinburgh, R. Morison.
Robinson, E. and McKie, D. (eds) (1970), *Partners in Science: The Letters of James Watt and Joseph Black*, London, Constable.
Rodger, R. (1988), 'Concentration and Fragmentation: Capital, Labour and the Stucture of Mid-Victorian Scottish Industry', *Journal of Urban History*, XIV, (2), 178–213; in Cooke, Donnachie, MacSween and Whatley, Vol. IV, 82–113.
Rodger, R. (1996), 'The Labour Force', in Fraser and Maver, Vol. II, 163–226.
Rose, J. (2002), *The Intellectual Life of the British Working Classes*, New York and London, Yale University Press.
Rose, M. B. (1986), *The Gregs of Quarry Bank Mill: The Rise and Decline of a Family Firm, 1750–1914*, Cambridge, Cambridge University Press.
Rose, M. B. (ed.) (1996a), *The Lancashire Cotton Industry: A History since 1700*, Preston, Lancashire County Books.
Rose, M. B. (1996b), 'The Rise of the Cotton Industry in Lancashire to 1830', in Rose, 1–28.
Rose, M. B. (2000), *Firms, Networks and Business Values: The British and American Cotton Industries since 1750*, Cambridge, Cambridge University Press.
Ross, D. (2002), *David Livingstone. Mission and Empire*, London, Hambledon.
Rubinstein, W. D. (1981), *Men of Property: The Very Wealthy in Britain since the Industrial Revolution*, London, Croom Helm.
Rubinstein, W. D. (1994 edition), *Capitalism, Culture and Decline in Britain 1750–1990*, London and New York, Routledge.
Saint Fond, F. de (1907, revised edition), *A Journey through England and Scotland to the Hebrides in 1784*, 2 vols, Glasgow, H. Hopkins.
Saunders, L. J. (1950), *Scottish Democracy, 1815–1840*, Edinburgh, Oliver and Boyd.
Scarfe, N. (2001), *To the Highlands in 1786: The Inquisitive Journey of a Young French Aristocrat*, Woodbridge, Boydell Press.
Schoeser, M. (1996), '"Shewey and Full of Work" – Design', in Rose, 187–209.
Shaw, J. (1984), *Water Power in Scotland, 1550–1830*, Edinburgh, John Donald.
Sinclair, Sir J. (1825), *Analysis of the Statistical Account of Scotland*, reprinted 1970, New York, Johnson.
Sinclair, Sir J. (ed.) (1791–9), *The [Old] Statistical Account of Scotland 1791–1799*, reissued 1973–83, Vol. II (The Lothians), Vol. IV (Dumfriesshire), Vol. V

(Kirkcudbright and Wigtownshire), Vol. VI (Ayrshire), Vol. VII (Lanarkshire and Renfrewshire), Vol. IX (Dunbartonshire, Stirlingshire and Clackmannanshire), Vol. X (Fife), Vol. XI (South and East Perthshire, Kinross-Shire), Vol. XII (North and West Perthshire), Vol. XIII (Angus), Vol. XVIII (Sutherland and Caithness), Wakefield, EP Publishing.

Slaven, A. (1969), 'A Glasgow Firm in the Indian Market: John Lean and Sons, Muslin Weavers', *Business History*, XLIII, 4.

Slaven, A. (1976), *The Development of the West of Scotland, 1750–1960*, London, Routledge and Kegan Paul.

Slaven, A. (1995), 'Entrepreneurs and Business Success and Business Failure in Scotland', in Aldcroft and Slaven, 59–92.

Slaven, A. and Checkland, S. G. (eds) (1986), *Dictionary of Scottish Business Biography, Volume I, The Staple Industries*, Aberdeen, Aberdeen University Press.

Slaven, A. and Kim, D. W. (1994), 'The Origins and Economic and Social Roles of Scottish Business Leaders, 1860–1960', in Devine, *Scottish Elites*, 152–69.

Sloan, W. (1994), 'Employment Opportunities and Migrant Group Assimilation: The Highlanders and Irish in Glasgow, 1840–1860', in Cummings and Devine, 197–217.

Smiles, S. (1863), *Industrial Biography: Iron Workers and Tool Makers*, reprinted 1967, Newton Abbot, David and Charles.

Smillie, R. (1924), *My Life for Labour*, London, Mills and Boon.

Smith, A. (1776), *An Inquiry into the Nature and Causes of the Wealth of Nations*, 2 vols, 1976 edition, Oxford, Oxford University Press.

Smout T. C. (1964), 'Scottish Landowners and Economic Growth, 1650–1850', *Scottish Journal of Political Economy*, XI, 218–34.

Smout T. C. (1969), *A History of the Scottish People, 1560–1830*, London, Collins.

Smout, T. C. (1970), 'The Landowner and the Planned Village in Scotland 1730–1830', in Phillipson and Mitchison, 73–106.

Smout, T. C. (1986) *A Century of the Scottish People, 1830–1950*, London, Collins.

Stewart, G. (1881), *Curiosities of Glasgow Citizenship*, Glasgow, James Maclehose.

Tann, J. (1970), *The Development of the Factory*, London, Cornmarket Press.

Tann, J. (ed.) (1981), *The Selected Papers of Boulton and Watt, Volume I, The Engine Partnership, 1775–1825*, London, Diploma Press and Cambridge, MA, MIT Press.

Tarrant, N. (1987), 'The Turkey Red Dyeing Industry in the Vale of Leven', in Butt and Ponting, 37–47.

Taylor, W. (1809), *An Answer to Mr. Carlile's Sketches of Paisley*, Paisley, Stephen Young.

Thom, W. (1880), *Rhymes and Recollections of a Handloom Weaver*, Paisley, Alexander Gardner.

Thompson, E. P. (1963, revised 1968), *The Making of the English Working Class*, London, Pelican.

Thomson, A. (1895), *Random Notes and Rambling Recollections of Maryhill, 1750–1894*, Glasgow, Kerr and Richardson.

Timmins, G. (1996), 'Technology', in Rose, 29–62.

Trainor, R. H. (1993), *Black Country Elites: The Exercise of Authority in an Industrialised Area, 1830–1900*, Oxford, Oxford University Press.
Trainor, R. H. (1996), 'The Elite', in Fraser and Maver, Vol. II, 227–64.
Turnbull, G. (1951), *A History of the Calico Printing Industry of Great Britain*, Altrincham, John Sherratt.
Turner, W. H. K. (1957), 'The Textile Industry of Perth and District', *The Institute of British Geographers' Transactions and Papers*, XXIII, 123–40.
Turner, W. H. K. (1958), 'The Significance of Water Power in Industrial Location. Some Perthshire Examples', *Scottish Geographical Magazine*, LXXIV, 98–115.
Tyson, R. E. (1995), 'The City of Glasgow Bank and the Crisis of 1857', in Aldcroft and Slaven, 151–70.
Tytler, S. (1884), *St. Mungo's City*, 3 vols, London, Chatto and Windus.
Unwin, G. (1924), *Samuel Oldknow and the Arkwrights: The Industrial Revolution at Stockport and Marple*, Manchester, Manchester University Press.
Ure, A. (1835), *The Philosophy of Manufactures*, 3rd edition, 1861, London, H. G. Bohn.
Ure, A. (1836), *The Cotton Manufactures of Great Britain*, 2 vols, London, Charles Knight.
Von Tunzelman, G. N. (1978), *Steam Power and British Industrialisation to 1860*, Oxford, Clarendon Press.
Von Tunzelman, G. N. (1994), 'Technology in the Early Nineteenth Century', in Floud and McCloskey, Vol. I, 271–99.
Wadsworth, A. P. and Mann, J. de Lacy (1931), *The Cotton Trade and Industrial Lancashire, 1600–1780*, Manchester, Manchester University Press.
Walker, G. (1991), 'The Protestant Irish in Scotland', in Devine, 44–66.
Walker, W. M. (1979), *Juteopolis: Dundee and its Textile Workers, 1885–1923*, Edinburgh, Edinburgh University Press.
Ward, J. T. (1987), 'Textile Trade Unionism in Nineteenth Century Scotland', in Butt and Ponting, 126–38.
Warden, A. (1864), *The Linen Trade, Ancient and Modern*, London, Longman.
Watson, M. (1990), *Jute and Flax Mills in Dundee*, Hutton Press, Tayport.
Whatley, C. A. (1988), 'The Experience of Work', in Devine and Mitchison, Vol. I, 227–51.
Whatley, C. A. (1995), 'Labour in the Industrialising City', in Devine and Jackson, 360–401.
Whatley, C. A. (1997), *The Industrial Revolution in Scotland*, Cambridge, Cambridge University Press.
Whatley, C. A. (2000a), *Scottish Society, 1707–1830: Beyond Jacobitism, Towards Industrialisation*, Manchester, Manchester University Press.
Whatley, C. A. (2000b), 'Altering Images of the Industrial City: The Case of James Myles, the "Factory Boy", and mid-Victorian Dundee', in Miskell, L., Whatley, C. A. and Harris, B. (eds), *Victorian Dundee: Image and Realities*, East Linton, Tuckwell Press, 70–95.
Whyte, I. D. (1989), 'Proto-industrialisation in Scotland', in Hudson, 228–51.
Whyte, I. D. (1994), *Scotland before the Industrial Revolution c. 1050 to c. 1750*, London, Longman.

Whyte, I. D. (1997), *Scotland's Society and Economy in Transition, c. 1500–c. 1760*, London, Macmillan.
Wiener, M. A. (1981), *English Culture and the Decline of the Industrial Spirit, 1850–1980*, London, Harmondsworth.
Wilson, J. (1812), *A General View of the Agriculture of Renfrewshire*, Paisley, Stephen Young.
Winstanley, M. (1996), 'The Factory Workforce', in Rose, 121–53.
Withers, C. W. J. (1986), *Highland Communities in Dundee and Perth, 1787–1891. A Study in the Social History of Migrant Highlanders*, Dundee, Abertay Historical Society.
Withers, C. W. J. (1998), *Urban Highlanders: Highland-Lowland Migration and Urban Gaelic Culture*, East Linton, Tuckwell Press.
Wolff, J. and Seed, J. (eds) (1988), *The Culture of Capital: Art, Power and the Nineteenth Century Middle Class*, Manchester, Manchester University Press.
Wright, L. C. (1953), *Scottish Chartism*, Edinburgh, Oliver and Boyd.
Wrigley, E. A. (1988), *Continuity, Chance and Change: The Character of the Industrial Revolution in England*, Cambridge, Cambridge University Press.
Young, J. D. (1979), *The Rousing of the Scottish Working Class*, London, Croom Helm.

Newspapers and magazines

Dundee Advertiser
Edinburgh Courant
Glasgow Chamber of Commerce Journal
Glasgow Courier
Glasgow Herald
Glasgow Journal
Glasgow Mechanics' Magazine, 1825
Glasgow Mercury
Manchester Mercury
Nottingham Journal
Perthshire Advertiser
Perthshire Courier
Scots Magazine
Weavers' Magazine and Literary Companion, 1818–19

Parliamentary papers

Report of Select Committee on the State of Children Employed in Manufactures, *Parliamentary Papers*, 1816, Vol. III.
Sheriff Returns on Parochial Schools, *Parliamentary Papers*, 1826, Vol. XVIII.
Report of Select Committee on the Bill to regulate the Labour of Children in Factories, *Parliamentary Papers*, 1831–2, Vol. XV.
Report of the Select Committee on the Factory Bill, *Parliamentary Papers*, 1831–2, Vol. XV.
Report of Select Committee on Manufactures, Commerce and Shipping, *Parliamentary Papers*, 1833, Vol. VI.

Factory Inquiry Commission Reports, *Parliamentary Papers*, 1833, Vols XX and XXI, and 1834, Vol. XX.

Report on the State of the Irish Poor in Great Britain, 1835, *Parliamentary Papers*, 1836, Vol. XXXIV.

Abstract of Education Returns Scotland, *Parliamentary Papers*, 1837, Vol. XLVII.

Reports from the Assistant Handloom Weavers' Commissioners, South of Scotland and East of Scotland, *Parliamentary Papers*, 1838–9, reprinted 1970, Irish University Press, Industrial Revolution, Textiles, Vol. IX.

Papers relating to Parochial Education in Scotland, *Parliamentary Papers*, 1841, Vol. XIX.

Report of the Select Committee on Distress (Paisley), 1843, *Parliamentary Papers*, 1843, Vol. VII.

Report of the Commissioners for Education (Scotland), 1867, *Parliamentary Papers*, 1867, Vol. XXV.

Return of Owners of Land, Scotland, 1872–3, *Parliamentary Papers*, 1874, Vol. LXXII, Part III.

Theses

Gauldie, E. E. (1966), 'Scottish Bleachfields 1718–1862', B.Phil. thesis, St Andrews.

Lockhart, D. G. (1974), 'Planned Villages in North East Scotland', PhD thesis, Dundee.

Nisbet, S. M. (2003), 'The Rise of the Cotton Factory in Eighteenth Century Renfrewshire', PhD thesis, Paisley (University of the West of Scotland).

Teviotdale, G. (1963), 'The Glasgow Parliamentary Constituency, 1832–1846', B. Litt. thesis, Glasgow.

Index